W0108039

SKETCHES FROM NIPAL

SKETCHES FROM NIPAL

HISTORICAL AND DESCRIPTIVE,

WITH

ANECDOTES OF THE COURT LIFE AND WILD
SPORTS OF THE COUNTRY IN THE TIME OF
MAHARAJA JANG BAHADUR, G.C.B.

TO WHICH IS ADDED

AN ESSAY ON NIPALESE BUDDHISM,

AND

ILLUSTRATIONS OF RELIGIOUS MONUMENTS,
ARCHITECTURE, AND SCENERY,

FROM THE AUTHOR'S OWN DRAWINGS

BY THE LATE

HENRY AMBROSE OLDFIELD, M.D.,
OF H.M. INDIAN ARMY,
MANY YEARS RESIDENCY SURGEON AT KHATMANDU,
NIPAL.

VOL. I

Published by

Gyan Publishing House
5, Ansari Road
Daryaganj, New Delhi-110002
Phone: 011-47034999, 9811692060
E-mail: books@gyanbooks.com

Distribution Network
gyanbooks.com
India, USA, Canada, UK, Australia, France

© **Publisher**

ISBN : 978-81-212-4027-7 (Set)
ISBN : 978-81-212-4897-6 (PB)
First Published, 1880

2nd Impression 2020

Printed at: Gyan Press, Delhi.

Sketches From Nipal Vol. I
Author: Henry Ambrose Oldfield

SKETCHES FROM NIPAL,

HISTORICAL AND DESCRIPTIVE,

WITH

ANECDOTES OF THE COURT LIFE AND WILD SPORTS OF THE COUNTRY
IN THE TIME OF MAHARAJA JANG BAHADUR, G.C.B.

TO WHICH IS ADDED

AN ESSAY ON NIPALESE BUDDHISM,

AND

*ILLUSTRATIONS OF RELIGIOUS MONUMENTS, ARCHITECTURE,
AND SCENERY,*

FROM THE AUTHOR'S OWN DRAWINGS.

BY THE LATE

HENRY AMBROSE OLDFIELD, M.D.,

OF H.M. INDIAN ARMY,
MANY YEARS RESIDENCY SURGEON AT KHATMANDU, NIPAL.

VOL. I.

LONDON:
W. H. ALLEN AND CO., 13, WATERLOO PLACE,
PALL MALL, S.W.

1880.

TEMPLE OF DEVI BHAGWANI, BHATGAON.
Built, A.D. 1703.

PREFACE.

The following pages were not written with an original purpose of publication, nor did they receive throughout the benefit of the Author's revision. During the earlier part of his Indian career Dr. Oldfield was engaged in duty as an Assistant-Surgeon in the Bengal Army. Before long he was appointed to the medical charge of the eligible station of Simla, where he attended on Lord Gough, then Commander-in-Chief. During the second Sikh war in 1848–9 he was ordered to join temporarily the 13th Irregular Cavalry, then serving in the Punjab; but was soon after recalled to his post at Simla, owing to the absence of his medical colleague at that station. He was transferred in 1850 to Khatmandu, as Surgeon to the British Residency in Nipal, then under the Honourable J. C. Erskine, of the Bengal Civil Service. In 1853 Mr. Erskine, who has since succeeded to the title of his grandfather, the celebrated orator and Chancellor, retired from India; and the post of British representative in Nipal was conferred on Colonel (now General) George Ramsay, a cousin of the Governor-General, the Marquis of Dalhousie. With these two Residents Dr. Oldfield remained at Khatmandu till the close of 1863. His duties there were, of course, primarily medical; but the lightness of these in so small a station enabled him to devote, by way of recreation and self-instruction, much study to the natural and social characteristics of Nipal, and to the private life, as well as the political relations, of its Court. In recognition of the knowledge and ability which he made in various ways available for the public service, the Indian Government, during the mutiny of 1857–8, nominated him Honorary Assistant to the Political Resident.

The suspicious policy of the Nipalese Government debarred any British officer from travelling freely throughout the interior of the country. But within the range allowed Dr. Oldfield visited, and noted with pen and pencil, whatever appeared of interest in its architecture, its magnificent mountain scenery, including the loftiest peak in the world, or the physical and moral peculiarities of its people. His pursuits. however, were not exclusively studious. He entered with ardour into the wild sports of the country, which his friendly relations with Jang Bahadur gave him special facilities for enjoying. To the use he made of his equal opportunities for observation and amusement the present volumes sufficiently testify.

From a boy he had been fond of drawing, and in such a neighbourhood he found inexhaustible material for elaborate water-colour sketches and studies, which unhappily it has not been found practicable to reproduce in their own proper hues within any reasonable cost. But his eye-sight was unfortunately not equal to his zeal; and in aiding it with too powerful glasses, to copy with greater exactness the intricacies of mountain form seen at fifty or a hundred miles distance, he overstrained and, as the result proved, irreparably injured his sight. Hence, during the last seven years of his residence in Nipal, he made little use of his artistic skill, beyond correcting and putting the finishing touches to the drawings of a native artist whom he had trained to copy his sketches. At a later period he held for a short time a post in the medical staff at Calcutta; but his health finally giving way, he returned to England in 1866, and retired altogether from the service in 1869.

He had begun, whilst at Khatmandu, to rearrange his notes, and put the essay on Buddhism in its present form, though rather for the use of himself and his friends than with any definite idea of a wider circulation. He also partially revised the hunting adventures and personal anecdotes; but the larger part of his manuscript was left as originally written. Since his decease various causes have for a time prevented any use being made of his papers. But his family now feel it to be due both to him and the Public no longer to withhold so much authentic and detailed information on a country abounding in curiosity and beauty, which borders our Indian dominions for not less than six hundred miles, and which, though not lying (happily for itself) in the highway of Russia, is in other respects not inferior in interest to Afghanistan.

E. O.

CONTENTS.

LIST OF ILLUSTRATIONS

To Dr. Oldfield's "Sketches in Nipal."

VOL. I.

SKETCHES FROM

NIPAL.

CHAPTER I.

GEOGRAPHICAL.

THE modern kingdom of Nipal is a narrow tract of country extending for about five hundred miles along the southern slope of the central portion of the Himalaya mountains.

It embraces nearly one-third part of that stupendous mountain barrier which, in one unbroken line, stretches for one thousand eight hundred miles—from the shores of the Indus north of Kashmir in a south-easterly direction to the great bend in the Brahmaputra river on the confines of China—and which separates the whole of British India, as well as the kingdom of Ava, from the highlands of Central Asia.

The territory of Nipal lies entirely within this mountain range, and extends from the 80th to the 88th degree of east longitude. Its length is about five hundred miles, and it has a varying breadth, which nowhere exceeds one hundred and forty miles, and averages in most parts from ninety to one hundred miles.

Its general direction is from west to east; its most southern and eastern corner, at the Michi river, reaches as low as the 26th, while its most northern and western angle extends up to the 30th degree of north latitude.

It is at the present time bounded on the north by Tibet, on the east by the little principality of Sikkim, on the south by Hindustan, and on the west by the British provinces of Rohilkand and Kamaon.

Previous to 1815 the kingdom of Nipal was very much more extensive, and included Kamaon and the whole of the hill country as far as the Satlaj river. Sir David Ochterlony, however, wrested those provinces from the Gorkhas; and by the treaty of Sigauli (1816), it was finally agreed that the river Kali should in future form the western boundary between the British and the Nipalese dominions.

Nipal is thus hemmed in on all four sides between the territories of the British and those of the Chinese governments; on its western, southern, and eastern sides it is circumscribed by the possessions either of the British or of their dependents, the Nawab of Oudh and the Rajah of Sikkim, while on its northern frontier the eternal snows form an insuperable barrier to any important extension of power in the direction of China.

The kingdom of Nipal covers an area of about sixty thousand square miles, and is therefore of about the same superficial extent as the Panjab.* No trustworthy census of its entire population has ever been taken,

---

* Not the Panjab of to-day, which has an area of 104,000 square miles.—(EDITOR.)

but it is believed to amount to about four millions. The Nipalese themselves reckon it at upwards of five millions; but there can be no doubt that their estimate is considerably, and perhaps intentionally, exaggerated.

Supposing it to be four millions, it would give an average of about sixty-six inhabitants to every square mile, which is quite as high as is likely to be correct in a *mountainous* country, especially considering that the census of the whole of France in 1827 gave only one hundred and fifty souls to each square mile. Of this population of four millions, at least one-quarter of a million live within the narrow limits of the Valley of Nipal.

It will give a clearer idea of the geographical position of Nipal if the nature of its frontier on each of its four sides is described a little in detail.

Along the whole extent of its northern side the snowy range of the Himalaya stretches in continuous and unbroken length, and forms the natural boundary between Nipal and the Chinese provinces of Central Tibet.

This portion of the Himalayas, which overhangs Nipal, varies in height from sixteen thousand feet to twenty-eight thousand feet; it is covered with perpetual snow, and embraces within its limits four of the highest mountains in the world. These are the Nanda Devi, the Dewaligiri, the Gosainthan, and the Kinchinjanga.

The *Nanda Devi mountain*, at the extreme western limit of the Nipalese Himalaya, is entirely within the British province of Kamaon; but it overlooks all the

1 *

western provinces of Nipal, and its rugged sides give rise to the streams which unite to form the Kali river, whose waters wash its eastern base and constitute the western boundary of the kingdom of Nipal.

The *Dewaligiri* is situated about two hundred miles to the east of the Nanda Devi, and due north of Gorakpur; it overlooks the whole of the central provinces of Nipal, and its towering peaks are clearly visible from the plains of Hindustan. It is said by Humboldt to be the loftiest mountain in the world, but its claims to that distinction are disputed by the Kinchinjanga.

The *Gosainthan mountain* is situated one hundred and eighty miles to the east of the Dewaligiri, and stands due north of the Valley of Nipal. It is distinguished alike for its sanctity and its elevation. While the sacred Tusk of Narayan, buried amid its snows, is an object of special worship to the pilgrim, the bold grandeur of its bluff peak is equally an object of admiration to the traveller.

The *Kinchinjanga,* which competes with the Dewaligiri for the sovereignty of the mountain world, is one hundred and thirty miles to the east of the Gosainthan. It forms the extreme eastern peak of the Nipal Himalaya, and belongs as much, or perhaps more, to Sikkim than it does to Nipal. It directly overhangs the whole country of Sikkim, as well as some of the eastern provinces of Nipal, and a lofty ridge or spur from its southern face forms part of the boundary between the territories of the two states.

These lofty mountains, the lowest of which is

upwards of twenty-four thousand feet high, divide the chain of the Nipal Himalaya into three not very unequal portions—the western, the central, and the eastern.

The western division extends from the Nanda Devi to the Dewaligiri, and is about two hundred miles in length. The central portion extends for one hundred and eighty miles from the Dewaligiri to the Gosainthan. The eastern division runs from the Gosainthan to the Kinchinjanga, which are distant from each other one hundred and thirty miles.

The long axis of the Himalaya mountains is not perfectly straight, but presents certain bends or angles, which, as it runs from the N.W. to the S.E., give to its direction a gradual curve, the convexity of which faces to the south.

The most elevated mountains in the range are situated at these angles, where they form so many joints or huge knots in the main chain of the Himalaya. They stand out in advance of their companions, with a forward direction to the south, like gigantic bastions, supporting, overlooking, and binding together all the lower mountains around them. From these and from the entire length of the central mountains numerous lofty ridges diverge, sometimes at right angles, but more generally at acute ones, to the Ghat line or main axis of the range.

These ridges, again, throw off smaller ones which divide and sub-divide, interlacing and dove-tailing with each other, until the whole tract of a country like

Nipal, which lies on the southern slope of the range, becomes intersected by mountains of various sizes and shapes. These usually run together into *ranges*, which are separated from each other by deep valleys, sometimes of very considerable extent, at others narrowed into mere gorges, which serve as the beds of torrents. These secondary ranges form a series of lateral and subordinate chains upon the flanks of the central or snowy peaks. *Individually* they appear to be under no fixed rules for their direction, but taken *collectively* they will be found to diverge from the Ghat line of the snow so as to be more or less parallel to each other, and to run out towards the plains like so many ribs given off from the backbone or spine of the Himalaya.

Whatever their original elevation or direction, they gradually subside as they approach the plains of India, and are ultimately lost altogether beneath the surface of the Terai. The immense elevation of these and of all the highest peaks in the Himalayas, and the vast scale on which even the subordinate ranges are constructed, render it easy to trace in them examples of the most important laws which regulate the structural anatomy of mountain masses. The Dewaligiri, in particular, affords a striking illustration of the fact that, however bold the outline of a mountain may be, however much its pre-eminent height may apparently isolate it from all the lower ranges above which it towers, yet it never is in reality a detached or solitary mass, and never consists of a single or simply-formed peak. Every first-class mountain—and such, and such only, are met with throughout the entire length of the snowy range—is composed of a mass or cluster of peaks, rising one above and within another, and supported by buttresses in the form of converging ridges, which spring from the lower hills as a foundation; all trend toward their common centre, and are mostly of sufficient elevation to be covered with perpetual snow.

This common centre is the highest peak of all; and around it, at varying elevations, the lower peaks, with their subordinate ranges and ridges, are clustered in greater or less proximity, and often in the greatest apparent confusion. This confusion is only apparent; but the series of these lower mountains is often so extensive, and their bulk so vast, that the eye becomes wearied in attempting either to follow out the details of their forms, or to reduce them to order as parts of a system. It is only when they are viewed as a whole, and from such a distance that their crests may be seen rising in succession one behind another until they are lost beneath the eternal snows, that it is possible to believe that there is any method in their arrangement, and that the eye can be taught to look upon them as mere outworks resting upon still vaster mountains,—as so many steps in the gigantic ladder which leads from ridge to ridge, and peak to peak, till it gains the snow-crowned summit of the range. Geology, however, has established it as an undoubted fact that all these huge secondary mountains—whether linked together into chains, or standing out boldly and alone—are but subordinate members of the great central chain upon which they rest, and whose granite peaks, in some places bare and black, in others covered with snow, emerge from under the mass of surrounding mountains like pointed rocks amid the waves of the sea.

The Nipal Himalaya is traversed by several passes leading into Tibet, but which, from their great elevation,—the lowest of them being higher than the highest mountain in Europe,—are only open to travellers during the warmer months of the year.

The most important of these passes are the following :—

1st. The *Takla Khar Pass*, or Yari Pass,—midway between the Nanda Devi and Dewaligiri mountains. The Karnali branch of the Gogra river, which rises on the north side of the Himalaya, not far from one of the sources of the Satlaj, quits Tibet and enters the western provinces of Nipal by this pass. The village of Thak, from which the pass derives its name, is situated near its southern or Nipalese entrance, and is the seat of considerable trade in the salt brought from Tibet.

2nd. The *Mastang·Pass* is about forty miles to the east of the Dewaligiri. It leads to a small principality of the same name at the foot of the Dewaligiri, but on its northern or Tibetan side. The Rajah is tributary to Nipal, and his being so induces the Nipalese to boast that from the Gosainthan westward their frontier line includes both slopes of the Himalaya.* It is an unfounded assumption of theirs; as the district of Mastang, though it pays a small annual tribute to Nipal, is *not* within its frontier, nor does it form any part of the Gorkha dominions. On the northern side of the pass and on the high road to Mastang is a large village called *Muktinath*, which is much visited by pilgrims, as well as by traders in Tibetan salt. Muktinath is. eight days' journey from Mastang, and four from Bini Shahr, the capital of the province of Malibum, which lies close under the snow, and is directly overlooked by the Dewaligiri. A good deal of Nipalese opium—grown in the western parts of the Terai—is smuggled into Tibet by the Mastang pass.

3rd. *Kerang Pass*, to the west; and

4th. *Kuti Pass*, to the east of the Gosainthan mountains. These being the passes nearest to the capital are most frequented by the Tibetan pilgrims and traders who come annually in large numbers to the Valley of Nipal during the cold months of the year.

The road from Kathmandu to Lhassa by Kerang joins the road by the Kuti pass at Tingri. The Kuti road is the shortest and most direct, by three or four marches, but it is not passable for ponies. For this reason the Chinese Embassy, on their way *to* China, always go by Kuti; but on their return *from* China,

* The principality of Mastang consists of an elevated mountain valley, lying between the first and second ranges of snowy mountains, and is approached from Nipal by the Muktinath Pass.

when they have with them eighty or one hundred valuable China and Poomee ponies, they come by Kerang, where the road is comparatively good. The Chinese army of invasion in 1792 came by Kerang for the same reason.

The Kerang pass is thirty-seven hill kos, or about one hundred miles from Kathmandu. The journey is made in eight stages, and the road lies by Nayakot. The Kuti pass is thirty-four kos, or about ninety miles from Kathmandu, and is also reached in eight marches.

The high road to Lhassa runs through the Kuti pass; and the traffic along it is therefore greater than along any of the other passes. The snowy peak to the *west* of the pass is called Kurdah-bhumi (copper soil); that on its east is the Tambakosi peak, from its base giving rise to the river of that name.

On the northern or Tibetan side of the pass is a level district or valley called Tingri, where the Gorkhas were defeated in a battle by the Chinese army of invasion in 1792, and the frontier post of the Nipalese at Kuti was taken and occupied by the conquerors. The Bhotia river, one of the seven branches of the Kosi, rises in the Kuti pass.

5th. The *Hatia Pass*, about forty or fifty miles to the east of Kuti. The Aran,—by far the largest of the seven streams whose union forms the Kosi river,— after rising by several sources on the north side of the Himalaya, quits Tibet and enters the eastern provinces of Nipal through the Hatia pass.

6th. The *Wallang Pass*, or Wallanchon Pass, is situated quite in the eastern extremity of the Nipal Himalaya, and but a little to the west of the Kinchinjanga mountains.

These different passes are used almost exclusively by the Tibetans (commonly called *Bhotias*, as they are inhabitants of the country of *Bhot*, or Tibet), who flock in large numbers to Nipal from all parts of Tibet, and especially from Lhassa and its neighbourhood during the cold months from November to March.

These Tibetans bring down with them for sale in Nipal blankets of various kinds, and other woollen manufactures, as well as ponies, watch-dogs, sheep, goats, crystals, agate, turquoises, yak-tails, gold dust, gold and silver ores, and large quantities of rock salt. The rock salt is packed in bags, forming loads of 15 lbs. each, which are brought across the snows fastened upon the backs of sheep. Whole flocks of sheep thus laden may be frequently met with entering the Valley of Nipal by the road from Nayakot and Kerang.

Besides the Tibetans, a few Niwar merchants, as well as some Kashmirians from Nipal, who have houses of agency at Lhassa, go to and from Tibet generally by the Kuti pass.

The roads through these passes, as well as all the roads leading to them in the Nipalese territory, are so very bad, that all loads of every description have to be carried on men's shoulders. When once, however, the Himalaya is passed, the roads thence to Lhassa, and generally throughout Tibet, are practicable for beasts of burden.

The *eastern* extremity of Nipal is about one hundred miles in width from north to south. It lies in 88° E. long., and extends from 26·50° to 28° N. lat. The frontier, which separates Nipal from the little principality of Sikkim, extends from the snows nearly in a straight line towards the plains of Hindustan. The boundary of the two states, *within the hills,* consists partly of the Kinchinjanga mountain, but mainly of a lofty range of mountains called the Singhilela ridge, which is given off from the Kinchinjanga, and runs due south towards the plains. This ridge near the snows is from ten thousand to fifteen thousand feet high, but it subdivides towards the south to an average height of seven thousand feet. At about sixty miles distance from the snows this ridge turns suddenly to the east, and at this point ceases to form the boundary between the two states. At the angle thus formed it gives rise to the Michi river, which flows in a southerly direction from its origin in the Singhilela ridge towards the Ganges, into which it ultimately falls.

For the first forty miles of its course below the hills, and until it enters the British territory, the Michi river separates the lowlands of Nipal from those of Sikkim, and forms part of the boundary to the kingdom of Nipal on its eastern frontier. The Singhilela range runs parallel to the Kankayi river, and about twenty miles distance from it, on its eastern or left side. This range is traversed by three narrow passes, the roads through which are bad, and practicable only for hill ponies.

The *southern* frontier of Nipal extends from the Michi river in the east, on the borders of Sikkim, to the Kali river in the west, on the borders of Kamaon, —a distance of about five hundred miles. For two-thirds of this extent the frontier of Nipal forms the northern boundary to the British province of Bahar; for the remaining or western third it runs along the northern border of the kingdom of Oudh.

The southern frontier of Nipal is divided into three distinct portions, forming an *eastern*, a *central*, and a *western* division. The eastern portion extends from the Michi river to the Oreka Naddi,—a small stream, which, rising in the Cheryaghati range of hills, and flowing in a southerly direction, about ten miles to the west of Bissaulia, on the high road to Kathmandu, —falls into the Sikrani river. This portion of the frontier is about two hundred and twenty miles in length in a straight line, and runs in a direction nearly due east and west. It separates the Morung and Terai of Nipal from the districts of Parniah, Tirhut, and Champaran in the British province of Bahar. It follows an irregular and wavy line, and is marked throughout its entire course by a series of pillars of masonry, to prevent the possibility of border disputes between the Nipalese and British zamindars. At the Oreka Naddi the boundary line of pillars falls back at a right angle, and runs due north for about twenty miles, at first along the left bank of the Oreka, then leaving that stream, passes across a strip of the Sal forest till it reaches the chain of low sandstone hills which is called Cheryaghati range. The eastern portion of the southern frontier is crossed by two large rivers as they quit the Nipalese territory,—the Kosi and the Baghmatti.

The *central* portion of the southern frontier extends from the Oreka Naddi to the borders of Oudh,—a distance of about one hundred and fifty miles. It separates the valley of the Rapti from the district of Ramnagar in Champaran, and the Terai of Butul Khas from the district of Gorakpur. For about forty miles the frontier runs along the crest of the Cheryaghati range, till it reaches the pass through which the great Gandak river debouches upon the plains at Tribani. At this point it dips into the plains, skirts the foot of the range for about ten miles, as far as Pali, and then, leaving the hills, extends in nearly a straight line, and with direction due east and west, till it meets the frontiers of Oudh at Tulsipur, at a point about twenty miles distant from the hills. The boundary line then falls back at a right angle from Tulsipur along the left bank of a small stream, and runs due north till it again joins the sandstone range of hills. By thus diverging into the plains, the frontier encloses a long narrow strip of lowland between it and the outer range of hills. This strip constitutes the Terai of Butul or Butul Khas, and lies due north of Gorakpur. The Gandak is the only large river which crosses this central portion of the southern frontier of Nipal.

The *western* division of the southern frontier of Nipal is formed throughout by the outer or sandstone range of hills, which here take a north-westerly direction, and along the crest of which the boundary line runs for one hundred and thirty miles, till it meets the Kali river on the borders of Rohilkand. The sandstone range separates the territories of Nipal from the kingdom of Oudh. It is crossed by two large rivers,—the Gogra and the Rapti (or Gorakpur), —as they escape from the western provinces of Nipal.

The *western* frontier of Nipal is formed by the Kali or Sarju river, which, rising in the snows, washes the eastern base of the Nanda Devi mountain, and flows in a southerly direction for about ninety miles within the hills, separating the territories of Nipal from the British province of Kamaon. After reaching the plains, through a pass in the sandstone range, it follows a south-easterly course, during about fifty miles of which it forms the boundary between Nipal and the British province of Rohilkand; it then enters the kingdom of Oudh, and falls into the Gogra or Karnali river.

The sandstone range of hills above referred to as forming part of the southern boundary of Nipal, extends, under different names, for nearly the whole length of the Himalayas. It is the lowest and outermost of all the mountain ranges and immediately overlooks the plains of Hindustan. It runs parallel with the Ghat line or long axis of the snowy range, at an average distance from it of eighty or ninety miles, and it separates the *dhuns* or valleys at the foot of the second or inner range of hills from the terais or lowlands which, with an average width of about twenty miles, skirt the outer base of the Himalaya mountains throughout their entire length from east to west.

The sandstone range is frequently interrupted by breaches or gaps. In some parts it almost disappears, subsiding or being half-buried beneath the vast alluvial plains on its northern and southern faces through which it has to penetrate. It has a varying height of from two thousand feet to three thousand feet above the level of the sea; and on the north-west, where it is known as the Sewalik range, has proved very rich in fossils of various kinds.

It is traversed by passes in several places, through which the rivers rising on the southern face of the Himalaya find their way into the plains of India.

The sandstone range has different names in different parts of its course. In Nipal that part of it which extends from the pass of the Gandak river in the west, to the Kosi river in the east, is called the Cheryghati range. The *western* part of the Cheryaghati range, is called the Ridge of Someshwar.

The Someshwar ridge separates the valley or *dhun* of the Little Rapti river from the British district of Ramnagar, and is of some interest as having in 1840 given rise to certain local disputes about the boundary, which very nearly involved the British and Nipalese Governments in war.

The central portion of the *Cheryaghati* range, between Someshwar ridge and the pass of the Bagh-matti river, lies to the south of the Valley of Nipal, and is crossed by the high road leading from the plains to Kathmandu.

Throughout the whole of its extent in Nipal both its northern and southern slopes are covered with a dense forest, chiefly of Sal trees.

Wherever the boundary line described as forming the southern frontier of Nipal is *not* identical with the range, but runs to the south of it,—as is the case below the Palpa and Betul hills, north of Gorakpur, and again from Oreka Naddi eastward to the Michi river, a distance of two hundred and twenty miles or more,— the portion of lowland intervening between the outer-most hills and the British frontier constitutes the Nipalese *Terai.*

CHAPTER II.

THE PROVINCES OF NIPAL.

THE territory of Nipal, *within the hills*, from Kamaon on the west to Sikkim on the east, is divided into three large natural provinces by four very lofty and massive ridges which respectively are given off from, or, more correctly, run up into, the high peaks of the Nanda Devi, Dewaligiri, Gosainthan, and Kinchinjanga mountains. These ridges stand out at right angles from the central axis or spine of the Himalayas, and from their origin in the snows run in a direction parallel to each other, and nearly due south towards the plains. They are much more prominent in elevation than any of the other subordinate mountains with which the sides of the snowy range are flanked, and by which the whole territory of Nipal is, to a greater or less extent, intersected.

Each of the three natural provinces into which Nipal is divided by these lofty ridges is walled in on all four sides by mountain barriers: on the north by the snowy range; on the south by the chain of sandstone hills; and on the east and west by one of the lofty ridges just referred to, which act as watersheds, subordinate to, but continuous with, the main Ghat line of the Himalayas, and which, running due north and south, throw off all their waters towards their eastern and western sides into the basins or valleys of which they form the lateral boundaries.

Each of these districts, thus walled in, forms a large mountain basin, having a gradual slope towards the south, and furrowed by numerous streams which rise on the sides of the surrounding mountains. All flow towards the plains, and all converge towards each other in their course through the hills, so decidedly that they unite into one large river in two out of the three provinces before they reach even the sandstone range of hills. These Himalayan rivers—the Gogra, the Gandak, and the Kosi — pass through gaps or breaches in the lowest range of hills, and then entering the plains, all flow on into the valley of the Ganges.

Each of the three great mountain basins derives its name from the river by which its waters are drained off ; and the limits of each of these basins are identical with the origin of the numerous feeders and tributary streams, whose uniform convergence towards each other in the hills, and ultimate union into one large river as they approach the plains, form a striking feature in the physical geography of the Himalayas.

The *three* natural provinces into which Nipal is divided may be distinguished respectively as follows :

1st. The *western* division, or mountain basin of the Karnali or Gogra river.

2 *

2nd. The *central* division, or mountain basin of the Gandak river.

3rd. The *eastern* division, or mountain basin of the Kosi river.

Besides these three grand geographical divisions of Nipal, there is a *fourth province or district*, of but comparatively limited extent, but of primary political importance, in consequence of its containing the Valley of Nipal proper, which is the capital of the modern empire and the headquarters of the reigning or Gorkha dynasty.

This district occupies an isolated tract lying between the country watered by the Gandak on the west, and that watered by the Kosi on the east. It is in the form of a triangle, the apex of which points to the snows, while its base rests upon the lower range of hills. It is interposed like a wedge between the neighbouring provinces of the Gandak and the Kosi, but is quite independent of each of them, being watered by a river —the Baghmatti—peculiar to itself, which drains the whole of the district, and follows a solitary course, not only within the hills, but also in the plains, until it falls into the Ganges opposite Monghir.

These four districts—the basins of the Karnali, the Gandak, the Kosi, and the Baghmatti rivers—embrace the whole territory of Nipal within the hills. Below the hills the lowlands constituting the Terai complete the remaining area of the kingdom of Nipal.

We will now describe each of these districts separately and a little in detail. The western division or basin of the Karnali extends from the Nanda Devi to the Dewaligiri mountain. It is divided into two unequal portions by the Kali river, which forms the boundary between Nipal and Kamaon. The territory on the right bank of the river belongs to the British, but it is not one-fourth of the extent of the whole basin. The Nipalese portion of this basin extends from the Kali on the west to the lofty ridge on its east which runs up into the Dewaligiri, and which acts as a watershed between this district and the adjacent basin of the Gandak. It is bounded on the north by the snowy range, and on the south by the chain of sandstone hills which form the boundary between Nipal and the kingdom of Oudh.

All the mountain streams whose ultimate union forms the Gogra river have their origin within the limits of this basin. Of these streams the most important are three in number—the Kali, the Karnali, and the Rapti. Within the hills these rivers all converge gradually towards each other, but they do not finally unite their waters till they have traversed a considerable portion of the plains.

1st. The *Kali* or *Sarju*. It arises by several streams frcm the eastern side of the Nanda Devi, flows in a southerly direction towards the plains, and forms the boundary between Nipal and Kamaon (see p. 15). All its tributaries are within the British territory, and the river is only of interest to the Nipalese as forming their western frontier.

2nd. The *Karnali* or *Gogra* river. The **former**

name is generally applied to it within the hills, the latter to it while in the plains. It is by far the largest river of the district; and it gives its name accordingly to this mountain basin. Its largest branch, named Karnali, rises on the *northern* side of the snowy range, near the Manassarowar lake, and enters the territory of Nipal through the Taklakhar pass. In its course towards the plains it traverses the central part of this mountain basin, gathering numerous tributary streams, most of which have *local* names, from all the ridges and intervening valleys by which the country is intersected. On crossing the sandstone range it enters the kingdom of Oudh, and is there known as the Gogra; after quitting the hills it receives numerous small tributaries from the adjacent plains through which it passes, and its volume is still further increased by the waters of the Kali and Rapti, both of which fall into it previous to its junction with the Ganges a little above Dinapore.

3rd. The *Rapti* or *Shingrak* river rises from the western face of the Dewaligiri mountain, converges in its course towards the Karnali, and receives several tributary streams from the adjacent ranges, as well as from the *dhuns* at the foot of the inner range of hills.

After quitting the hills, which it does by a separate pass in the sandstone range, it traverses the north-eastern corner of Oudh, then runs through the centre of the Gorakpur district, having the station of that name on its left bank, and at last pours its waters into the Gogra river.

The western division or basin of the Karnali includes the modern provinces of *Jumla*, *Doti*, and *Suliana*. Until the close of the last century this district was divided into twenty-two separate principalities, which were known *collectively* as the Baisi* Raj, and were all tributary to the Rajah of Jumla.

The names of these Baisi Raj were :—

Jumla.	Darimeka.
Jagwikot.	Doti.
Cham.	Suliana.
Acham.	Bamphi.
Rugam.	Jehari.
Musikot.	Kalagaon.
Roalpa.	Ghoria Kot.
Mallijanta.	Gutam.
Balhang.	Gajur.
Dailik.	

Jumla lies to the N.W. of this division, and extends towards the snows. It is watered by the Karnali river ; and its capital, Chinnachin, stands in a valley somewhat smaller, but of greater elevation above the sea, than the Valley of Nipal. Barley is its staple produce, as rice is that of the Valley of Nipal.

At the present day Jumla is a place of very little importance. It has a rajah, however, who is a man of considerable wealth, and who married a sister of

* From *Bais*, " twenty-two."—(ED.)

the present King of Nipal. Previous to the conquest of the western hills by the Gorkhas, Jumla was the chief of the forty-six principalities into which the country lying between the Kali and the province of Gorkha proper was divided, and all of which were tributary to the Jumla Rajah. The tribute was often only nominal, or consisted of fish, game, &c.; but still it was offered to him as head of the clan, and as a mark of homage and subjection.

These forty-six principalities—twenty-two lying in the basin of the Kali, and twenty-four in the basin of the Gandak—were all conquered and annexed to Nipal by Bahadur Shah towards the close of the last century. The Rajah of Jumla was confined at Kathmandu, and the allegiance of all the tributary chieftains, all of whom were Rajputs, was secured either by hostages at the capital, or by marriages between them and the royal family of the Gorkhas.

The different rajahs of both Chaubisia* and Baisi are still recognised as of royal blood, and receive royal titles. They are all now jagirdars or pensioners of the Gorkha Government, some of their *jagirs* being as large as four or five lakhs of rupees, while others are only worth as many thousands. They have followers of their own, whom they may at any time be called upon to levy and assemble for the public service. Some can collect four hundred or five hundred, others only forty or fifty.

---

* From *Chaubis*, "twenty-four."—(ED.)

Doti is a large and populous province lying to the south-west of Jumla. It is watered by the Karnali river, and is separated from Oudh by the sandstone range, and from Rohilkand by the Kali river.

Its capital—named Doti or Dipait—stands on the inner or second range of hills, and is the headquarters of the governor of the province. The town contains between four hundred and five hundred houses, and is on the left bank of the Sweti-Ganga, one of the tributaries of the Karnali river.

Generally two regiments of infantry and a few guns are stationed at Doti. The town is eighty-five miles N.E. from Bareilly, and about seventy miles S.E. from Almora, and one hundred and sixty-two cos, by the military road, from Kathmandu.

Suliana. This province, with a capital of the same name, lies to the east of Doti, and is watered by the river Rapti.

The town of Suliana is a military station or outpost on the Oudh frontier, and is one hundred and twenty miles due north of Lucknow.

There is an extensive *dhun* connected with Suliana, and lying to the north of the sandstone range, and watered by a branch of the Rapti river, and called Sulianmari.

The town of Pentana is situated towards the interior, fifty miles N.E. of Suliana, and eighty-six kos west of Kathmandu. It is one of the principal Nipalese magazines for manufacture of arms and ammunition. Salpetre abounds in the neighbourhood.

The central division or basin of the Gandak river is bounded on the north by that portion of the snowy range which extends from the Dewaligiri to the Gosainthan mountain, and which is crossed by the Mastang and Kerang passes leading into Tibet. It is bounded on the south by the sandstone range of hills, from the borders of Oudh to the pass of the Baghmatti river, and on the west by the lofty ridge of the Dewaligiri, which separates this division from the basin of the Karnali. Its eastern boundary is formed partly by the Gosainthan with the Dhaibung ridge, which runs due south from it, and partly by the elevated mountain plateau which lies at the base of the Gosainthan, and in the centre of which is the Valley of Nipal proper. This region has been known among the Nipalese, from time immemorial, by the name of Sapt Gandaki, or the country of the Seven Gandaks, in consequence of its containing within its limits all the seven mountain streams which unite, even before they quit the hills, to form the Gandak river. By means of these seven tributaries the Gandak drains off every drop of water from all the hill country lying between the Dewaligiri and the Gosainthan.

These seven streams all arise either directly among the snows or in their immediate neighbourhood. They flow in a southerly direction, converging towards each other rapidly as they approach the plains, and finally unite in the *dhun* or valley which runs on the north side of the sandstone range, into one very large river, which quits the hills at Trebani through a pass called, after it, the Pass of the Gandak, whence it follows a south-easterly course through the British province of Saran, and falls into the Ganges immediately opposite to Patna.

These seven rivers, which are known collectively as the Sapt Gandaki, are, taking them successively from west to east, 1st, the Barigar; 2nd, the Narayani or Saligrami; 3rd, the Sweti-Gandaki; 4th, the Mar-syangdi; 5th, the Daramdi; 6th, the Gandi; and 7th, and most easterly, the Trisulganga.

1st. The *Bharigar river* rises from the eastern face of the Dewaligiri mountain and flows in a S.E. direction, separating the province of Khachi and district of Gulmi on its south from Malibum on its north, till it meets with the Narayani river, with which it unites.

2nd. The *Narayani river* is also called the Salik-rami or Salegram river, in consequence of the number of the sacred stones called salegrams which are found in its bed, and which are particularly abundant near its origin.

The Narayani arises from several sources in the Dewaligiri mountain. Its principal and largest feeder arises either at Muktinath or a little to its north, on the road towards Mastang. It flows southward through the province of Malibum,* till it unites with the Bari-

---

* It flows close past Bini-Shahr, the capital of Malibum; at this place the river is thirty yards wide. There is a large fair held annually (on the 1st of the solar month of May, or about middle of January), at Deo Ghat. It is a sacred spot, and numbers resort there at that time to bathe, &c.

gar. Their united waters, under the name of Kali Gandak, follow a S.E. course, forming the northern boundary to the province of Palpa, and separating it from the district of Garrhun, till they reach the *Dhun* or Valley of Chitaun, where they join the confluence of the other Gandaks at Deo Ghat.

3rd. The *Sweta* (or *Saita*) *Gandaki river* rises in the snowy range to the east of the Mastang pass at a mountain called Machia Puchar, or the Fish's Tail. It flows nearly due south, having the districts of Satahung and Garhung on its western or right bank, and those of Lamjung and Tanhung on its eastern or left bank. It joins the Trisulganga at Kaiphul Ghat near Deo Ghat.

4th. The *Marsiangdi river* rises in the Rui Bhot ridge of the snowy range, at Lakwa Bassiari, north of Lamjung and N.W. of Gorkha, and follows a southward course, nearly parallel to the Swetiganga, till it falls into the Trisulganga near Deo Ghat. The Marsiangdi forms the western, as the Trisulganga river does the eastern, boundary to the province of Gorkha, which is separated by it from the districts of Lamjung and Tanhung.

5th. The *Daramdi river* rises in the snow, on Mount Taku, to the west of Mount Mala, north of Gorkha, and flows southerly through that province till it joins the Gandi river at Dhurbang Ghat.

6th. The *Gandi river* rises in the snowy range at Mount Mala, flows through Gorkha, and, after its union with the Daramdi, falls into the Trisulganga.

7th. The *Trisul* or *Trisulganga river* is the most easterly of the seven branches of the Gandak river. It arises from the largest of twenty-two lakes or *kunds* which lie embosomed in a hollow or valley immediately below the highest peaks of the Gosainthan mountain, and at an elevation of not less than thirteen thousand or fourteen thousand feet above the sea.

On the north side of this gorge the rocks rise precipitously from the edge of the lakes, and their crests are sprinkled with perpetual snow; while on the opposite side is the wide-spreading base of the lofty Jibjibia, the main spur or ridge of which runs due south, acting as a watershed between the most eastern sources of the Gandak and the most western sources of the Kosi river, till it terminates in the bluff and rugged mountain, about fifteen thousand feet in height, which directly overlooks the Valley of Nipal. The largest of these lakes is called Gosain-kund, or sometimes Nilkhiat-kund, after Mahadeo Nilkhiat (Blue neck), to whose honour it is sacred. To worship a rock which is thought by the pious to represent that deity, and to bathe in the sacred lake in which that rock is sunk, many hundreds of pilgrims annually resort to Gosainthan in the months of July, August, and September, at which period the passes are open in consequence of the greater part of the preceding winter's snow having melted away during the summer heats. The journey, however, to Gosainthan is always a difficult, and sometimes a dangerous one. Avalanches are not uncommon from the melting of the snow; and many a pilgrim has been buried beneath them. The road is narrow, precipitous, and in many places exceedingly slippery. The cold is often intense, and there is no kind of accommodation on which travellers can rely, as the huts of the Bhotiyas who live in these districts are quite insufficient for the numbers who throng towards the sacred lakes. They have to sleep in caves, under trees, or in temporary sheds, and many who are old or infirm either perish during the journey, or die from its effects soon after their return to Nipal.

The name " Gosainthan " ought to be confined to the rocky gorge or hollow in which the Nilkhiat-kund and other lakes are situated. But it is commonly applied to the whole mass of peaks and ridges, including Dhaibang and Jibjibia, which lie due north of the Valley of Nipal, and which embrace that part of the snowy range which extends between the Kerang and Kuti passes. The highest peak of this vast mountain mass is called Deoralli, and it is twenty-four thousand seven hundred feet above the level of the sea. It is very distinctly visible, not only from Nipal, but from the adjacent plains of India.

In one of the large rocks on the northern edge of the Gosain-kund are three deep clefts, from each of which a spring pours its waters in a perpetual cascade into the lake which lies about thirty feet below. The three cascades are called Trisul-dhara (*dhara* means a *small* stream or jet of water; *chehro* a *large* one).

These three springs and the lake beneath them are fabled to have been formed by Shiva Mahadeo, who, when the gods churned the ocean in order to obtain from it the water of immortality, had drunk the poison which arose from the sea during the operation. This made him fall into a swoon, which would have proved fatal had not Durga revived him by the use of certain incantations.

This poison, though it did not destroy the god, produced the most excessive pain and thirst, and caused a permanent blue discolouration of his neck, whence he received the name of Nilkhiat, or the Blue-throated. Hoping to relieve his sufferings, and allay the burning fever which consumed him, Mahadeo repaired to the snow in this secluded region, and thrusting his trident or *trisul* into the mountain side, three streams of water immediately gushed forth.

Their waters collecting in the hollow beneath, produced a lake, which was called, after the god, the Lake of Nilkhiat. Mahadeo stretched himself along its edge, and assuaged his thirst by drinking its waters.

Near the centre of the Gosain-kund, or Lake of Nilkhiat, is a large, tawny-coloured rock, of an oval shape, the rounded top of which can be seen sunk a foot or more beneath the surface of the tranquil and transparent water. The pious worshippers of Shiva, as they stand on the edge of the sacred lake, look on this unhewn rock as a divinely carved representation of Mahadeo, and fancy they can trace out in it the figure of the deity reclining full length upon a bed of serpents. This rock must have been deposited in its present position when the lake was filled by an ancient glacier; and sunk as it is in the centre of the ice-cold waters, it can never have been touched by mortal hands.

The only sculptured figures of any kind at Gosainthan are a small figure of Naraga (about eighteen inches high); a small bull, kneeling; and the pillars which originally supported a bell, but the bell itself is gone. These all stand together at the edge of the water on the south side of the lake. There is no kind of carving or representation of Shiva in any part of the whole Gosainthan. On the road, near Chandanbari, is a small *uncarved* stone, a foot high, which is worshipped as Ganesha, and is called Lauri-Vinnaik.

The Betravati river rises from one of the lakes of Gosainthan, to the north of Surajkund; it flows between Dhaibang and Jibjibia, turns round along the southern base of the former, and falls into the Trisul, opposite its western shoulder, and eight miles above Nayakot.

In consequence of the tradition that the three springs were caused by Mahadeo's *trisul* (or trident), the river which rises in the lake is called the Trisulganga, or Trisulgandaki.

From its origin in the Gosainthan the Trisulganga follows generally a south-westerly course, flowing between the province of Gorkha on its right, and the territory of Nipal proper on its left bank. It receives a tributary stream—the Rassua Naddi—from the neighbourhood of the Kerang pass, and is joined by the Bura-Gandak river, just below Ramcha; while three or four miles below that town it is joined by its sister stream, the Tadi. The Tadi, also called the Suryavati, rises in the Surya-kund, or Fountain of the Sun, which is the most easterly of all the twenty-two lakes of Gosainthan, and is between two and three miles distance from the Gosainthan-kund, in which the Trisul has its source. The Tadi follows at first a somewhat easterly course, then turns to the west, washing the southern base of Jibjibia; while by its tributaries—the Likhu and Sindura streams—it drains the northern face of Sheopur and Bhirbandi, and winding through the Valley of Nayakot, falls into the Trisulganga at Devi Ghat. Its length, from its source to Devi Ghat, is about thirty miles, and it runs for the greater part of its extent through richly cultivated, though malarious, valleys. The Tadi is a rapid but shallow stream through the greater part of its course, but as it approaches Devi Ghat it becomes confined within a deep and rocky channel, through which it dashes with resistless force.

A bridge has several times been constructed over the Tadi near its confluence with the Trisul, but it has in every instance been swept away during the rains by the violence of the swollen torrent; and the attempt is not likely to be renewed.

In the neighbourhood of Nayakot the Trisulganga is a narrow but deep and very rapid stream. It flows

in a rocky channel between thickly wooded mountains, which rise almost precipitately from its shores,
and not, like the Tadi, through wide and cultivated
valleys. Three or four miles above its confluence
with the Tadi, at Devi Ghat, it is crossed by a *sangah*
or wooden bridge, over which runs the high road
from Kathmandu to Gorkha. The bridge, however,
is most strictly guarded by a company of sepoys, and
no one from Gorkha or Nipal is allowed to cross it
without previously obtaining a passport of permission
from the Minister. In the rains the waters of the
Trisul, as well as of the Tadi, rise very quickly, and
the huge boulders and masses of rock, evidently
rounded by friction and the action of water, which
lie strewed about the shores of both rivers at Devi
Ghat, show the enormous power of the swollen torrents
which lodged them in their present situation. At Devi
Ghat there is a small hamlet, consisting of a *powa* and
a few cottages, which is deserted from April to November by all but a few fishermen and potters (Manjhis, Kumhars, &c.) who belong to a race that dwells
all the year round with perfect impunity in the most
malarious valleys of the Himalayas. There is a ferry
over the river, but no passengers, travellers, or merchants are allowed to cross from one side to the other
without a passport from the Minister. A good many
people pass backwards and forwards during the day,
paying one pice a-piece, both here and over the *sangah*
on the Trisul; but they are the inhabitants of the
little villages in the immediate neighbourhood, going

on local business, and are all personally known to the master of the ferry.

Although Devi Ghat is a very holy spot, and is under the special protection of Devi Bhairavi, the guardian deity of the district, yet it contains no temple to the goddess. At the point where the waters of the two rivers unite, there is merely a rude and primitive shrine in her honour, composed of a heap of unhewn stones, which is temporarily walled in each season by some planks of wood, to protect it from the gaze of the profane. The Temple of Bhairavi stands in the town of Nayakot, having been erected there instead of at the confluence of the sacred streams, by the express desire of the goddess herself, in order to save her worshippers from being exposed to the violence of the deluge which occasionally bursts over Devi Ghat when the Tadi and Trisul overflow their banks.

The Valley of Nayakot is elevated only two thousand feet above the level of the sea, and Devi Ghat must be somewhat lower still. As the lakes from which the Tadi and Trisul arise are situated only just beneath the line of perpetual snow, there must be upwards of ten thousand feet of descent for those rivers in a distance of only thirty miles, from their origin in the snow to their junction at Devi Ghat. This will account for the rapidity of their stream, and for the sudden manner in which they sometimes swell into vast torrents, either from any excess of rain or from the melting of the glaciers beneath which they arise.

From Devi Ghat the Trisulganga flows in a south-westerly direction towards the plains, and forms the eastern boundary to the province of Gorkha, from which it receives the Gandi and Marsiangdi rivers; while it is also joined in its course by several feeders (among others, by the Kulpu and Mahais streams, which arise on the western face of Mount Nayarjun) from the western side of the hills of Nipal proper, which lie along its left or eastern bank. After a course of from eighty to ninety miles from Devi Ghat, the Trisulganga unites at or near Deo Ghat with the Sweta-Gandaki and Narayani in the common confluence of all the branches of the Great Gandak river.

There is a road leading to the plains from Devi Ghat to Deo Ghat, which runs along the left or eastern bank of the Trisulganga. The jealousy of the Nipalese, and their fear lest in case of war it might be used as a mode of approach to the capital from the Gorakpur direction, makes this road a closed one, and no general traffic is allowed along it. Shikaris, who in the autumn bring quail and other game from the Gorakpur terai for the use of the *darbar*, travel along this road as being the shortest and most direct.

From Deo Ghat the Great Gandak river, having united the waters of its seven mountain branches, flows nearly due south, and quits the hills at Trebani through a pass in the sandstone range to the west of the Someshwar ridge. Before reaching the sandstone range it receives tributary feeders from the *dhuns* or valleys which run east and west between the first and second ranges of hills, and which are crossed by the Gandak in its passage towards the plains.

The most important of these is the little Rapti river, which, rising near Bhamphedi, flows in a westerly direction past Hatowara, through the Valley or *Dhun* of Chitaun, and falls into the Gandak river fifteen miles north of the Someshwar ridge.

The hill country watered by these seven branches of the Gandak river occupies the central of the three natural divisions of the kingdom of Nipal. Till towards the close of the last century it included within its limits, besides the kingdom of Gorkha proper, twenty-four other independent principalities, collectively called the Raj Chaubisia, all ruled over by Rajput princes, and all tributary to the Rajah of Jumlah.

The names of the Chaubisia Raj were—

Lumjung, or Lamjung.	Gulmi.
Tannahung.	West Nayakot.
Gulkot.	Khanchi, or Khachi.
Malibum.	Isma. ⎫ On southern
Satahung.	Dharkot. ⎬ or right bank
Garrhung.	Musikot. ⎭ of Barigar R.
Pokhra.	Thilli.
Bharkot.	Saliana.
Resing.	Wigha.
Ghering.	Paison.
Dhoar.	Lattahun.
Palpa.	Kashki.
Butul.	Dang.
Tansen.	Parthana.

These petty states were all quickly over-run and
absorbed by the Gorkhas shortly after their conquest
of the Valley of Nipal. The exact and ancient limits
of each principality are now unknown, and the knowledge, if we possessed it, would not be of either interest
or value.

The Gorkhas have divided the whole tract of country
forming the basin of the Gandak into four large provinces, in one or other of which all the ancient principalities are included. These provinces are—1st,
Malibum, to the north-west; 2nd, Khachi, to the
south-west; 3rd, Palpa, to the south; 4th, Gorkha,
to the north and east.

1st. *Malibum* is a large province lying close below
the snowy range, and overlooked directly by the Daula-
giri mountain. It extends southwards to the banks of
the Barigar river. Its capital is Bini-Shahr, a large
town on the Narayani river, and four days' march
from Muktinath in the Mastang pass. Malibum is
watered by the Narayani; towards the east it includes
the ancient chiefdoms of Satahung and Garrhung,
which lie on the right or western bank of the
Sweta-Gandaki river.

2nd. *Khachi* lies to the south-west of this division,
between the sandstone range on the south, which
separates it from the Nipalese western terai, and the
Barigar river on its north, which separates it from
Malibum. On the east it adjoins the province of
Palpa, and on the west that of Suliana, in the basin
of the Gogra river. A considerable portion of Khachi

lies in the *dhuns* or valleys which extend east and west between the first and second ranges of hills.

3rd. *Province of Palpa*, the most important, if not the most extensive, district in either of the three great divisions of Nipal. It lies along the borders of the British territory of Gorakpur, and is bounded on the north by the Narayani or Kali Gandak river, which separates it from the districts of Garrhung and Pokhra, which are situated between Palpa and Gorkha. On the south it is bounded by the sandstone range of hills, from the borders of Oudh to the Pass of the Great Gandak river. On the west it adjoins Khachi; and on the east it is limited by the Great Gandak river, which separates it from the district of Chitaun.

It has a considerable tract of lowland, forming the Terai of Betul, or " Butul Khas," attached to it. This slip of terai is bounded on the north by the sandstone range, and extends from Pali, a few miles to west of the Gandak, eastward to Tulsipur, on the frontier of Oudh. It lies due north of Gorakpur.

The Sal forest clothes the southern face and foot of the hills; but beyond it and to south of it the country is comparatively open and swampy, and is covered by extensive plains of long grass and occasional large patches of cultivation. It is intersected by numerous *nallahs* or beds of streams which in the rains flow down from the outer hills and fall into the Rapti. For some miles on each side of the Gandak river after it enters the plains the country is open and mostly covered with grass; its level is low, but there is no continuous forest either upon or below the hills. Patches even of sal forest and bamboo jungle do not appear for several miles either to the east or west.

The town of Butul is situated in the mouth of a pass leading across the sandstone range, and connecting the lowlands of the Terai with the *dhuns* and lower hills forming the province of Palpa.

Palpa and Butul were originally two separate principalities; they were afterwards united under one independent Rajput prince, who, having conquered Butul, added it to his hereditary possessions of Palpa. The lands of Butul, though conquered and annexed, were yet held in fief, or paid an annual sum, first to Oudh, and afterwards, by transfer, to the British.

During the regency of Rani Rajendra Lachmi towards the close of last century the hill country of Palpa was conquered and annexed to Nipal. The rajah retreated to Butul, but was subsequently induced, under false promises of redress, to visit Kathmandu, where he was put to death, and his territories in Butul seized and occupied by the Gorkhas. Their ill^gal occupation from 1804 till 1812 of the Terai of Butul, which was under British protection, was one of the aggressions which led to the Nipal war in 1814.

Several of the ancient small principalities are included within the limits of the modern province of Palpa. Of these Gulmi is one. The town of Gulmi lies seven kos (twenty miles) north-west of the city of Palpa, and is situated on a branch of the Barigar river. On the conquest of Gulmi the daughter of the rajah was married to Ran Bahadur, while Bahadur Shah married a daughter of the conquered Palpa rajah; in each case the victor making his bride a hostage for the loyalty and allegiance of her father.

West Nayakot, a district on the west bank of the Gandak, and so called to distinguish it from East Nayakot on the Trisul and Tadi below Gosainthan, was another of the principalities of the Chaubisia which is now included within the province of Palpa. It is of some historical interest as having been the country in which the Rajput ancestors of the present race of Gorkhas first settled when they were driven by Musalman persecution from the plains of Hindustan in the twelfth century. From Nayakot they advanced towards Lamjung on the Sweta-Gandaki, whence they swarmed eastward, and spread over and permanently established themselves in the country of Gorkha. The town of Palpa, the capital of the district, stands on the second or minor range of hills. It is sixty-three kos from Kathmandu, and nine kos N.N.W. of town of Betul.

Five miles east of Palpa is the city of Tansen, formerly a petty chiefdom, now the chief military station of the province of Palpa. It is the headquarters of three regiments of one thousand five hundred sepoys, who are under the command of the governor of the province. The governorship, being a responsible and lucrative appointment, is always conferred upon a sirdar of some importance, and generally upon a near relation of the Premier of the day.

Tansen has a *darbar* and a market-place, and also a mint, where copper pieces are coined. Cotton cloths of various sorts are made and sold in considerable quantities in this neighbourhood by the Gurangs, a tribe who abound throughout the province of Palpa.

CHAPTER III.

PROVINCES OF NIPAL (*continued*).

THE province of Gorkha is situated in the north-eastern portion of the basin of the Gandak. It includes the whole tract of country lying between the Marsiangdi and the Trisulganga rivers. These two streams, rising in the snows, a considerable distance apart—one near the Mastang pass, the other near that of Kerang—and converging towards each other in their course through the hills, until they unite with the Kali Gandak near Deo Ghat, enclose between them a delta or triangle, the northern side or base of which is formed by the snowy range, while the Marsiangdi bounds it on the west and separates it from the districts of Lamjung, Tanhang, and Pokhra, and the Trisulganga on the east flows between it and the territories of Nipal proper. The Daramdi and Gandi rivers both flow through the province of Gorkha in their course to join the Trisulganga. The *city of Gorkha*, the capital of the province, is situated on the Hanumanbanjang mountain on the eastern or southern or left bank of the Daramdi river. It contains about two thousand houses, and is twenty-six kos from Kathmandu by the ordinary or Nayakot road. It has a palace or *darbar*, but it is just falling into ruins.

The ancestors of the present race of Gorkhas derived their national name of *Gorkhali* from this province or district, in which they first established themselves as an independent power. The term *Gorkha* is not limited to any particular class or caste; it is applied to all those whose ancestors inhabited the country of Gorkha, and who from it, as a fatherland, subsequently extended their conquests far and wide over the eastern and western hills.

The men of Doti, Jumlah, Malibum, and other western districts in the Nipal and *Kamaon* hills are "Parbattiahs" or Highlanders, but they are not Gorkhas.

Among the *Gorkhas*, or descendants of those who quitted Gorkha with Prithi Narayan, are men of all castes, and some of no caste at all. Besides Brahmans, Kshatriyas, Magyars and Gurungs,—who constitute the military classes,—the *Damais*, or tailors and bandmen, the *Kamais*, or ironmongers, and the *Sarkis*, or shoemakers, though all *out*castes, are admitted as *genuine Gorkhas*, because their ancestors were natives of that district. ‑

The term "Parbattiah" is applied only to the tribes dwelling to the *west* of the Valley of Nipal; the

Niwars, Kiruts, Limbus, and other eastern tribes are never called Parbattiahs.

It is a mistake to call the inhabitants of Kamaon, and the other western hills, from whom our Sarmur and other battalions are mostly recruited, *Gorkhas.* Their fatherlands were parts of the Gorkha dominions, having been annexed by conquest; but the inhabitants of those hills were Parbattiahs, never Gorkhas.

To the south-west of the province of Gorkha, in the direction of Palpa, and not far from the foot of the inner range of hills, is the *Valley of Pokhra,* with a capital city of the same name, which is fourteen marches distant from Kathmandu.

Pokhra is situated on the Swetagandaki river, and lies between Satahung on its west and Tanhung on its east. Previous to its conquest by the Gorkhas it was one of the twenty-four petty but independent principalities which occupied the greater part of the country of the seven Gandak rivers.

The city of Pokhra is large and well inhabited; it is famous for its copper manufactures, and it has a large annual fair, at which these, as well as supplies of grain and all productions of the district, are sold.

The Valley of Pokhra is much larger than the Valley of Nipal. It contains several large lakes, from which circumstance it derives its name—the term Pokhra, or Pokhri, meaning a tank, or piece of *standing* water. The largest of these lakes is said to be two days' journey round. Unfortunately the level of the water in these lakes is so much below that of the surface of

the valley (generally from one hundred and fifty feet
to two hundred feet) that they cannot be used for
purposes of irrigation. The surface of the valley is
more level than that of Nipal, and is not so much cut
up by ravines or watercourses ; but from the scarcity
of water for irrigation these natural advantages cannot
be much made use of, and a large part of the valley
is under little or no cultivation.

Jang Bahadur calculated that if, by power of steam
in working pumps, &c., the water of these lakes were
made available for general irrigation, and the whole
valley were brought under regular cultivation, it would
yield an annual income of five or six lakhs of rupees.
Jang would willingly have incurred the expense of
bringing this about ; but it would require an accu-
rate survey made by an engineer on the spot, who
would have to superintend the entire operations, and
this is a measure to which Nipalese jealousy, and their
fear of the resources of the country being exposed to
foreigners, would never consent.

The *dhuns* or valleys at the foot of the hill country
of the seven Gandaks are very extensive.

All these sub-Himalayan valleys or *dhuns*, in the
western hills as well as in Nipal, lie along the north
side of the sandstone range, running parallel to it,
and between it and the second or inner range of
hills. They have an average breadth of from five to
ten miles and an average length of from twenty to
forty miles. Each is traversed by a stream which rises
generally in the lower hills, winds its way through the

centre of the valley during its entire length, and ultimately falls into the main river of that mountain district at or a few miles to the north of the pass by which that river quits the hills for the plains. The soil of these *dhuns* is alluvial and is covered with a rich coating of vegetable mould, which is susceptible of very high cultivation. In Nipal the *dhuns* have been mostly allowed to fall into a state of jungle, and are consequently clothed with forests of sal and cotton trees, and are inhabited only by wild beasts. The Nipalese are averse to the " clearing " of these forests, as they look upon the malarious jungle at the foot of their hills as the safest and surest barrier against the advance of any army of invasion from the plains of Hindustan.

To the west of the Great Gandak river, previous to its quitting the hills, is the *dhun* or valley which lies between Palpa on the inner and Betul on the outer or sandstone range, and which is called Gongtali-mari, from the name of the stream by which it is drained.

To the east of the Gandak is the *dhun* of Chitaun (known as Chitaun-mari); and still further northward, and continuous with it, is the *dhun* or valley which lies below Makwanpur, which is called Makwan-mari. Both these *maris* or *dhuns* are watered by the Little Rapti river and its tributaries.

The *Little Rapti river* (called *Little* to distinguish it from the *Great* Rapti to the west, on which Gorakpur is situated) rises from the inner or second range of hills, in a glen below the Sisapani mountain, a little to the east of Bhimphedi, from which place it is separated by a low ridge of hills.

It follows a very tortuous course, winding through a narrow valley, having steep and thickly wooded hills on each side, till it reaches Hetowara, where the hills fall back, and the valley, as well as the river, acquires a considerable breadth. From its source to Hetowara —a distance of fifteen miles—it is a shallow, narrow, but very rapid stream, flowing over a rocky bed, and constantly fretted and interrupted by large boulders and masses of stone. During the periodical rains the Rapti quickly swells into a deep and impetuous torrent.

About a mile and a half below Hetowara, which stands on its left or south-eastern bank, it is joined by the Karrah river. The Karrah is a shallow and narrow stream, which rises in the low range of hills on which the fort of Makwanpur is situated, descends into the valley or *dhun* which lies below the fort, and which is called Makwan-mari, and winds through the entire length of that valley—a distance of about ten miles— till it joins the Rapti below Hetowara. The Karrah stream contains numbers of fish, but the water, though very clear, is not considered by the natives to be good or wholesome. This, they say, depends partly on its channel lying in an alluvial and not in a rocky soil ; but mainly on its banks being for the most part so over-hung by jungle, that its waters are constantly impreg-nated with decomposing vegetable matter. The waters of the Rapti, which flow in a rocky channel, are remarkable for their coldness, purity, and wholesomeness.

After being joined by the Karrah stream, the Rapti flows due west through the district of Chitaun (Chitaunmari), and falls into the Gandak river about fifteen miles to the north of the Someshwar ridge of the Cheryaghati range of hills.

The *dhun* of Chitaun (Chitaunmari) is of considerable extent, and derives its name from the town of Chitaun, which is situated on the right bank of the Rapti, about twenty-five to thirty miles below Hetowara, at or near the point where it is joined by the Mantaura river, a tributary stream of considerable size, which flows through the lower hills to the north-east of Chitaun.

The district about Chitaun is open, and covered with long grass jungle rather than forest, and is very much infested with rhinoceros. It is the best shooting ground for the rhinoceros in the whole of the Nipalese *dhuns*.

Previous to the first Nipal war, the *dhuns* of Chitaun and Makwanpur were extensively cultivated; but since the peace of 1816 the Gorkha Government, from motives of policy, have caused the inhabitants to abandon the greater part of them, and they have been allowed to revert to their natural state of forest and grass jungle.

A continuous high road, along which troops can march and light guns be carried, traverses the whole extent of the central and western provinces of Nipal,

4

connecting together the principal towns which lie scattered among the hills from the capital to the borders of Kamaon. Starting from Kathmandu, this road runs through

  Nayakot;
  Gorkha;
  Tannahung, with branch to Lamjang, on the north ;
  Pokhra;
  Satahung;
  Tansen;
  Palpa, with branch to Betul, on the south ;
  Gulmi;
  Pentana ;
  Saliana ;
  Doti or Dipaet, with a branch to Jagarkot and
    Jumlah.

The *eastern* of the three great natural divisions of Nipal includes the whole of the region watered by the mountain tributaries of the Kosi river. In consequence of its containing within its limits, and having the whole of its waters drained off by, the seven branches of the Kosi, it is called the Sapt Kosiki, or country of the seven Kosis. This division is bounded on the north by that portion of the snowy range which extends from Gosainthan to Kinchinjanga, and which is crossed by the Kuti, Hatia, and Wallang passes. Its western boundary is formed by the Dhaibang ridge of the Gosainthan (which acts as a watershed between the basin of the Kosi and that of the Gandak) and by the whole of the district of Nipal proper. On the east it is separated from Sikkim by the Singilela ridge of the Kinchinjanga, and by the Michi river; and on the south the sandstone range of hills separates it from the Terai and the district of Morung.

The seven Kosi rivers are the following, taking them successively from west to east :—

1st, the Milamchi; 2nd, the Bhotia Kosi; 3rd, the Tamba Kosi; 4th, the Likhu; 5th, the Dudkosi; 6th, the Aran; and, 7th, the Tamor. These streams all rise in the neighbourhood of the snows; in their course through the hills they run nearly parallel to each other, but as they approach the lower range they suddenly converge towards a common point of confluence at Varsha Kshattra or Bara Chattra, from which place their united waters roll on in one large river, which enters the plains through a pass in the sandstone range. On leaving the hills the Kosi separates the Terai proper, which lies on its right bank, from the Nipalese province of the Morung, which lies on its left, and then entering the British territory, it flows through the district of Parniah, and falls into the Ganges a little below Baglipur, and opposite to the north-east shoulder of the range of Rajmahal hills.

1st. The *Milamchi*, or *Indiani river*,* rises from the eastern side of Gosainthan and from the Jibjibia

---

* It is called by the Gorkhas at present the *Indiani*.

4 *

ridge. It flows in a south-easterly direction to the west of Mount Sipa, and washing the base of the hills which form the eastern boundary of the Valley of Nipal, receives a tributary stream from the Banepa valley, and unites with the Bhotia Kosi at Dholat Ghat.

2nd. The *Bhotia Kosi river* rises in Tibet, in the plain of Tingri; it flows, first, in a south-west direction through the Kuti pass, whence it turns towards the south, and unites with the Milamchi. The river formed by their union is called the Sankosi; it flows south-east till it joins in the confluence of the Aran and Tambur at Bara Chattra Ghat.

3rd. The *Tamba Kosi;* 4th, the *Likhu;* and, 5th, the *Dud Kosi,* all rise in the snowy range between the Kuti and Hatia passes; they flow in a south-westerly direction, nearly parallel to each other, and all fall into the Sankosi river, which thus unites into its single stream the waters of five out of the seven Kosis of the country.

6th. The *Aran river* is by far the largest of all the rivers in this mountain basin. It rises from several sources, some of which are on the north or Tibetan, as well as on the southern side of the snowy range.

On the north or Tibetan side of the first range of snowy mountains it has one source in the Valley of Tingri, not far from the origin of the Bhotia Kosi. This branch follows a very circuitous course before it reaches the Hatia pass. It has several other branches, which arise from the wilderness of Damsen,—a wild and rugged region, which Hooker estimates at from sixteen thousand to eighteen thousand feet above the sea, and which stretches east and west between the first and second ranges of the snowy mountains, and lies to the south, or immediately beneath the Kambela or great range which forms the southern boundary of the vast valley of the Yaru' or Sanpu river, on the banks of which Digarchi and Lhassa are situated.

While still in Tibet these branches unite into one river,—the Aran,—which enters Nipal through the Hatia pass, flows through the hills in a southerly direction, receiving numerous tributaries in its course, and finally, when it approaches the plains, unites with the Sankosi and Tamor rivers at Bara Chattra Ghat, twenty miles north-west of the town of Bijapur.

7th. The *Tamor* or *Tambur river* rises from the western base and the Singilela ridge of the Kinchin-janga mountain. It flows in a south-westerly direction, and unites with the Aran and Sankosi at Bara Chattra Ghat.

The hill country constituting the basin of the Kosi river, is divided into two provinces or districts by the Aran river. The district lying on the right bank of the Aran, and extending between it and the Dud Kosi, is the country of the Kirantis,—a hill tribe of low-caste Hindus, who once possessed considerable power and territory in these eastern hills, but were speedily reduced to submission by Prithi Narayan after his conquest of Nipal.

The country of the Kirantis and Limbus at the

present time is divided into fifty-two small subahships ; each subah governing and being responsible for four or five villages, and able to raise generally, if required for the public service, about ten men from each village under his control.

The district lying on the eastern or left bank of the Aran, and extending from it to Sikkim, is Limbuana, or the country of the Limbus, another tribe of low-caste Hindus. It formerly belonged to Sikkim, but it was conquered and permanently annexed to Nipal by Prithi Narayan. Previous to the Gorkha conquest of the Valley of Nipal, the territories of the Niwar kings of Bhatgaon extended eastward to the Dud Kosi river, which formed the boundary between the country of the Niwars and the country of the Kirantis.

Below the inner hills, and on the northern face of the sandstone range, is the *dhun* of Bijapur, called Bijapur-mari, from the town of Bijapur, which is situated on its southern border. It is traversed lengthways by a stream which falls into the Kosi before it quits the hills.

The sandstone hills east of the Kosi river subside in elevation, and are so much interrupted, that they no longer form a continuous range.

The sandstone range separates the hill country of the seven Kosis from the long narrow strip of forest and lowland which constitutes the Terai of Nipal, and which stretches along the foot of the hills for upwards of two hundred miles.

This Terai extends from the Oreka Naddi on the west to the Michi on the east,—a distance of about two hundred and twenty miles. It is bounded on the north by the Cheryaghati range of hills, and on the south its limits are marked by a series of eight pillars erected along the whole length of the frontier line which separates the territory of Nipal from the British district of Parniah, Tirhut, and Champaran. Its greatest breadth nowhere exceeds thirty miles; in its narrowest part, where it is traversed by the Kosi river, it is only twelve miles across; its average breadth is about twenty miles. The Terai consists throughout its entire length of two very distinct portions,—these are the Sal forest, and the open and cultivated lowland to which the name of Terai proper should be restricted.

The *Bhavar* or *Sal forest* is a long belt of tree-jungle which covers the southern side of the Cheryaghati range throughout its entire length from the pass of the Gandak to the pass of the Kosi river. It varies in depth in different parts, but has an average width of from five to ten miles.

Westward of Bissaulia the forest rapidly diminishes in width, until, as it approaches the Gandak river, it disappears for a time altogether. The forest is almost uninhabited.

Along the foot of the hills, sometimes on the edge, sometimes on banks of streams, in the heart of the forest, small patches of cultivation are scattered about where the jungle has been cleared and little hamlets

or villages have been formed, which are thinly inhabited by certain tribes of low-caste Hindus, who
manage to live here throughout the year, and who
brave with impunity the deadly malaria and the
savage beasts with which these districts are infested.
These people follow the calling of agriculturists, of
potters, and, where the neighbourhood of rivers allows
it, of ferrymen or fishermen. They live " from hand
to mouth"; they grow a little rice and grain, but
scarcely enough for their own consumption; and they
get occasional but uncertain supplies of animal food
from. the carcases of cattle which die, as well as by
catching fish, and hunting the wild pigs and deer
which abound in the forest. Though they probably
belong to the same original stock as the natives of the
adjacent plains of Hindustan, yet their continued residence for many successive generations in the most
unhealthy and malarious districts, as well as their
scanty food and their system of only marrying among
themselves, has caused the "breed" to deteriorate
most painfully; and whoever their early ancestors may
have been, these aboriginal inhabitants of the Terai
are, at the present day, a puny, badly developed, and
miserable-looking race. Living almost in a state of
nature, they never appear to suffer from any exposure
to the weather, and to be entirely exempt from all
danger of jungle fever; and though they look half-
starved, and as if they were deficient in muscle and
bone, yet they are capable of undergoing very considerable exertion and fatigue. This is shown by their

supplying not only the class of dale runners, but also the mahouts and others who during the hot and rainy months are employed in the dangerous and difficult business of catching wild elephants. They seem to combine the activity of an animal with the cunning and craftiness so characteristic of the human savage.

The Sal forest, as its name implies, abounds chiefly in sal trees, but it contains also very many sissu and lemel trees, as well as a considerable number of firs (the *pinus longifolia*, or *chil* of the North-West Provinces, and *dhup* of Nipal), many of large size, along the sides and crest of the Cheryaghati range.

On the outskirts of the forest portions of jungle are, from time to time, "cleared," and the hitherto uncultivated land becomes absorbed into the open terai.

By this process of "reclaiming" land, which is constantly going on to a greater or less degree, not only does the forest become gradually diminished in its width, but the amount of land under cultivation in the open terai is steadily but slowly increasing in extent, and consequently in value also.

Between the Gandak on the west and the Michi on the east, the forest is crossed by several rivers. The Baghmatti, the Kosi, and the Konkayi, or Konki, are the only ones of any considerable size. Except the Kosi, all the rivers which cross the terai are fordable during the dry months of the year. The Kosi is never fordable at any season. Numerous small streams rise in the Cheryaghati range, and flow

through the forest into the open terai, where they
fall into one or other of the larger rivers. During the
rains these streams often acquire a very considerable
volume; but during the greater part of the year they
are either altogether dried up, leaving their channels
as mere empty nullahs or ravines, or else their waters
are so much reduced in bulk, that, after trickling
along the descent of the hills, on reaching the verge
of the forest they disappear, and finding their way by
subterranean courses, reappear on- the inner edge of
the open terai.

This is the case with the Bichaliola Naddi, which
rises a little to the west of the principal pass in the
Cheryaghati range, trickles down its wide and stony
bed, along which the high road to Kathmandu runs
for about six miles, and about two miles after it has
passed Bichako disappears in the sandy soil, and
emerges again at the outer margin of the forest, about
a mile's distance to the north-east of Bissaulia, whence
it flows on as a rather wide stream, and falls into the
Sikrana river.

During the greater part of the year the open channel
of this stream is a mere dry nallah; no water passes
along it, until, from the swelling of the stream during
the rains, the underground passage is overflowed, and
then the surplus waters flow along the open bed of the
river through the forest.

The *Terai proper*, consisting of the lowlands lying
outside and to the south of the Sál forest, has an
average width of from ten to fifteen miles. It is

widest towards the west, between the Oreka and the Kumla streams; from the Kumla eastward to the Kosi it gradually becomes narrower; and in the Morung, from the Kosi to the Michi river, it does not exceed five miles in breadth.

Strictly speaking there is no open terai in the Morung,—the open land to the south of the forest, and which has now an average width of five miles, originally having formed part of the forest itself, and having been gradually brought under cultivation by steady and constant efforts at clearing and reclaiming the jungle.

The whole Terai, including the Morung, forms, for administrative purposes, one large "non-regulation" province, and is under the government of a single high officer of state—usually a near relative to the Premier—at the present day* a brother of Jang Bahadur. His residence is at Khatta Banga, a few miles east of Bissaulia, where two regiments of the line are stationed under his command. The Kosi river, which flows from the hills in a direction north and south, divides the Terai into two provinces—a western and an eastern. That portion which lies on the right bank of the river is the Terai proper, and extends from the Kosi westward to the Oreka stream. That which is on the left bank constitutes the Eastern Terai, or the Morung, and extends from the Kosi eastward to

---

* Viz. 1858.

the Michi river. With the exception of occasional patches, as around ruins of Simraun, or spurs running out from the forest, the whole Terai west of the Kosi is cleared of jungle. It is thickly inhabited throughout the year by Tharus, &c., and swarms with cattle which are brought there to graze. The majority of its population are migratory; they dwell in the Terai during the cold months, and retreat either to the hills or to the adjacent plains of Hindustan during the unhealthy period of the year. The Terai west of the Kosi river is divided, for fiscal and judicial purposes, into four *zillahs* or districts.

These are, from west to east:—

1st. *Barah and Parsa.* Through this district the high road runs to Kathmandu from the plains. Parsa, where a detachment under Captain Sibly was defeated with the loss of two guns in January 1815, is close to the present Bissaulia.

2nd. *Rochat* extends from the limits of the Barah-Parsa district eastward to the right bank of the Baghmatti river.

In the district of Rochat, on the left bank of the Jamni Naddi, and upon the frontier, fifteen miles west of Baghmatti, and the same distance from the foot of the hills, are the ruins of Simraun. At the present day they are very extensive, but are buried among thick jungle, which it is considered sacrilegious to attempt to clear away. Simraun was the ancient and fortified capital of the powerful Hindu kingdom of Mithila (modern Tirhut), which extended from the

Gandak to the Kosi, and from the Ganges to the hills of Nipal.

It is said to have been built A.D. 1097 by Rajah Nanyupa Deva, and his descendants occupied the throne for several generations. The last of his dynasty, Rajah Hari Singha Deva, was conquered and driven into the hills, A.D. 1322, by Ghaias-u-din Toghlak Shah, Emperor of Delhi. The kingdom of Mithila was annexed as a province to the Musalman dominions, and its capital, Simraun, was reduced to ruins. On retiring to the hills Hari Singha Deva conquered Nipal, and his descendants continued on the throne of Nipal till they were displaced by Prithi Narayan.

On the right bank of Baghmatti, and very near to the frontier, is the village of Baharwar, on a high, dry, and healthy spot. In the first Nipal war, when the division under Major Bradshaw invaded the Terai, their first action was at the outpost of Baharwar, which they attacked and carried, November 1814.

3rd. *Salaya Saptari* extends from the Baghmatti eastward to the right bank of the Kumla. In this district, near the frontier, are the ruins of the old city of Janikpur.

4th. *Mohtari* extends from the Kumla stream to the right bank of the Kosi river. On the right bank of the river, and close to the frontier, is an outpost named Bhanurwa, on a dry and somewhat elevated spot, well adapted for a military station.

The Terai east of the Kosi river, and extending thence to the Michi, constitutes the district of Morung.   The Morung is remarkable for its extreme flatness, in many places giving it the character of a swamp, its stiff, clayey soil, and for its pestilent climate.   It is the most malarious and unhealthy district in the whole Terai.   The water, also, of the streams which run through it is very bad, and often almost of a poisonous quality.

There is no continuous range of sandstone hills in the Morung.   Between the foot of the inner hills and the inner margin of the forest it is quite flat, and is more or less swamped all the year round.

With the exception of the Morung, the soil of the Terai generally is a rich alluvium consisting of a varying mixture of black loam, clay, and sand, and is well adapted for every kind of crop, including sugar-cane, poppy, and tobacco.

Elephants are fast disappearing from the Terai to the west of the Kosi; and even in the Morung the numbers are much less than they were formerly.

RUINS OF A BUDDHIST TOPE, CALLED KATRISAMBHU, IN KATHMANDU.

Erected, A.D. 1427.

CHAPTER IV.

HAVING described the general geographical characters of the western, central, and eastern divisions of Nipal, with the belts of terai which skirt their southern borders, it remains now to notice more particularly the small but important district in which the capital of the kingdom is situated, and which comprises the Valley of Nipal and the hills in its immediate vicinity. This district lies directly to the south of the Gosainthan mountain, and consists of an elevated plateau surrounded by hills, and situated between the country of the seven Gandaks on the west, and that of the seven Kosis on the east.

It is of a triangular shape; its apex points towards the north, and rests below the bluff and lofty extremity of the Dhaibang ridge. Its western boundary is formed by the Trisulganga river, which separates it from the province of Gorkha. On the east it overlooks the country of the seven Kosis, from which it is divided by the Milamchi or Indiani river. Its base is towards the south, and is formed by the range of Sesapain and other lower hills which lie to the north of the valley and district of Makwanpur. According to the system on which the three great divisions of Nipal were described, and by which their limits were fixed, this district would include only that region which is watered by the Baghmatti and its tributary the Panauni, and would then consist merely of the large valley of Nipal and the small valley of Chitlong, with the hills which form their immediate boundaries. But as the flanks of the mountains which enclose these two valleys are bordered by several smaller valleys which lie in the immediate vicinity of the great valley of Nipal, and are closely connected with it, it will be convenient to look upon the whole series as forming part of the district of Nipal proper, although they are not strictly comprised within its geographical limits, as their waters are drained off by tributaries, not of the Baghmatti, but of the Gandak and Kosi rivers.

The following valleys are comprised within the district of Nipal proper, and are all situated around the large central valley of Nipal, from which they are separated by an intermediate range of hills.

1st. The valley of Chitlong, to the south-west of Nipal, with its subordinate valley of the Panauni river, a tributary of the Baghmatti.

2nd. The valleys of the Duna and of the Kulpu

rivers on the west of Nipal, watered by tributaries of the Trisulganga.

3rd. The Valley of Nayakot, to the north of Nipal, with its subordinate valleys of the Tadi, Likhu, and Sindura rivers, all tributaries of the Trisulganga.

4th. The Valley of Banepa, to the east of Nipal, watered by a tributary of the Sankosi river.

The Valley of Nipal proper, around which these subordinate valleys are collected, is a gently undulating plain, of nearly oval shape, having an average length of about fifteen miles, and encircled by mountains which, rising more or less abruptly from its margins, form its natural boundaries. It lies at an elevation of four thousand seven hundred feet above the level of the sea, and the chain of hills which surrounds it has a varying height of from five hundred to three thousand feet above the surface of the valley, or of from five thousand to eight thousand feet above the level of the sea.

It is bounded on the north by Mount Sheopuri, the loftiest and most massive of all the mountains by which the valley is enclosed. Its pointed summit, crowned with a forest of sál and oak trees, is elevated fully eight thousand feet above the level of the sea.

Sheopuri is flanked and supported on the west by Mount Kukanni, with which it is connected by the " Sangla " pass, and on the east by Mount Manichur; each of which hills is about seven thousand feet in height. The eastern boundary of the valley is formed by Mount Mahadeo Pokhra, six thousand seven hun-

5

dred and eighty-six feet in height, and which is joined to Mount Manichur by an intermediate and lower range of hills.

On the south-east is Mount Phulchoah, a lofty, richly wooded, and widely spreading mountain, about eight thousand feet in elevation. It sends out an arm or spur, called Ranichoah, towards the Mahadeo Pokhra hill, with which it is joined by the pass leading to the Valley of Banepa. Another steep and rugged ridge, called Mount Mahabharat, runs to the south and overhangs the pass of the Baghmatti river.

The highest peak of Phulchoah consists of a mass of rock, overshadowed by some very fine oaks. In this rock are shrines to Devi Bhairavi and to Mahenkal, as also a small Buddhist shrine, with small relief of Manjusri (Saraswati), to which the Niwar women flock in spring, taking their girls as soon as they have learnt to use the "kirkha" or thread machine, the handle of which is presented, with fruit, flowers, &c., as an offering to the deity, as Manjusri is considered especially to preside over all kinds of handicraft. The summit of Phulchoah commands a view of the plains as well as of the snowy range.

Due south is Mount Mahabharat, its western extremity forming one side of the pass through which the Baghmatti river quits the Valley of Nipal. This pass is the only break or gap which occurs in the continuity of the chain of mountains by which the valley is surrounded.

On the south-west of the valley is Mount Chanda-giri, six thousand six hundred feet in height, the eastern shoulder of which, called Hathibun, is washed by the Baghmatti river, and whose south-eastern peak is called Mount Champa Devi.

Due west of the valley is Mount Indra Than,* a rounded hill not more than one thousand or one thousand five hundred feet above the level of the valley. This range of low and rounded hills, continuous on the east with Mahabharat, on the west with Deochoah, and on which are situated the cities of Keshpur and Chabbar, cuts off or detaches from the east of the large valley a small or subordinate valley, which lies below Thankot, and extends east and west along the base of Mount Chandagiri. It is crossed at the village of Narkab by the high road from Thankot to Kathmandu.

On the north-west is Mount Nagarjun, seven thousand feet in height, a boldly formed and richly

---

* "Deochoah" is the name of the mountain. Indrathan, or Indrastan, is the name of a small piece of dense tree jungle, near its summit, on its southern face, in the centre of which is a small shallow tank, with a couple of shrines, each containing a figure of Indra and Indriuni, seated on an elephant. Indra is said annually to visit and bathe in this tank, and when this is supposed to take place numbers of the pious bathe there also. At its junction with Mount Nagarjun the Deochoah mountain turns round somewhat upon itself, and sends off a spur in a south-easterly direction, which becomes elongated into a low range of hills which stretches across the valley from west to south, and which is continuous with a similar spur from Mount Mahabharat to the south-west of Mount Phulchoah.

5 *

wooded mountain, which, by sending forward two large
spurs or arms towards the east—one the hill of Shambunath, the other that above Balaji—not only encroaches considerably upon the extent or area of the
valley, but also destroys the regularity of what would
otherwise be a nearly oval outline. Towards the
south Nagarjun is connected with Mount Deochoah,
while on the north a low ridge connects it with a spur
from the west of Mount Kukanni, and thus completes
the continuity of the girdle or circular chain of mountains in whose hollow lies spread out the richly
cultivated plain which constitutes the Valley of Nipal.

To the north-west of the valley, overlooking it but
not forming part of its immediate boundaries, are two
mountains—Mount Bhirbandi and Mount Kumhara.
The former is the loftiest mountain in the district
of Nipal proper; its rounded summit, called Kaulia
peak, covered with brushwood jungle of hollyoak and
rhododendron, is elevated between eight thousand
and nine thousand feet above the level of the sea, and
full four thousand feet above the surface of the
valley.

It is continuous towards the east with Mount Kukanni; the pass between the two mountains is six
thousand feet in height, and over it runs the high road
from Nipal to Nayakot, Gorkha, and Tibet. Mount
Kumhara is situated to the west of Bhirbandi, with
which it is connected by an intervening ridge.

These two mountains towards the north overhang
the Valley of Nayakot; while on the south and east

they look towards the Valley of Nipal, from which they are separated by the valley of the Kulpu river and by the low connecting ridge which runs between Mount Kukanni and Nagarjun.

The six mountains, Mounts Kumhara, Bhirbandi, Kukanni, Sheopuri, Manichur, and Mahadeo Pokhra, stretch as a continuous range from the banks of the Trisulganga on the west to those of the Milamchi river in the country of the Kosis on the east. This range forms the northern boundary to the entire district of Nipal proper. It runs parallel with, and directly opposite to, the southern face of Mount Jibjibia, whose rugged crest, elevated fifteen thousand feet above the sea, stands as an eternal barrier between the populous and cultivated valleys which lie at its base and the snowy peaks of the Gosainthan which rise immediately in its rear. All the mountains immediately surrounding the Valley of Nipal are of secondary formation, but the stratified rocks of which their masses are composed are very rarely exposed to view. Everywhere these mountains are covered with a deep coat of rich soil which gives rise to the most luxuriant vegetation. The Chandagiri, the Phulchoah, Manichur, the Sheopuri, the Nagarjun, are clothed with oaks and rhododendrons up to their very summits. Even the most precipitous parts of the northern sides of these mountains are concealed beneath a mass of forest and shrub jungle, which is in many places so dense as to be quite impenetrable to man, while it affords admirable cover for leopards, bears, and wild hogs. In

some places, as on the north side of Bhirbandi, on
the southern slope and about the base of Sheopuri
and Manichur, large masses of naked rock jut out
upon the surface, sometimes of a bare hill, sometimes
in the heart of a mass of jungle. But these masses
are not part of the internal structure of the mountain,
but are mere detached and solitary boulders, buried in
past ages among the earth on the mountain side, and
now accidentally exposed to view in consequence of
the denuding influence of the periodical rains.

All the mountains surrounding the Valley of Nipal
are·very much steeper on their northern than they are
on their southern sides.

The ascent of the Chandagiri, of the Sheopuri,
and of Bhirbandi, on their southern sides, is comparatively an easy one, in consequence of the slope
being long and gradually inclined; the descent on the
north side of all these mountains is abrupt and precipitous. This is caused by the layers of rock and softer
material, of which these mountains are composed, all
trending towards the central ghat line of the snows
with a uniform and moderate inclination. The plane
surfaces of these layers face towards the south, while
their truncated extremities are directed to the north;
and as usually is the case with stratified mountain
masses, the declivity of the edges of their strata is
abrupt and severe in proportion as the acclivity of their
surfaces is gentle and moderate.

There is another curious characteristic of most of
these hills, which is observable more or less through-

out the whole length of the Himalayas. As a general rule, vegetation is very much more luxuriant on the northern than it is upon the southern side of the mountains.

In many instances the south side of a mountain is perfectly free from all kinds of jungle, and has merely a thin coating of short grass, while the north side of the same mountain is covered with a mass of forest trees. In such cases, the upper boundary line where the jungle ceases coincides exactly with the crest or watershed of the hill, and is often so abruptly marked that it is difficult at first to believe that it has not been produced by artificial means.

The same thing occurs even in the subordinate ridges and spurs of these hills; their southern sides are often naked, while their northern faces are clothed with vegetation.

This does not appear to depend upon any original difference either in the quantity or the quality of the soil with which the opposite sides of the mountains are covered.

It is caused by the absence of moisture on the southern sides of the mountains, in consequence of their constantly being exposed to the direct and scorching rays of a tropical sun. The thin layer of earth which is strewed over the surface of the mountain side is so quickly dried of its waters by the sun, that enough moisture is not left in the soil for the production or support of any considerable extent of vegetation.

The *north* side of the mountains is not exposed to
this direct heat, and it consequently retains its
moisture sufficiently to make its soil fertile and pro-
ductive.

For the same reason the snows which fall upon the
higher hills, during the winter months, disappear on
their southern and sunny, much sooner than they do
upon their northern and shady sides.

According to the tradition of all Hindus, what is
now the Valley of Nipal was, in the early ages of the
world, a large and very deep lake, of an oval form,
and encircled by lofty mountains, which rose more or
less precipitously from its edges.

Manjusri Bodhisatwa has the credit of having converted this lake into a dry valley, by cutting through
Mount Kotbar on its southern side with his sword,
and so making a passage through which all the waters
escaped. The cleft in the mountain, caused by Manjusri's sword, remains to the present time, and constitutes the pass or channel between the Phulchoah
and Champadevi hills, through which the Baghmatti
river leaves the Valley of Nipal. There is good reason
to believe that this legend is based upon truth, and
that Nipal was in remote ages a mountain lake, enclosed in the hollow of the same circular range of
hills by which the valley is surrounded at the present
day. It is probable that in consequence either of
one of those subterranean convulsions common to all
mountain districts, or of the gradual but continuous
elevation of its bottom, or from both causes combined,

the lake burst its boundaries on its southern side, and that a large portion of its waters escaped into the lower hills through the channel which is now the bed of the Baghmatti river.

At the same time that its waters were being slowly drained off, the hollow of the lake must have been gradually filled up by the soil constantly brought into it by numberless streams from the sides of the surrounding mountains.

These processes of draining off and filling up must have gone on slowly, steadily, and simultaneously, so as to allow of the uniform deposition along the bottom of the lake of all the soil and solid ingredients which were contained within its waters.

In the course of time these deposits became more and more consolidated, until at length, the waters having dried up or drained away, the entire mountain hollow became filled up with a mass of alluvial soil, the extent of which corresponded with the limits, as its surface did with the level, of the former lake.

This view of the formation of the valley is confirmed by numerous facts which can hardly be explained by any other theory.

At the present day the continuity of the mountain barrier around the valley is so perfect, that were it possible by any means to block up that one pass through which the Baghmatti river flows towards the plains, not one drop of water could escape by any other channel, and, in the course of time, the accumulation of its pent-up waters would convert the valley again into a lake.

Throughout its entire extent the soil of the valley is purely alluvial, and is mostly arranged in strictly conformable or horizontal strata, such as can only have been formed by gradual deposition from a large mass of standing water.

This alluvial soil consists almost entirely of clay and sand, and is so evidently formed of débris from the surrounding mountains, that, all around the confines of the valley, its composition corresponds in quality and even in colour with that of the nearest adjacent hill. It is remarkable for the utter absence in it of all and every kind of rock formation; even pebbles are hardly ever seen on the surface, and stone can only be obtained from quarries in the sides or spurs of some of the surrounding mountains.

The abrupt manner in which many of the boundary mountains emerge from under this alluvial soil; and the almost perfect uniformity of level of all the high lands, not only on the edges but throughout the whole extent of the valley, wherever they have not been subjected to the wearing influence of running streams, are additional evidences in favour of the belief that the modern valley now occupies the hollow of an ancient lake.

The only fact opposed to this belief is the negative one, that fossil aquatic shells have not yet been observed in this alluvium; but as the soil has never yet been examined by a geologist, it is very probable that such remains may yet be discovered.

The shape of the Valley of Nipal is irregularly oval, but its outline is a good deal interrupted by the numerous spurs which project into it from the surrounding hills. This is particularly the case on its western side, where the spurs of Mount Nagarjun and of Mount Indra-Than stand forward so boldly that they encroach upon the extent of the valley, and not only diminish its width from east to west, but, by causing its southwest and north-west portions to bend round the projecting bases of these hills, they destroy the regularity of its oval shape, and give to its general outline a form closely resembling that of a kidney.

The long axis of the valley runs from north to south, and its average length is about fifteen miles.

Thus the distance from Sanku in the north-east to Thankot in the south-west,

> or, from Barranilkhiat at the foot of Mount Sheopuri, in the north, to the pass below Phirphing, through which the Baghmatti leaves the valley;
>
> or, from Jaitpur at the foot of Mount Kukanni, in the north-west, to Godaura at the foot of Mount Phulchoah in the south-east,

is, in all these which are the longest diameters of the valley, as nearly as possible fifteen miles in a direct line.

The width of the valley is somewhat less, and

averages from twelve to fourteen miles. In its narrowest or most constricted part, from Balaji at the foot of Nagarjun in the west, to Chargu Narayan, on the south of Lanku, or a spur from Mahadeo Pokhra on the east, the distance is not more than nine or ten miles. The circumference of the valley, at the level of the above-mentioned places, and allowing something for the irregularity of its outline, is probably about fifty miles, and it embraces an area of about two hundred and fifty square miles.

The valley is most abundantly supplied with water by numberless streams of various sizes, which rise in the sides of the surrounding hills, and in their courses converge more or less directly towards the central long diameter of the valley, where they all terminate by joining the Baghmatti river, which by means of its tributaries drains the whole district of Nipal proper.

The Baghmatti rises as a small streamlet at a spot called Bhagdwar, from a spring on the northern face of a spur, which forms the eastern shoulder of Sheopuri, whence, winding its way through the deep gorge or hollow between Sheopuri and Manichur, it descends by a bold cascade into the valley, which it traverses with a serpentine course from north-east to south-west. Having cut a passage by a narrow and precipitous gorge through a spur of Mount Sheopuri at Gaokarran,* it passes to the south of the ancient

---

* Before arriving at Gaokarran it receives a considerable tributary—called the Shujalmatti, or Jackal stream—from the southern base of Sheopuri.

Buddhist temple of Keshachait, and skirts three sides
of the sacred wood of Pashpatinath, beneath the
shrines of which it flows in a narrow channel, which is
almost concealed in places by the shade of the trees
which overhang it.

On leaving Pashpatinath, it flows at first in a south-
westerly direction, between the cities of Patan on its
left, and Kathmandu on its right bank; then turning
towards the south, it passes through a gorge lying below
the ancient city of Chabbar, and crossing the south-east
portion of the small valley, it extends along the base
of the Chandagiri, and quits the valley by the pass
below Phirphing, between Mount Champa Devi on
the west, and Mount Mahabharat on the east. In its
course through the valley, the Baghmatti passes
through four different gorges,—first, at Gaoharran;
second, that of Gajeswari at Pashpatti; third, that
below Chabbar; fourth, that of Kotbar below Phirphing.

Manjusri has the credit of having formed them all
with his talwar when he let the waters of the valley
escape.   The Sheomarghi Niwars and Hindus say
that Vishnu was the operator, not Manjusri.

For the first few miles of its course, the Baghmatti
is a very narrow stream, but it soon increases in
breadth from the many tributaries which flow into it
from all parts of the valley. Its bed is sandy, except
in such places as Gaokarran and Pashpatinath, where,
having forced its way through the substance of a hill,
its channel is strong, and is interrupted by masses of

detached rock. Its waters are esteemed to be not only sacred, but peculiarly pure and wholesome. The Baghmatti is always shallow, but, during the rains, it swells into a wide and rapid stream.

The following legend describes the mode in which the Baghmatti and Bishnmatti rivers were first produced :—

Kaskat Sand, the fourth mortal Buddha, during a pilgrimage to Nipal, ascended Mount Sheopuri. Some of his followers, struck with the beauty of the place, wished to be initiated into the Buddhist religion, that they might permanently reside in the country ; but no water could be found for the performance of the ceremony of baptism. Kaskat Sand, having implored Divine guidance, thrust one of his thumbs against the rock, when forthwith the waters gushed forth and his disciples were duly baptised. The spring thus formed gave rise to a river, which he named Varimatti, or Baghmatti.

The hair which was cut off from the heads of the disciples on being tonsured, he divided into two portions ; one part was placed in the stream and became instantly converted into a rock, which he called Keshchaitya, which exists to the present day, and from beneath which the sacred source of the Baghmatti issues.

The other portion of hair was scattered to the winds, and as it fell upon the earth it gave rise to a river, which was named Keshnvati or Bishnmatti.

The following are the principal tributary streams

which fall into the Baghmatti during its course through the valley.

The *Bishnmatti*, the *Dhobi-Kola*, the *Manhaura*, and the *Hanumanmatti*.

The *Bishnmatti* or *Keshnvati*, rises on the southern face of Mount Sheopuri, to the north-west of Bara Nilkhiat. At the point where it leaves the mountain and enters the valley, is a small hamlet named *Bishnnath*, to which pilgrimages are annually made. It flows in a southerly direction along the base of Mount Nagarjun, past the village of Balaji, and having the Buddhist temple of Swambhunath on the high land on its right bank. It washes the western side of Kathmandu, which is built upon its left bank, and unites with the Baghmatti river a little to the south of the city. In the north-west of the valley it is joined by the Sanglakola, from the Sanglabanjan or pass between Sheopuri and Kukanni. About half a mile before reaching Balaji, it is joined by the Mahadeokola stream, from the district below Jaitpur.

Two pucka* bridges connect the city with the right bank of the river; over one the road leads to Swambhunath, over the other to Kirtipur and Thankot.

At the confluence of the two rivers several temples have been built; and there is an extensive *ghat*, which is a favourite spot for burning the bodies of the dead.

The Bishnmatti is joined by several small streams

---

* "Pucka" (or *paka*—from pakána, to cook) refers to kiln-baked bricks—as opposed to kachá, "raw" or sun-dried ones.—ED.

and feeders from the high land on each side of it; among them may be named the Badrimatti and the Subanumatti.

The *Badrimatti* rises near the foot of Mount Nagarjun, and falls into the Bishnmatti opposite to Swambunath. It is only remarkable as being the stream on the right bank of which, close to its junction with the Bishnmatti, all public executions take place.

The *Subanumatti* rises in the hollow between the Nagarjun and Deochoah hills, and falls into the Bishnmatti near its confluence with the Baghmatti.

The Bishnmatti, by its feeders, drains the northern and western portions of the valley. It flows through a broad and level plain, on the high ground to the left of which stands the British Residency.

The *Dhobikola* or *Rudramatti* rises on the south side of Mount Sheopuri, flows in a southerly direction, about one and a half miles to the east of Kathmandu, and falls into the Baghmatti, about a mile to the east of the junction of that river with the Bishnmatti.

Between the town of Harigaon, which stands near its right bank, and the high ground on which is the town of Deo Patan, the Dhobi Kola is crossed by a pucka bridge, over which lies the main road from the capital to Pashpatinath and Kastachait.

The Dhobikola drains the northern and central parts of the valley, its basin lying between the valley of the Bishnmatti on the west and that of the Baghmatti on the east.

The *Manhaura* or *Manumatti* rises in a glen at the

north-east base of Mount Manichur, considerably to the north of the town of Sanku, to the east and south of which town it flows, passes round and below the wooded hill of Changu Narain, and then flowing in a south-westerly direction through a rather extensive plain or valley of its own, falls into the Baghmatti river opposite to and north of the city of Patan. It drains the north-eastern portion of the valley.

The *Hanumanmatti* rises in a small and sacred tank on the crest or watershed of Mount Mahadeo Pokhra. This tank, from which the hill derives its name, is remarkable as giving rise to two rivers, one of which (the Hanuman) flows westward and falls into the Baghmatti, while the other flows eastward, through the valley of Banepa, and joins the Sankosi river. Descending into the valley, the Hanuman river is joined by several streamlets from the wide-spreading base of the Mahadeo Pokhra hill, it winds round the southern side of the city of Bhatgaon, a little to the west of which it is joined by the Kishn-Kushn, or Kansavati streamlet, from the southern base of the Changu Narain, and then flows due westward till it unites with the Manhaura, a short distance before that stream falls into the Baghmatti. It drains the eastern portion of the valley.

CHAPTER V.

THE VALLEY OF NIPAL—*continued.*

THE south and south-eastern portions of the valley are watered by several small streams which rise on the side or in the base of Mount Phulchoah, and flow in a more or less northerly direction to join the Baghmatti river. Of these may be noted the Tukcha and the Nikhu.

The Tukcha or Kukhumatti rises near Godauri, at the foot of Phulchoah, and flows due north to the east of Patan, and within a quarter of a mile of the city walls; falling into the Manhaura close to its confluence with the Baghmatti.

The Nikhu is a small stream which rises among the low hills at the foot of Mount Mahabharat, and falls into the Baghmatti just before that river enters the gorge below the city of Chobbar.

The small or subordinate valley between the base of Mount Chandagiri and the low range of hills on

which Keshpur and Chobbar are situated, is drained
by a stream which rises near Thankot, and, flowing
eastward, passes below and to the west of the city of
Kirtipur, and then joins the Baghmatti a little below
its junction with the Bishnmatti.

The Baghmatti river having by its numerous tributaries collected into one stream the waters from
the whole extent of the valley, winds round the base
of the eastern shoulder of Mount Chandagiri, passing
below Phirphing, and escapes from the valley by the
pass or hollow between Mount Champadevi on the west,
and Mount Mahabharat on the east. After quitting the
valley, the Baghmatti is soon joined by the Panauni
stream, which waters the valleys of Chitlong, Marko,
and Tumbakhana; it flows in. a southerly direction
through the lower hills, passing a few miles to the
east of Malwanpur, and close to Hariharpur, and then
enters the plains through a pass in the sandstone
range.

Crossing the Sal forest and Terai, it pursues a
solitary course through Tirhut, where it is joined by
the Little Gandak (on which is Mozaffarpur) and
falls into the Ganges opposite to, and a little below,
Monghir.

Little is known of the character of the country
through which the Baghmatti passes after it leaves the
valley, until it reappears in the Terai. A road accompanies it, which is said to be not only the shortest
of all the roads leading to the plains, but to be practicable for beasts of burden; to have an easy and

gradual level; and to be free from all formidable ascents or descents. It is, however, and always has been, most strictly closed against foreigners, and it ·may be fairly inferred that it is in consequence of its being known to be the easiest and most direct of all the roads which lead to the valley, that the Nipalese have adopted such jealous precautions to prevent any European from entering their territory by this route.

The surface of the plain constituting the Valley of Nipal has a gradual and gentle slope from the higher lands around its circumference towards the central lowlands through which the Baghmatti river winds its serpentine course from north-east to south-west.

It is, however, rendered irregular and very much cut up by the numerous streams and their attendant valleys, which traverse it in all directions. The broken and undulating character of its level is probably due to the following causes.

In those remote times when by the draining off or drying up of its waters the Lake of Nipal was converted into a valley, the surface of the alluvial plain which was then exposed, was, at first, nearly, if not perfectly level.

The streams, however, which continued to flow into the valley from the surrounding hills must soon have destroyed this uniformity, by cutting through and washing away the rich and soft alluvium of which the soil consisted, and so hollowing out a number of troughs or watercourses considerably below the level of the original surface of the plain.

The constant action of these streams, continued through a succession of ages, has gradually but steadily carried away a vast quantity of soil; and as in their course through the valley they became increased by numberless little streamlets from the districts through which they passed, their channels have been constantly increasing in width as the lands on either side of them have been worn away, until at length a series of valleys have been produced, the sides of each of which slope down, more or less abruptly, towards the stream which traverses its centre, and by which all its waters are drained off. These valleys are separated from each other by tracts of higher lands, which retain their original level, in consequence of never having been exposed to the wearing and disintegrating influence of running streams.

In consequence of a process of this sort constantly going on, each of the numerous streams which traverse the Valley of Nipal now runs in an attendant plain or subordinate valley of its own; and the general surface of the great valley is broken up into a succession of more or less extensive plains, separated from each other by plateaus of high and level land, and each of which is watered by one of the tributary streams of the Baghmatti river.

As all these streams converge in their courses more or less directly till they unite with the Baghmatti, the attendant plains which accompany them, and which have been formed by the disintegrating action of their waters, also have a general direction from the circumference of the valley towards the hollow or lowland plain which runs through its centre from north-east to south-west, and in which is the bed of the Baghmatti river.

These different subordinate valleys, like the main streams which flow through them, mostly run from north to south in a direction nearly parallel with that of the Baghmatti, and uniting with that river in the central part of its course where it crosses the valley from east to west.

Each of these valley streams rises either in a glen or from a spring near the base of one of the surrounding hills. Near its source the stream cuts for itself through the highlands a mere shallow channel; this soon widens until it becomes a deep and broad ravine, which rapidly increases in breadth and depth as it is joined by other ravines bringing down streamlets from the adjacent highlands. As it advances it opens out, and gradually assumes the character of a more or less extensive plain, traversed by a winding river, and bounded on each side by high banks, which in some places terminate abruptly in overhanging cliffs, in others are connected with the plain by a gradual slope.

Each stream usually follows a serpentine course, winding backwards and forwards from side to side of the valley through which it flows. The size and direction of the stream regulate not only the form and extent of the plain which accompanies it, but the character and slope of the high banks by which its valley is bounded.

Where the bed of the stream lies at the edge of the plain, and immediately beneath the higher land, its waters slowly but steadily eat away and encroach upon the soft alluvial soil of which these banks are composed. In such places the plain is bounded by precipitous cliffs, which are continually crumbling and breaking down, as their foundations are undermined and washed away by the river which flows along their base. On the other hand, where the stream flows across or in the middle of its valley, the banks ascend from the plain with a gradual and uniform slope, which is covered with richly cultivated fields, divided, for purposes of irrigation, into a succession of terraces, rising one above another from the lower to the higher level.

These plains or valleys which accompany the tributary streams of the Baghmatti river are mostly of considerable extent, but their width varies very much in different parts of their course. In no part do any of them exceed a mile in breadth, and in some places they are not more than from one to two hundred yards across. The plain which accompanies the Bishenmatti, where it spreads out between Balaji at the foot of Mount Nagarjun on the west, and the highlands on which are the British lines on its east, is fully a mile in breadth. Near its confluence with the Baghmatti, where it flows beneath the city of Kathmandu on its left and the artillery parade ground on its right bank, it is little more than one hundred yards across.

The Dhobi Kola stream flows at first through a rather wide plain, but where the river is crossed by the bridge and road leading from the capital to Pashpatinath, and flows between the high land on which stands the town of Harigaon on the west, and the hill leading to Deopatan on the east, its valley is not more than two hundred yards in breadth. It spreads out again into a wide plain, fully a mile across. before it joins the Baghmatti river. Where the valley or plain of the Dhobi Kola joins that of the Baghmatti, the high ground on which stands Shappatalli is situated; it is an isolated plateau, of a triangular form, its apex pointing to the north. On the east and west is the level plain of the Dhobi Kola, while on the south it is washed by the Baghmatti.

The Baghmatti river, by having to flow through the narrow gorges at Gaokarran and Pashpatti, has its attendant valley divided into three distinct and different portions.

It flows through a first distinctly defined valley between Baghdwar, where it leaves the Sheopuri mountain, and the pass of Gaokarran. It flows through a second equally distinct valley in its course from Gaokarran to Pashpatti. Here it has the woods of Gaokarran and Pashpatti on its left, and the high land on which are the temples of " Baddhnath " and " Dandeo " on its right bank. After emerging from the wood of Pashpatti, it flows through a third extensive and very circuitous plain before it finally leaves the Valley of Nipal.

The wood and temples of Pashpatti are situated on a plateau which forms a sort of elevated isthmus, stretching across the valley of the Baghmatti and connecting the high banks of the Dhobi Kola on the east with those of the Manhaura on the west. It is cut right through by the narrow gorge in which the Baghmatti river flows. The valley of the Manhaura river near its commencement is very narrow, where it runs between the high land on which is the town of Sanku on its right, and the hill of Changunarain on its left bank. It spreads out afterwards into a plain nearly a mile across, where it has the wood of Pashpatti on the west and the high land of Timmi on the east.

The valley of the Hanuman Kola is nowhere very wide, nor is that of any of the other smaller streams which converge from all parts of the circumference of the valley towards the Baghmatti, and each of which is accompanied during part of its course by an attendant valley of greater or less extent. All these lowland plains or valleys consist of very rich soil, which can at any time be brought under irrigation, either from the main stream or from some of its numerous feeders in their course to join it from the higher land on its sides. These lowlands are mostly appropriated to the cultivation of rice, and but very thinly inhabited—all the cities and towns in Nipal being situated on the higher and drier lands.

The highlands by which these plains are separated from each other vary considerably in width, but they are all of nearly the same level, and have an average height of from eighty to one hundred and twenty feet above the surface of the plains which lie below them. They appear to have retained the original level of the ancient bed of the lake; as it must have existed when first exposed by the drying up or draining away of its waters, and before it had been cut up into a series of valleys and ravines by the disintegrating action of running streams. The broad plateaus which separate the river plains are promontories of varying extent, which are sent forward, with a general convergence towards the centre of the valley, from the high and level lands which lie along the base of all the surrounding mountains.

Near the edge of the valley these highlands rise with a uniform, but gentle, and often almost imperceptible slope towards the foot of the adjacent hills, with which they become continuous. In some few places the high grounds immediately at the foot of the hills (as below Mount Kukanni for instance) are so very much intersected and re-intersected by ravines, each of which during the rains brings down a streamlet to the plain beneath, that the general appearance of the surface becomes so rugged and broken, that unless seen from a considerable distance, all uniformity of level is apparently destroyed. As they sweep up the broad hollows or bays which exist between two projecting spurs, their slope increases, and their surface is divided into tiers of terraces, which, rising one above another, often extend to a considerable height up the mountain side.

From the above description of the surface of the Valley of Nipal it is evident that it has two distinct and very well marked levels. These are,—

First, the level of the upper or high lands, which extend round the base of the mountains, and project as promontories towards the centre of the valley.

Second, the level of the lowlands or plains which lie along the banks of the numerous streams which unite to form the Baghmatti river.

As a general rule, all the lowlands of the valley, from their facility of irrigation, and certainty of flooding during the rains, are appropriated to the cultivation of rice. Here and there a few cottages, or a powa or a temple may be seen upon them, but usually these lands are very thinly inhabited, as their lowness and dampness make them unhealthy, while their extreme fertility and productiveness cause them to be too valuable to be much used for building purposes. Nearly all the inhabitants of the valley live on the high level lands. All the cities, towns, principal villages, &c., are situated upon them, as well as the scattered cottages of the soldiery and other parbattiahs, who never congregate together in masses, but always, when they can manage it, have their dwellings separate and detached.

The surplus high ground which is not required for human habitation is devoted to the cultivation chiefly of cereals, and such dry crops as are independent of irrigation.

Wherever there is a plateau, however small, there is usually a cottage, or a small cluster of dwellings on its top, while on the slope, or in the plain below it, the ground, where susceptible of irrigation, is laid out in terraces for the cultivation of rice. The high ground round the edge of the valley at the base of the hills, and especially that which runs up between the mountain spurs, combines to a considerable extent the advantages and peculiar character both of the upper and lower levels. Its proximity to the streams in their courses from the mountain to the valley enables the inhabitants to command a constant supply of water, which they easily divert into narrow channels for the purposes of irrigation, while the height of the land itself above the river-plain makes it always dry, cool, and healthy.

These districts round the edge of the valley are, accordingly, very thickly inhabited. Many large villages are situated upon them, and their surface is studded with the picturesque thatched cottages of the soldiery, prettily situated near some spring or temple, or clustered together in small groups around a large and sacred tree.

These lands round the margin of the valley are granted almost exclusively in *jagir* to the soldiery, and they are very much coveted, from their productiveness, healthiness, and proximity to the capital.

CHAPTER VI.

KATHMANDU.

THE principal cities in the Valley of Nipal are Kathmandu (the present capital of the kingdom), Patan, Bhatgaon, and Kirtipur, which were the capitals of their respective principalities until the Gorkha conquest in 1767.

Besides these cities there are several large towns and numberless villages of various sizes, situated in different parts of the valley. Many of these villages are mere hamlets, but some of them possess an interest and importance disproportioned to their size, in consequence of their having been built in the immediate neighbourhood of some of the principal temples or most sacred spots within the valley.

The following. list includes all the cities, towns, villages, and hamlets which are deserving of any especial notice :—

The city of Kathmandu.

The city of Patan.

The city of Kirtipur.

The city of Bhatgaon.

The hamlet of Bara Nilkhiat.

The hamlet of Balaji or Chota Nilkhiat.

The hamlet of Shambhunath.

These are all situated on the high ground watered by the Bishnmatti river.

The town of Harigaon, on the high land which overhangs the valley of the Dhobikola.

The village of Chabiar
The hamlet of Badhnath } Both situated on the high land which extends between the Dhobikola and the Baghmatti.

The town of Gaokarran
The village of Deo Patan
The town of Chobbar
The town of Phirphing } Situated above the four gorges or narrow passes through which the Baghmatti river flows in its course through the valley.

The town of Sanku
The village of Changu Narain*
The town of Timmi } In the neighbourhood of the Manhaura river.

---

* There are four small hamlets, each containing a shrine sacred to Narayan, in different parts of the valley; to visit all four in one day is a religious feat often performed. They are, Changu Narayan, Bishanku Narayan, Sikur Narayan, and Echengu Narayan. The circuit from Kathmandu is twenty-two kos, or forty-four miles.

The hamlet of Godauri, at the foot of Mount Phul-choah.

The town of Thankot, at the foot of Mount Chan-dagiri.

The following remarks are applicable to each of the four capital cities in Nipal:—Kathmandu, Patan, Kirti-pur, and Bhatgaon. During the time of the Niwar Rajahs each city was surrounded by a high wall, in different parts of which were large gateways, which generally remained open, but in times of danger or disturbance could be closed and defended.

Since the Gorkha conquest of the valley the walls have been allowed to decay, and have now nearly dis-appeared, while many of the gateways are in ruins. The limits of each city are, however, still strictly marked along the line where the ancient walls stood, and no Hindus but those of good caste are allowed to dwell within its precincts. This rule does not apply to Mussalmen, several of whom reside within the city of Kathmandu, but it is strictly enforced against Hindu outcastes, such as sweepers, butchers, executioners, &c., all of whom are obliged to live in the suburbs of the city. It is much more attended to in Kathmandu than it is in the other cities. The number of gateways corresponded exactly with the number of squares (*tols*) within the city,—each gate-way being associated with a particular square, and placed under the municipal control of the same local authorities, who were as much responsible for the repairs and defence of the gateway as they were for the general management of the square.

In each city the largest and most important bu'lding is the royal palace or darbar. It is situated in a central part of the city, and opposite to its principal front there is an open irregular square, which allows free access to the palace, and round which temples of various kinds are clustered together.

In all the cities there are a number of small squares irregularly scattered about. There are thirty-two in Kathmandu ; and there ought to be thirty-two gateways. The principal public buildings, courts of law, &c., are generally situated on one or more of the sides of these squares.

In Kathmandu, Patan, and Bhatgaon, most of the principal temples are in the immediate vicinity of the darbar ; many are within its precincts, and many more are crowded around or opposite to its principal façade. At Kirtipur the darbar was on the highest part of the crest of the hill on which the city is built ; it is now completely in ruins, but around its remains several temples more or less decayed are still standing.

The darbars are usually of an irregular quadrangular form, one side towards the rear being generally left open, and communicating with the gardens, stables, &c.

The outer façade of one or more of the other sides is open to the streets. The inner quadrangle is always private, and is usually divided into a number of smaller courts of various sizes with buildings on all four sides.

THE DURBAR, PATAN, NIPAL.

These inner courts communicate one with another by small doorways only, which can easily be secured, so that, in case of danger or disturbance, by closing them the inmates of the palace may shut themselves into the different parts of the building, and defend themselves with ease against a large number of assailants. These inner courts are appropriated to different purposes; some contain temples for the private use of the inmates of the palace, some are inhabited by the royal ladies, others are employed for public receptions and spectacles, while one or more are often used as stables for elephants.

To any person not acquainted with their relative positions and different outlets, the mass of small quadrangles, detached buildings, temples, &c. within the precincts of any of the palaces would appear to be a confused labyrinth of courts, passages, and doorways. These remarks apply especially to the darbars at Kathmandu and Bhatgaon. There are from forty to fifty different courts of various sizes, each having a separate name, in the darbar at Kathmandu; while in that at Bhatgaon there are, or rather originally were, ninety-nine distinct courts within the precincts of the palace. During the dynasty of the Niwars the darbar at Bhatgaon was the largest and most costly of any in Nipal. Since the Gorkha conquest, that of Kathmandu, as being the residence of the king, has been enlarged in every direction, and kept in thorough repair, and it is now accordingly the most extensive, though by no means the most ornamental or picturesque. The darbar at Patan was never so large as those of Bhatgaon or Kathmandu. The darbar at Patan was of simpler construction, and did not contain so many divisions ; while that at Kirtipur, which was very much less extensive than the others, is now in such a state of ruin that it is impossible to tell what was originally the form or even the outline of the building. The streets through the different cities are mostly narrow, crooked, and dirty. In Kathmandu alone is there a street leading to the darbar along which a four-wheeled carriage can be driven. In the other cities, and through the greater extent of Kathmandu itself, the streets leading to the darbar, as well as those which traverse the towns in all directions are mere lanes, adapted only for foot passengers, horses, and elephants. The streets do not appear to have been laid out on any particular system. Two or three of the principal streets radiate from some of the gateways on the circumference of the city towards the darbar, which is usually situated near its centre, and in their course they pass through some of the small squares (or *tols*) with which each capital abounds. Other smaller streets connect the different squares and leading thoroughfares together, and these again are intersected by numerous narrow lanes, which ramify about the city in all directions. Even where the streets are wide enough for a carriage, as they are in some places, both at Patan and Bhatgaon, the pavement is so irregular that it is not adapted to wheeled vehicles. The wheels would soon be knocked off by jolting over gutters and drains; and where the brick and tile pavement, which is used throughout all the streets and lanes, has been kept even and in good order, it is too slippery to be safe for draught cattle.

There is an utter absence in all the cities of any system of drainage; nearly stagnant gutters on each side of the street, running immediately below the house-fronts, do the duty of sewers, and into them most of the filth and refuse of the adjacent buildings find their way.

Numerous temples—Buddhist and Hindu—are situated in different parts of the cities. The Hindu temples are generally placed near some of the principal thoroughfares; but all the important Buddhist temples are situated a little off the road, and stand in the centre of squares or quadrangles which have been built around them, and which are inhabited exclusively by Buddhist Niwars.

None of the houses consist of less than two floors, and they are mostly three, four, or even five stories high. They are strongly built of red burnt brick, and have overhanging pent tiled roofs, the projecting eaves of which rest upon a number of short wooden supports, which slope upward from the walls of the house, and are often curiously and elaborately carved into the shape of grotesque monsters, &c. The frame-work of the roof consists of wood, and it is covered with red tiles (resting upon a layer of adhesive clay), which are ingeniously curved, so that they mutually

7 *

overlap and support each other, and are so grooved
that when in apposition they form a series of little
continuous channels, by which all rain is quickly
carried off from the surface of the roof. The ground
floor of the house, towards the street, usually consists
of an open balcony, which serves either for a shop, or
for a convenient lounging and sitting place for the
inmates of the house. This balcony communicates
in almost all houses, by a low doorway,.with a quadrangle behind, which is open to the sky above, and is
closed in on all four sides with buildings, the windows
of which look into it. Almost every house of any
size, public or private, contains a central quadrangle
of this kind, round which the rest of the house is
built. The size of the quadrangle of course varies in
accordance with the extent of the house. In most
cases the lowermost or ground floor is an open sort of
verandah running round the court, supported by wooden
posts, and. having one or more step-ladders on it,
which lead, through trap-doors, to the floor above.
In this open verandah servants live, in company with
the live-stock of the house, such as horses, cows,
goats, dogs, &c. In the dwellings of the poor the
central court is too often a common receptacle for all
the washings and filth of the surrounding buildings,
and it is doubtless often a fertile source of fever and
disease, especially where, as frequently happens in
some of the larger houses, some. twelve, twenty, or
even more different families of the poorer and working
classes, but of the same caste and trade, inhabit the

same range of buildings running round one single central quadrangle.

In all houses the ceilings are low and the doorways small, and as the windows (which consist of very massive frames, often beautifully and elaborately carved on the outside) are without glass, and can only be closed by wooden shutters, the rooms are confined and badly lighted. Staircases are unknown, and the communication between the different floors of which a house consists is effected by means of stepladders leading to narrow trap-doors, which can be quickly closed and easily defended.

Kathmandu, from being the capital of the kingdom, is the most important city of Nipal.* It is situated towards the western side of the valley, about a mile from the base of Mount Nagarjun, and stands on the east or left bank of the Bishnmatti, near the confluence of that river with the Baghmatti.

It is of an oblong form, and is said by the Buddhist Niwars to have been built after the shape of the sword of its great founder, Manjusri, while the Hindus profess that it resembles the sword or scimitar of Devi.

The handle or blunt extremity of this traditionary

---

* Under the dynasty of the Niwar Rajahs, the principality of which Kathmandu was the capital included *within* the valley-the towns of Sanku, Changunarain, Gaokarran, Harigaon, Deo Patan, and all the villages and hamlets along the northern and western sides of the valley..

sword is directed to the south, towards the confluence of the Baghmatti and Bishnmatti rivers, while its apex points to the north, where it terminates in the suburb of Timmale, which stretches round or rests upon it, say the Buddhists, as the chattra of cloth does upon the point of Manjusri's sword. The greatest length of the city from north to south is about a mile, and its breadth varies from one-fourth to one-third of a mile.

On the west Kathmandu is bounded by the Bishnmatti, and its streets, or those of its suburbs, slope down rather steeply from the higher level on which the greater portion of the city is built, to the very edge of the river, which flows in some places directly below its walls.

The Bishnmatti is crossed by two pucka bridges, over one of which goes the road from the city to the arsenal, and artillery barracks and parade-ground, and over the other the direct road to the temple of Shambunath.

On the east and south the city overlooks the lowlands which lie along the courses of the Dhobikola and Baghmatti rivers.

The earliest name by which the city was known was Manju Pattan, having been so called after himself by Manjusri, its traditional founder. Its modern name is said to be derived from an ancient building, which stands in the heart of the city near the darbar, and which was originally and is still known among the Niwars as *Kathmandu*, from *kath* " wood " (of which material it is chiefly composed), and *mandi*, or *mandon*, "an edifice, house, or temple."

This building was erected by Rajah Lachminna Sing Mall, A.D. 1596, not as a temple (though there are some figures of Shiva inside it), but as a house of accommodation for fakeers, and it always has been and is still used solely for that purpose. Though old, it is in good preservation, having been always kept in repair by Government.

In consequence of the extension of the suburbs of the city, especially towards the west and north, the walls of the city have been allowed to fall into decay, and in many places are now hardly distinguishable. Many of the gateways, of which originally there were thirty-two, are still standing, but the gates themselves have long since disappeared. There are said to be thirty-two small squares or *tols* in the city, but the following are the only squares which are now of any interest or importance.

Assan Tol, at the northern end of the city (near the Rani Talao).

Indra Chok, between Assan Tol and the darbar.

The square in front of the darbar.

The Kathmandu Tol, to the south-west of the darbar.

The Toba Tol, in south-west of city, near the bridge over the Baghmatti.

Laghan Tol, in south-east of city, close to another small square (Laghan Taubian), which has a Buddhist temple in its centre. Two streets, one from gateway to north-east, another from gateway to north of

city, meet at the Assan Tol; thence one street runs
through Indra Chok to the darbar, whence one
street runs south-west to the Bishnmatti through
Kathmandu Tol and Toba Tol, and another runs
south-east to Laghan Tol, and thence on towards
the magazine and high road to the Baghmatti and
Patan. Several other streets traverse the city,
mostly running more or less directly from gateways on its circumference towards the neighbourhood of the darbar. Innumerable lanes, narrow,
dirty, and crooked, intersect the city, and connect
these different thoroughfares with each other. The
pavement throughout the city is of brick tiles; in
most places a gutter runs on each side of the street,
leaving a narrow space between it and the houses;
but as this space, though paved, is not wide enough
for a footpath, all the traffic is carried on along the
middle of the road. The most important building in
the city is the darbar, which is situated in its centre.
It is a low, rambling, and by no means imposing-
looking structure, its architecture exhibiting a strange
mixture of the most discordant styles. The ancient
parts were built by the Niwars, and their carved
windows and grotesque monsters supporting the roofs
have been so disfigured by the Gorkhas with thick
coats of paint and plaster, that their primitive and
characteristic features are almost destroyed. Modern
wings have been added also during the present century, which are built after the European fashion, with
plain glass windows and green Venetian blinds, and

in which stucco is used instead of stone, and gaudy colours but imperfectly conceal the absence of costly carving.

The darbar covers a considerable extent of ground, and is of an irregular quadrangle form. To the north it is partly open to the city, and is flanked by the lofty Talliju temple. At the southern end is the council-chamber, the Basantpur, and the long modern darbar or public reception room. On the east it encloses the royal garden and stables, and on the west, which is its principal front, it is open to the street, and forms one side of a rambling irregular square, in which are clustered together a number of Hindu temples, originally built by the Niwars, and which have therefore the usual form and elaborate carvings by which all Niwar temples are distinguished. In consequence of their vicinity to the palace they have been kept in good repair by the Gorkha Government, but their ornamental carvings have been so disguised and daubed over with paint, gilt, and tinsel (à la mode Gorkha), that they have lost all their original beauty, and may almost, without caricature, be compared to those wooden models of Chinese pagodas (which they resemble distantly in form) which are to be found in every London toy-shop. Besides those which are around, there are several temples within the precincts of the darbar; but their lofty gilt roofs rising one above another, and tapering to pinnacles above, are the only parts of them which are visible from the streets.

Opposite the north-west corner of the darbar is the
Kot, or military council-chamber, in which was
enacted the massacre of 1846.   The Kot Ling,
Dhunsar, and other courts of law are also situated
around the western front of the darbar.

Near the south-western angle of the darbar is the
little square now used as a fruit market, which is
called Kathmandu Tol.   The old building, Kathmandu, from which the city derives its name, is situated on its northern side; the old Dhunsar court of
law, now deserted and in ruin, on its eastern; some
fakirs' houses on its south, and some old and half-
ruined temples on its west.   It is one of the most
curious and characteristic places in the whole of the
city.

Several of the sardars have during the last few
years built large houses in different parts of the city.
The sites on which they stand having been well
selected, the ground levelled, and the surrounding
buildings cleared away, give to them rather an imposing appearance, and make them contrast very
strongly with the humble and dirty, but still very
picturesque exteriors of the mass of the old Niwar
dwellings in their neighbourhood.

Their exteriors are in the pseudo-classic, or carpenter's Gothic style of architecture, profusely covered
with paint and plaster, instead of with rich carvings
and fancifully cut wooden reliefs.

In their interiors the private apartments retain the
low ceilings and doorways, step-ladders, and trap-

THE MARKET PLACE, KATHMANDU.

The building (from which the City derives ... name) was erected A.D. 1596.

doors, which are characteristic of most native houses; but they have one or more large public reception rooms, built in the English fashion, with lofty ceilings and glass windows, the walls of which are ornamented with mirrors and pictures, and the floors covered with Brussels carpets. These rooms are filled with the most curious medley of useful and ornamental articles of English and French furniture. Steel fire-places, with marble mantlepieces; sofas, couches, easy chairs, billiard tables, and four-posted beds; candelabras, pianos, organs, glassware, vases, &c., are crowded together in the most curious confusion, and in a manner which shows that though their present owners may value them as curiosities, they are utterly ignorant of or incapable of appreciating their real use. Still the presence of these European luxuries and ornamental furniture has introduced an appearance at least of elegance and comfort into the interior of the houses of the Gorkha sardars, which was never dreamt of, even by royalty, at the time when the Niwar dynasty was on the throne.

Numerous as are the different Hindu temples in Kathmandu, there are none of them of any peculiar interest or beauty. The Talliju temple is the most important, and the most imposing in its appearance.

There are several Buddhist temples in different parts of the city; of these the most interesting are "Kathisambhu," and Buddhmandal, in a square of its own, near the square called Laghan Tol. The number of Buddhist Niwars in Kathmandu is small compared with that in Patan, and the Buddhist remains and temples are not therefore so numerous in the former as in the latter city. It is believed that the Buddhists in Kathmandu scarcely amount to half of the Niwar population, whereas in Patan fully two-thirds of the Niwars are Buddhists.

It is almost impossible to estimate the population of Kathmandu or any other large city in Nipal with any accuracy, as no regular or scientific census has ever been taken. In Kathmandu the population is probably not less than sixty thousand nor more than eighty thousand; of these the great bulk are Niwars, the Gorkhas forming but a very small minority.

Outside the city, on the east, is a level grassy plain, one-third of a mile long, and from two hundred to three hundred yards wide, which is the grand parade ground, and is called the Thandi Khel.* On its eastern and northern sides are barracks for some of the regiments which are stationed at the capital. In its centre is a peculiarly ugly stone column supporting a gilt figure of Jang Bahadur, which was erected by himself, and inaugurated with great pomp and ceremony in 1853.

Between the parade-ground and the city is a palace, built and fitted up by General Bhim Sen as his own residence when he was Premier, but which, since the murder of his unfortunate nephew, Martabar Singh, who also lived in it, has been appropriated for the

---

* This parade-ground and barracks, as well as the artillery cantonments and arsenal, were built by General Bhim Sen.

use of some of the members of the royal family. Although the house itself is kept in repair, yet the flower-gardens have been neglected, and are now over-run with jungle; and the fountains can no longer play, in consequence of the fish-ponds from which they sprang having been allowed to dry up. Close to this palace is a lofty stone column, about two hundred feet high, which was erected by Bhim Sen. It gradually tapers from its base to the summit, where it does not support any kind of statue, but ends in a sort of lantern pinnacle, very similar in appearance to the celebrated pepper-boxes of the British National Gallery. It was not raised to commemorate any particular epoch or event, but apparently merely for the purpose of "astonishing the natives," and it well deserves the name of "Bhim Sen's folly."

At the south-western angle of the Thandi Khel is the magazine, where is the Government foundry for the manufacture of cannon, as well as of many other articles which are worked in the hard metals.

Close to the magazine is a temple to Jagannath, built in 1852 by Jang Bahadur. The temple was commenced on a very grand scale by Bhim Sen; but when little more than the foundations had been laid, that minister died, and the work was abandoned, in consequence of the general belief in Nipal that it is unlucky to carry on or resume an undertaking which has been interrupted by the death of the party who commenced it.

Jang, however, disregarding this prejudice, has completed the present building on the very foundations which were left unfinished on the death of his great uncle Bhim Sen.

It is only to be regretted that he was not as liberal with his money as he was with his religion, and that his good taste did not induce him to erect a building of durability and architectural merit, as Bhim Sen had intended to do, in the national style of the Niwars, instead of constructing a cheap brick-and-plaster imitation of one of the most common and least ornamental temples of Hindustan. On the high road near the northern end of the Thandi Khel, is a small but richly endowed temple, of great antiquity, and having a larger number of worshippers than any temple in the valley. It is certainly the most popular and fashionable "chapel-of-ease" in Nipal, and its votaries are found among the highest as well as the lowest in the land. It is called the Temple of "Mehenkal," under which name the Hindus worship Mahadeo or Shiva; while the Buddhists maintain that the sacred figure represents, not Mahadeo, but the Bodhisatwa Padma-Pain, and that this is proved by the little stone figure, which they consider to be Amitabha, which is rising out of the forehead of the idol. It is one of those points on which "a great deal may be said on both sides of the question"; but the result of the doubt is very curious, as it has led to the temple becoming a sort of neutral ground on which the rival Hindus and Buddhists meet to pray before one common God, whom the former worship as Shiva, and the latter as Padma-Pain.

In the north-east outskirts of the city is a large square tank, called the Rani Pokhra, or Queen's Tank, having been constructed by a former queen of Nipal. In its centre is a small temple to Devi, which is connected with the western side of the tank by a bridge or viaduct of several arches. The old temple and bridge, being much decayed and partly overgrown by wild ivy, were very picturesque objects, especially if looked at from the southern side of the tank, when the background of the view was formed by the snowy peaks of the Gosainthan, as they glistened in the sun high above the bluff and forest-crowned head of Mount Sheopuri. They were pulled down in 1851 by Jang Bahadur, who replaced them by the present ugly brick-and-plaster structure, while at the same time he destroyed the pretty appearance of the tank by surrounding it with a high brick wall, which completely shuts it out from the road. Whenever the trial "by ordeal of immersion" takes place, the ceremony is performed in this tank. Close to the north-west and south-west corners of the tank were two of the ancient city gateways; the former is still standing, but the latter has disappeared. A high road runs from each of these corners of the tank to the Assan Tol.

Near the north-east angle of the tank is a small temple to Narayan, prettily situated among a group of very fine Nipal elm trees. A spring of water rises close to it, from which the place is called the Narain

Hitti (Hitti meaning a spring or watering-place). Opposite to the temple is a large modern stucco house, which was formerly the residence of Fathi Jang Chauntra. After his death at the Kot massacre in 1846, the house rem......ed unoccupied till 1852, when it was repaired, and is now tenanted by Gul Ranudat Singh. Outside the city, towards the north, are the suburbs of Timmale, which contain two or three large houses belonging to sardars, and formerly occupied by Generals Badrinat Singh and Jai Bahadur. Timmale extends towards the British Residency, from which it is separated by a parade-ground, attached to which is a building containing the headquarters of two Gorkha regiments.

A large powder-magazine formerly stood in the centre of this parade-ground, but it was struck by lightning in 1834, and completely destroyed by the explosion of one hundred and sixty thousand pounds of gunpowder which it contained at the time. Twenty-seven men were killed by the accident, and the British Residency, which was only four hundred yards distant, had a narrow escape, as all its windows, blinds, &c. were smashed by the concussion, but no other injury was sustained.

Adjoining this parade-ground, on its north side, is the British Residency, with the barracks, occupied by a company of sepoys. The British lines occupy an area of about forty acres, and are situated on the high grounds immediately overlooking the plain of the Bishnmatti river.

To the west of the city of Kathmandu, and separated from it by the Bishnmatti river, are the cantonments and parade-ground for the two regiments of artillery; they are situated on the high grounds, on a plain immediately beneath the south side of the hill of Sambhunath.

The barracks are ranged along the north side of the parade-ground; on the south side are the gun-sheds, in which nearly all the guns in the neighbourhood of the capital are stored, and among them are the two guns captured from the British in 1815, on the defeat of Captain Sibley's detachment at Parsah in the Terai. The arsenal is a large detached building at the south-west angle of the parade; it contains all the musketry, swords, and ammunition which are kept in store by the Nipal Government. It is an extensive building running round the four sides of a central square; the walls are of brick; the roof is tiled, but the floors and a great part of the interior consist merely of wood.

To the south of Kathmandu, a level delta-shaped plain extends from the city walls to the point of confluence of the Baghmatti and Bishnmatti. Several Hindu temples are clustered about this sacred spot, and on the right bank of the Baghmatti General Bam Bahadur has recently completed a handsome and useful ghat, two or three hundred yards in length, and leading by a flight of stone steps down to the water's edge.

CHAPTER VII.

PATAN.—BHATGAON.—KIRTIPUR.

Patan, or *Lallit Patan*, is the largest city in Nipal.
It is situated on the high ground to the south of the
Baghmatti, about half a mile from the left bank of
that river and about one mile and a half to the south-
east of Kathmandu. Previous to the Gorkha conquest, Patan was the capital of one of the three independent principalities into which Nipal was divided ;
it was the residence of one of the Niwar kings, and
was at that time a wealthy, powerful, and important
city.*

At the surrender of Patan to Prithi Narayan in

---

* The King of Patan possessed a larger territory *within* the
valley than belonged to the kings either of Bhatgaon or Kathmandu. His jurisdiction extended over Kirtipur, Chobbar, Thankot, Phirphing, Godauri, and all the towns and villages to the
south of the Baghmatti and Hanumankola streams.

1768, the city was given up to plunder, the nobility
and principal men were murdered, and the greatest
barbarities were practised on the unfortunate inhabitants, who, being mostly Buddhists, received but little
mercy at the hands of their Hindu conquerors.

The royal palace was dismantled; the dwellings of
the wealthy citizens were robbed of everything valuable that they contained, and even the temples were
not spared. Their accumulated wealth was seized,
and the revenues of the Church lands which were
attached to all temples for their support, and which
had from time immemorial been regarded as sacred,
were appropriated either wholly or in part by the
rapacity of the Gorkha Government.

Patan has never recovered from the blow it then
received. Although still a very populous city, containing probably not less than sixty thousand inhabitants, it has lost all its social as well as political
importance. The spirit of its inhabitants appears
to have been completely crushed by the loss of their
independence, the overthrow of their royal house, the
murder of their leading citizens, and the plunder or
destruction of all which they held most sacred.

The consequence is that the city of Patan has
gradually but steadily declined; its darbar, public
buildings, and most of its temples have fallen into a
ruinous and dilapidated state; while the poor Niwars
hove not the means to restore them, and seem stricken
with a sort of apathy which prevents their attempting
even to check the progress of further decay.

8 *

It is not the Newars who are to blame for the neglected and ruinous condition of so many of their temples and public buildings. Under the Niwar dynasty every temple had a liberal jaigir permanently attached to it, the produce of which mainly kept it in repair and paid the expenses of the festivals connected with it. On the Gorkha conquest of the valley such of the temples as the new Government thought it would be desirable to keep in good repair for the use of the Gorkha invaders were allowed to retain a moiety, seldom more, of their church-lands; these temples are to this day in very fair preservation. But in the majority of cases Prithi Narayan confiscated the entire jaigir; and in many instances, where he had spared the sacred revenues, Ran Bahadur, and afterwards Bhim Sen, appropriated them. Such temples having been left to the precarious support of the "voluntary system" among a people whose poverty is greater even than their piety, have naturally decayed, and are now fast falling into ruin. Although a most curious and interesting city—rich in Buddhist monuments and Hindu temples, and full of ;picturesque views of buildings once profusely ornamented with elaborate carvings and grotesque sculptures in wood and in stone, but now broken into ruins or overgrown with jungle—yet there is an air of sad solemnity, and almost of gloom, hanging about everything connected with the place.

The city looks much too large for its inhabitants; its streets as well as its buildings appear to be half empty; there is none of the bustle and activity and palpable prosperity which are visible throughout Kathmandu and Bhatgaon. Ruined buildings and deserted shrines, broken archways and mutilated sculptures, meet the eye at every turn; and while these remains are evidences of its former grandeur, they still painfully proclaim the melancholy fact that Patan's "glory has departed." The city is of a circular form, and is said to resemble in shape the wheel or chakra of Buddha. Its ancient walls and gateways in most places are ruinous, and in many have quite disappeared.

The darbar is situated in the centre of the city, and towards it numerous streets converge, more or less irregularly, from all those sites in the circle of the ancient walls where gateways formerly stood, and where some of them are standing at the present day.

The streets in Patan, although wider, are much dirtier than those in Kathmandu, and they are not generally kept in such good repair. The darbar originally consisted of three sides of a quadrangle; the side facing to the north is now in ruins; that facing to the west was the principal front, and forms one side of the large irregular square round which are collected a number of Hindu temples and columns of various ages and in different styles. This side of the darbar is still in very good preservation, and its architectural effect is greatly enhanced by the lofty five-storied temple, named Deo-Talli, which rises from its centre, and which, by its prominence and height, gives an appearance of dignity and elevation

to the whole building, which are very much wanted
in many of the principal edifices in Nipal.

The side of the darbar which faces to the south
is now completely destroyed. The fourth or eastern
side was open and formed part of a private garden to
the palace. Within the precincts of the darbar were
several small courts of different sizes, but they were
not so numerous as in the darbars of Bhatgaon or
Kathmandu. In some of these courts on the western
side of the darbar were temples which are now falling
into ruin. The courts communicating with these
temples were most elaborately ornamented with
carvings and sculptures of various mythological subjects; many of these are still in very good preservation, though the temples themselves are crumbling
into ruins.

Although the Niwars of Patan were mostly Buddhists, the royal family were Hindus; and the sym-
pathies of the court therefore were in favour of
Hindu rather than purely Buddhist worship. Accordingly most of the principal Hindu temples in
Patan are clustered together round the immediate
vicinity of the palace, while all its Buddhist temples
are scattered about in different parts of the city, and
some of those that are the most ancient are situated
in its outskirts.

There are several squares in different parts of the
city, and some of them are much larger than any
either in Kathmandu or Bhatgaon. Some of these
hardly deserve the name of squares, for they are

mainly irregular open spaces formed by the meeting
at one point of three or four streets coming from
different directions. In the centre of such open
places there is commonly either a temple, or a column,
or a peepul tree; or two or three temples or powas
are sometimes built around its sides. The most
notable of these irregular squares is situated a short
distance from the south-east angle of the darbar;
though of but limited extent, it is of importance as
being one of the halting-places for the car in the
annual festival in honour of Machendranath, and it
is besides remarkable for a very ancient *hithu* or
watering-place on its south side. The water issues
by three ornamental mouth-pieces, and falls into a
stone reservoir. The purity of the water and antiquity of the spring (the first hithu having been constructed here A.D. 880) combined with its position in
one of the principal thoroughfares in the city, make
this watering-place a sort of "Aldgate Pump" of
Patan.

There is a large square in the western part of the
city, built round an extensive tank, on the west side
of which is an ancient Buddhist chaitya, and on the
south side one or two Hindu temples.

To the north of the darbar is another irregular
square, on the east side of which stands a lofty-
roofed temple, within the inner quadrangle of which is
a sacred tank.

There are, besides the above, several smaller squares
containing Hindu temples sacred to different divini-

ties ; but they none of them possess any peculiar interest.

By far the most curious and ancient of these squares are the quadrangular ranges of buildings which are built around the most important of the Buddhist temples with which Patan abounds. These quadrangles are called " Vihars " (pronounced " Biar "), and in ancient times were monasteries, which were occupied solely by Buddhist monks, their followers, and pupils. In the course of ages, however, as Buddhism in Nipal has declined from its primitive purity, the religious character of these institutions has entirely passed away. There are no longer monasteries in Nipal, and the establishments formerly devoted exclusively to religious purposes are now mere guilds of trade, occupied to overflowing, not by pious monks and tonsured ascetics, but by families of the prolific Niwars, who hereditarily follow certain avocations which, with their quarters in the vihar, they have inherited from their ancestors.

This practice of certain families, who follow the same trade, all clustering together into the same ranges of buildings, where they enjoy by inheritance peculiar privileges in consideration of their performing peculiar duties, has had great influence in encouraging, if it did not help to originate, the system of caste, founded on the exclusive exercise of certain hereditary trades, which has been universally adopted by all the Buddhist Niwars in Nipal, although it is utterly opposed to the spirit as well as the law of the orthodox Buddhist scriptures.

There are in Patan fifteen large and distinct vihars at the present day, and as each of these was originally a monastery, we may imagine how the streets of the city must in bygone ages have swarmed with the teachers and followers of Buddhism, and how great an influence in religious matters the pious monks of Patan must have exercised over the rest of the valley. Patan ever has been, and is still, the stronghold of Buddhism in Nipal. Two-thirds of its Niwar inhabitants are Buddhists; it abounds in Buddhist monuments and temples; and by far the most important and grandest festival in Nipal, that of Machendranath, is a purely Buddhist one, and is celebrated in its streets.

Besides these fifteen principal vihars, there are a large number, more than one hundred, of other smaller vihars, which are mere offshoots from one or other of the fifteen original ones. The inhabitants having outgrown the limits of an old vihar, some of its members migrate and found another, which, however, is always looked upon as a colony, closely connected with the parent establishment.

The same applies to Kathmandu, in which there are not above eight or ten, if so many, of the original vihars; but there are said to be no less than eighty-eight vihars altogether now in Kathmandu, including all the subordinate colonies. Some of them are very small; they vary in size and decoration, according to the means of those who founded them.

All the vihars are inhabited solely by Banhra Niwars, at least as a general rule. The Tafu, Udas, and heterodox Buddhists live scattered about in streets and lanes through the city; they never congregate in masses as do the Banhras. An individual Tafu or other Niwar may be allowed to reside in a vihar from charity, or as an exception; but he has no hereditary right to residence. The Banhras occupying the same vihar usually follow the same avocation.

One of the most extensive of these fifteen vihars is situated in the western quarter of the city, between the darbar and the large tank square. It contains a number of small Buddhist temples of various sizes, the largest of which stands in the centre of the square. The most important Buddhist square in Patan is that which contains the temple of Machendranath. It is situated in the southern quarter of the city. Perhaps the most interesting vihar is that which is said to be the most ancient building in the city, and which is situated near the much-frequented hithu to the southeast of the darbar. It is called "Unko Vihar." Close to it is another small vihar containing a very curious Buddhist temple, called Maha Buddh, dedicated to Sakya Singa. The other vihars and Buddhist temples within the limits of the city do not require any peculiar mention.

All these vihars, not only in Patan, but in the

other capital cities and towns in Nipal, possess the same general architectural characters.

They are double-storied, and built after the ordinary Nipalese fashion, of burnt red bricks with massive wooden window-frames and doorways, and overhanging tiled roofs, the eaves of which rest upon boldly carved wooden supports. The ornamental carvings of their windows and doorways are generally very elaborate, and on the stone gateways which form the entrances to some of them, are bold bas-reliefs of various mythological subjects. Although surrounding Buddhist shrines and containing within their limits many sacred objects of Buddhist worship, yet these vihars must not be mistaken for temples. In former times they were monasteries, inhabited by mendicant monks and ascetics, but they were never temples to the Supreme or any other Deity; at the present day they are merely secular establishments or corporations, intimately associated with the existing corrupt system of caste, and are maintained ₁by the Niwars as separate institutions solely for the encouragement of trade and not for the support of religion.

Although the greater part of every vihar is occupied by families of trading Niwars, yet a certain portion of the quadrangular range of buildings is set aside for the use and habitation of those priests and their attendants and companions who are in immediate charge of the temple or temples to which the vihar is attached. In this part all such supernumerary ornaments, trappings, &c. connected with the temple as are only used on certain occasions, are stowed away; and in some cases where a locomotive god belongs to a temple, and is only displayed to his worshippers in procession on peculiar high-days and holidays, the image of the deity himself—with the clothes, masks, and paraphernalia worn by those who officiate in such religious festivities—is carefully kept *perdu* in the vihar under the charge of certain responsible parties.

Outside the walls of Patan are four large Buddhist temples, one opposite to each of the four cardinal points of the compass. The south-eastern and western are each about a quarter of a mile from the city walls, but the northern one, by the extension of the suburbs around it, has become included apparently within the city itself, although it is really outside the boundary line of the ancient walls.

These four temples are remarkable from being of a different character to any of the other Buddhist temples in the valley. They have the usual hemispherical dome or "garb," and round their bases are the shrines and images of the celestial Buddhas, but they have no kind of spire or pinnacle; the summit of the dome supporting merely a wooden kind of ladder-scaffolding, which, on certain festive occasions, is crowned with a temporary chattra or pinnacle. In their general appearance and architectural character they much more nearly resemble the ancient Buddhist topes of Central India and Afghanistan than the ordinary chaityas or spire-crowned temples of Nipal.

Outside the city, near the eastern of these topes, is a three-roofed Hindu temple of Devi, having four entrances, each guarded by a pair of lions. It is chiefly remarkable as being a most favourite spot for the incremation of the dead, it being calculated that fully half the corpses of Patan are burnt in its immediate vicinity.

Between the western tope and the city walls is an old and rather pretty tank. Beyond and to the north-west of the western tope is a small conical hill on which is situated a vihar, surrounding several Buddhist temples.

The southern tope is much the largest of them all; between it and the city walls is a fine Nipal elm, round the trunk of which the car of Machendranath is dragged at the Ruthjatra, and under the shadow of which the god receives a preliminary washing before the festival commences.

Kirtipur in the early history of Nipal was the capital of a small independent principality, but it was afterwards annexed, by right of conquest, to the possessions of the King of Patan. It stands in a commanding position upon the level crest of one of the low rounded hills which form a continuous range across the south-western quarter of the Valley of Nipal, running parallel to the base of Mount Chandagiri, and connecting a spur from Indra Than in the west with one from Mahabharat in the south.

Kirtipur is raised between two hundred and three

hundred feet above the level of the surrounding plain. It overlooks the city of Kathmandu on the north, and that of Patan towards the east, from each of which capitals it is distant about three miles. Towards the south it commands the small valley which skirts the base of the Chandagiri from east to west. The stream by which that valley is drained flows round the western shoulder of the hill of Kirtipur in its course to join the Baghmatti. Towards the east it is connected by a low ridge with the hill on which stands the town of Chabbar.

Kirtipur has never been an extensive city; but its almost impregnable position gave it an importance, disproportioned to its size, during the early period of Nipal history, while in modern times it has been rendered memorable not only for its gallant resistance through three protracted sieges to the invading army of Prithi Narayan, but for the brutal manner in which the Gorkhas, after its fall, wreaked their fury upon the heroic Niwars, who, though exhausted by three years' warfare (1765-67) and with part of their town betrayed into the hands of the enemy, had still refused to surrender their citadel and strongholds, until they were cajoled by false promises of a general amnesty.

Having obtained by treachery what they had failed to carry by force of arms, the Gorkhas murdered most of the principal citizens and cut off the noses and lips of all the male inhabitants; those only being spared who could play on wind instruments, and who therefore might be of use as musicians in the army of the conqueror.*

The name of the town was ordered to be changed from Kirtipur into Naskatapur, or "the City of Cut Noses."

Since those days the city has rapidly fallen into decay, no attempt having been ever made to restore its temples or repair any of its public buildings. The ancient walls and some of the gateways are still standing, but they are very much dilapidated. The city generally is in a melancholy state of ruin and decay. It is inhabited solely by Niwars, and it is doubtful whether it contains five thousand inhabitants. The air is very healthy, and the water is said to be so pure that cases of goitre very rarely are seen among those who dwell in Kirtipur.

The principal approach to Kirtipur is by a winding road, which ascends the north-eastern face of the hill on which the city stands; but there are besides several foot-paths leading from the plain below to different parts of the town. The city is traversed throughout its entire length from east to west by a rather narrow, crooked, dirty street, which leads from its eastern entrance to the darbar, which is at the western end of the town.

The ruins of the darbar and some adjacent temples

---

* Father Giuseppe, who was then in the country, wrote an account of this siege—since published in the "Asiatic Researches." Thirty years later, Colonel Kirkpatrick saw many of the ill-fated victims. (See Wright's "History of Nepal," ch. i.)—ED.

are situated on and around a small conical hill, which
rises out of the western extremity of the town,
whence they overlook and command the whole of
the city. In its best estate the darbar was never
a large one, but it is now so utterly in ruins that
even its form and extent cannot be traced. The
body of a ruined temple (built of a peculiar purple
or lake-coloured brick, which is not now manufactured) still survives, unroofed and overgrown with
jungle, on the highest part of the hill, and some of
its ornamental stone figures of elephants, lions, &c.,
are still in very fair preservation in front of its
eastern entrance. It appears originally to have stood
in the centre of a sort of square or quadrangle (probably part of the Basantpur), with which the level
summit of the hill was crowned.*

The base of this little conical hill was strengthened
and supported by terraces built of stone, and running
up its sides, one above the other; and the ascent
was, and is still, by a steep flight of steps, which
in ancient days could easily have been defended
against attack.

Most of the temples in Kirtipur are more or less in
ruin, but there are some whose revenues have been
partially spared by the Gorkha Government, and these
are, therefore, still in good preservation. ·

---

* This temple was built A.D. 1555. It was sacred to Parbati and
Maha Deo combined.

The principal temple stands upon the edge of the hill, near the centre of the north side of the town. It is a four-roofed temple of Bhairab,* and has a large number of worshippers, many of whom, on certain occasions, come from distant parts of the valley to perform their devotions at the shrine of the most popular deity in Nipal. 'Inside the temple is a painted image, not of a man, but of a tiger†—that animal being looked on as a symbol of the god. Close to the quadrangle which contains the temple of Bhairab is a small square, in the centre of which is a tank of very dirty water, and on the north side of which are two or three ruined temples.

On the northern edge of the town, at the top of one of the foot-paths by which the hill is ascended, is a small shrine of Ganesha, which has a beautifully carved and very picturesque stone gateway, covered with designs of different mythological subjects. This shrine was built, A.D. 1665, by a Sherista Niwar, a Jaisi by caste. On the toran above is, in the centre, Ganesha; on his right hand, on a peacock, is Kumari‡; on his left, on Garuda,§ is Vishnavi; next to Kumari, seated on a buffalo, is Varahi; next to Varahi, on a demon or man, is Chamunda or Kali;

---

* This temple was built by one of the royal family, A.D. 1513.

† From which the temple is called Bagh Bhairab.

‡ The Virgin, Siva's consort, otherwise known as Kali, Durga, &c.—(ED.)

§ A being, half bird, half man, on whom Vishnu is sometimes represented as riding.—(ED.)

next to Vishnavi, seated on an elephant, is Indraini;
next to Indraini, seated on a lion, is Mahalachmi;
above Ganesha, in the centre, is Bhairab, having on
his right hand Brahmaini seated on a goose, and on
his left Rudraini (consort of Mahadeo) seated on a
bull. Below the Gryphons on each side are Kalsas,
supporting a Siri Baksh. Above, at the lower angle
of the toran, is a double trikon with a binda or point
in the centre. The eight female deities represented
on this toran are collectively called " Ashtamatrika,"
or the eight divine mothers. They stand in the following order of precedence towards each other :—
1st, Brahmaini, on a goose; 2nd, Rudraini, on a
bull; 3rd, Kumari, on a peacock; 4th, Vishnavi, on
Garuda; 5th, Varahi, on a buffalo; 6th, Indraini, on
an elephant; 7th, Chamunda or Kali, on a demon
(wife of Bhairab); 8th, Mahalachmi, on a lion. Above
them all is often placed, as in the present instance, Bhairab as lord of all. Ganesha and his
brother Kumar being sons of Bhairab or Maha Deo
are often, as in this case, introduced into these sculptures.

    In the south-eastern quarter of the city there is a
Buddhist temple, called Chillandeo, which, though
comparatively small, yet on account of the number
of sculptured objects of Buddhist worship which it
exhibits, and the accuracy with which the various
deities and their respective symbols and vehicles are
figured, is one of the most perfect and valuable
monuments of Buddhism in the whole valley.

THE "GOLDEN GATE" IN THE DARBAR, BHATGAON
Built, A.D. 1754

There are no other buildings of any particular interest in Kirtipur.

The city of *Bhatgaon* is situated on the eastern side of the valley at a distance of about three miles from the foot of Mount Mahadeo Pokhra, and of between seven and eight miles in a south-eastern direction from Kathmandu. It is built upon the northern or right bank of the Hanuman stream, which flows round its eastern and southern sides. It stands upon a promontory of high table-land which stretches from the base of Mount Mahadeo Pokhra, and extends between the plain of the Hanuman stream on its south and east, and that of Kashn Kushn or Kansavati stream on its north and west; these two streams, with their attendant plains or valleys, uniting with each other a short distance below or to the west of Bhatgaon. The city is said to resemble in shape the conch or shell of Vishnu Narayan; the rounded and broader end of the shell being towards the north-east, and having its point directed to the south-west. Bhatgaon is not so extensive as either Kathmandu or Patan; but its streets are wider and cleaner, its general appearance more imposing, and its temples and public buildings are in better preservation than similar edifices in any of the other cities in the valley. It is supposed to contain about fifty thousand inhabitants, and of these the large majority are Hindu Niwars, the Buddhist Niwars hardly amounting to one-third of the population.

For two hundred years previous to the Gorkha conquest of Nipal, the King of Bhatgaon had generally maintained a decided ascendency over the two principalities of Patan and Kathmandu.

The three kings of Nipal were independent sovereigns, but being descendants of the same common ancestor—Jai Ekshah Mall—the two junior branches usually acknowledged the supremacy of the elder House, or that of Bhatgaon.

The jurisdiction of the King of Bhatgaon, *within the valley*, was comparatively limited, as—with the exception of Timmi—it extended over no large towns. *Beyond* the valley, however, his territories spread eastward to the Dudh Kosi river, and northward to the Kuti pass, and were much more extensive than those of either of his brother sovereigns. His royal residence, although smaller, was always more handsome, costly, and ornamental than either of the other capital cities in Nipal.

At the time of the Gorkha conquest of the valley, Bhatgaon was surrendered to Prithi Narayan without a struggle, and it escaped in consequence a good deal of the plunder and maltreatment which were experienced by the other cities of Nipal at the hands of the conquerors.

The great majority of its inhabitants being Hindus, the Gorkha King—himself a bigoted Hindu—appears to have respected their temples, and to have restrained his followers from committing any flagrant or open violence against the public buildings with which the city abounded. Prithi Narayan may also have felt some sympathy for the fallen fortunes of his former ally, Ranjit Mall, whose applications for assistance against the Kings of Kathmandu and Patan had been the immediate cause of bringing the Gorkhas into the territories of Nipal.

From these various causes the aged King of Bhatgaon was treated by Prithi Narayan with considerable leniency; his capital was respected, and though the Gorkhas, of course, *suo more*, appropriated the entire revenues of the state, and the greater portion of those of the church, yet they fortunately spared enough of the latter to enable the Niwars to keep the majority of their temples in a state of very good repair.

It is in consequence of this unusual moderation on the part of the Gorkhas that, in comparison with Patan or Kirtipur, Bhatgaon still presents a flourishing appearance; its streets and inhabitants have a cheerful aspect, and its religious edifices generally are, even at the present day, in fairly good preservation.

The mass of the Niwars of Bhatgaon being Hindus, most of the religious edifices which adorn the city are sacred to Hindu deities. The Buddhist temples and vihars are but few in number, and are none of them remarkable for either their size or their decoration. For description of darbar and temples, &c., see other note-books.

The ancient walls and gateways of Bhatgaon, like those of the other capital cities, are fast crumbling into ruin. The principal streets trend from the gateways either to the darbar (which is situated on the northern edge of the town), or to the small square called Taumari Tol (containing the temples of Bhowani and Bhairab), which is a little to the south of the darbar, and which stands in the centre of the city.

Outside the city, on its western side, is a very large and handsome tank, called Siddha Pokri, three hundred yards long and one hundred yards wide, surrounded by a stone gateway and enclosing wall with partis at the four corners and in the centre of the four sides. It was built by Rajah Partab Mall, 1640–50, and thoroughly repaired and stocked in gold fish, imported from China by General Bhim Sen during his Premiership.

About a quarter of a mile to the west of this tank is another large tank, of similar shape but smaller dimensions. It was built by Partab Mall at the same time as the other tank. It is now neglected and fast going to ruin. There is also a small tank, called the "Queen's Tank," on the opposite side of the road. Between these two tanks is an open plain, overlooking the valley of Kashn Kushn to the north, and that of the Hanuman stream to the south. It is used as a parade-ground for the troops now quartered in Bhatgaon.

To the south of the city, at the distance of rather more than a mile, is a very curious shrine of Ganesha

—called Ganesha Than,*—very prettily situated, at the summit of a steep flight of stone steps, on one shoulder of a richly wooded hill which runs out into the valley opposite to Bhatgaon.

There are no other objects of particular interest in the immediate neighbourhood of Bhatgaon. The suburbs of the city, which lie chiefly on its southern and eastern sides towards the river, are very dirty, and infected with pigs and buffaloes and their respective herdsmen.

The Hanuman stream is crossed by three pucka bridges; over the southern one the road passes towards Ganeshthan; the two other bridges lead towards the east.

---

* It is commonly called "Suraj Banaik." There are four favourite banaiks or shrines of Ganesha in the valley:—1, "Suraj Banaik," near Bhatgaon; 2, "Sidhi Banaik, at Sanku; 3, "Assu Banaik," in Kathmandu; 4, "Bigna Banaik, near Chobbar.

CHAPTER VIII.

REMARKS ON THE ROUTES BY WHICH AN INVADING ARMY
COULD APPROACH THE VALLEY OF NIPAL.*

FROM the Oudh frontier to the old Tenavi Naddi, the
country situated between the parallels of Bansi and
Sharwa is covered with dense forest jungle and intersected by deep nullahs.   North of Sharwa and to
within ten miles of the lower range of hills it is
comparatively open and swampy, and is covered
with extensive plains of long grass, and occasional
large patches of cultivation.

Between the old and new Tenavi Naddis is an immense swamp, impassable at most places, extending
from Irwah to Tilokpur, and from Sipur nearly to
Betul. From Tilokpur to Palia the appearance of
the country is much the same, but the ground is in

---

* Condensed from a Report to Government by Mr. Ross Bell,
C.S., dated Delhi, March, 1839.

general lower, and the scenery varied with patches of
sal forest and bamboo jungle. Eastward of Pulia,
as far as the Gandak, the country alters; it is no
longer intersected by nullahs, and the jungle entirely
disappears.

The above tract of country, lying to the north of
Gorakpur, is admirably adapted for defensive operations; but many of the reasons which render it so
would deter the Gorkhas from using it as a passage
into our provinces, for the following reasons :—

1st. Because the numerous and deep nullahs, the
swamps—many of which are impassable—and the
dense and extensive forest jungles, render rapid
movements either of advance or retreat impracticable
except to a very small party.

2nd. From the Gorkha custom of never carrying
supplies, and the country through which they would
be obliged to pass not furnishing grain in any quantity.

3rd. Because to the distance of thirty miles from
Betul, in the direction of either Gorakpur or Bansi,
the water of the numerous nullahs is of a poisonous
quality; the few wells are far apart, and even their
water is unwholesome.

4th. Were they to march to Gorakpur, either by
Bichaul or Lotan, they would expose themselves not
only to be taken in flank by any cavalry sent against
them, but also to have their communications cut off
even by a small force on the road leading from the
Bagha ghat through Nauringhi and Mirrhedia.

5th. Because their most advantageous points from whence to attack our territory in that quarter are the passes of the Gandak and Cherya Ghatti.

The country stretching under the hills from the Gandak to the Cherya Ghatti pass is uninhabited, and no good water, except from the Rapti, is to be found in it.

There are three principal passes by which an army may enter within the lower range of hills from the side of Bettiah and Tirhut, viz., in the centre, that of Cherya Ghatti by Bichakoh ; on the left or west, that of the Gandak ; on the right or east, that of the Baghmatti. The route of the Baghmatti is probably the easiest, as it is by this route that crowds of buffaloes and other cattle come to Nipal. Some may infer the same from the extreme and jealous precautions taken by the Nipalese to prevent any foreigner ever entering Nipal by that route.

Mr. Bell would recommend, however, that only a feigned attack be made in that quarter to act as a diversion, the principal attack being made by the Gandak and Rapti. The reasons for this are that we know exactly what difficulties are before us in the latter route, and that we have lots of good guides (the dak runners, Danghars, who came originally from Chota Nagpur), whereas we know nothing of the Baghmatti route, and could not get a single guide.

The Gandak is navigable for large boats as high up as the Mutabanni, and for small boats within a few miles of its junction with the Rapti, during the whole year. Stores may, therefore, be conveyed to the pass of the Gandak with great facility and little expense. This is not the case with the Baghmatti.

The army should advance in two divisions, one through the Cherya Ghatti, the other by the Gandak pass.* The effect of this would be to turn the position of the Cherya Ghatti and to force the Gorkhas to evacuate the lower hills and jungles which are bounded by the Rapti on the north, and by the Ramnagar and Bettiah districts on the south. The road passes by Bichakoh, a small post situated in the bed of a ravine at the junction of two streams, one of which has its source to the northward, the other to the west. Were opposition offered here, the post might easily be turned by following down the bed of the stream which flows in front of Bichakoh, or by crossing on the left of the post to the Delta which is formed by the junction of the two streams and then ascending the bed of that on the right. From Bichakoh the road lies up the bed of the stream on the right.

The Cherya Ghatti pass itself is the first really strong, defensible position. It could not be stormed

---

* The approach from our territories to Cheryaghatti lies through Bissaulia, a Nipal village, twelve miles from the frontier, and on the skirts of the Sal Forest; here the jungle is very thick, from the Nipal Governor never having allowed any timber to be cut. It could offer no effectual resistance.

in front without great loss, but could be turned in flank by the Gandak pass and so rendered indefensible, as it would require to be evacuated by the Nipalese to save themselves from being attacked in rear. The division would then march to Hetowara.

The division which enters the lower range of hills by the Gandak pass should proceed to the junction of the Gandak and the Rapti, there cross the former stream below the junction, and then proceed up the left bank of the Rapti to Hetowara, where it would join the other division.

The valley of the Rapti is of considerable extent. Until the commencement of the first Gorkha war it had been extensively cultivated, but the then policy of Nipal led to the inhabitants being removed to the villages on the surrounding hills, since which time the lands have gradually reverted to a state of jungle.

On the occasion of calling one day at the Residency in 1851, Mr. Erskine rather pressed Jang on the subject of making a good road from the plains to the Valley of Nipal. Jang stated that the prejudices of his countrymen were very strong against it, as they thought that while the roads remained in the present state no invading army could make its way to the valley. For his own part, he said, since he had been to England and seen our railroads and tunnels, &c., he knew our power and skill so well that he was convinced if we could not make a road over a mountain, we should make a tunnel under it, so that no mountain could stop our progress. "But," added he, "though the cat cannot fight on even terms with the lion, yet if the lion drives him into a corner the cat will scratch his eyes." On another occasion Jang said, "I know my nation is not equal to yours, nor our power to yours; but there is one thing in which we are and ought ever to be equal, namely—*justice, mutual justice!*"

Proceeding from Hetowara to Bhimphedi, Ross Bell proposes to turn the fort of Chisa Garhi (which is situated north-west of Bhimphedi) by ascending a spur of the mountain which rises from the valley to the east of Bhimphedi, and leads, by a gradual ascent, to the top of the ridge, arriving at the top of the range about four miles to the east of Chisapani. Then turning westward, they would march upon Chisapani (where a spring is), along the crest of the hill, and from that spot command the fort and destroy it by shells in half an hour. Having surmounted this mountain, he anticipates no more difficulties, as there are no more defensible positions. The water of the Rapti is perfectly wholesome along its whole course; with the exception of the spring at Chisapani, there is no water between Bhimphedi and Tumbha Khana; from Tumbha Khana to Kathmandu there is no scarcity.

CHAPTER IX.

ON THE NIPAL TERAI.*

THERE are two routes by which the Terai may be traversed from Bissaulia to the Mechi or Machi river. One runs through the Cachar, *i.e.* for the most part close to the foot of the outer range (Cherya-ghatti), rarely leaving it for a greater distance than four miles. This rock, generally speaking, is through thick forest without under-jungle; it is but thinly inhabited by a few Tharus, Dhanwars, and Manjis (Masahis), who, having cleared a few spots along the road, grow rice and bajra, and eke out a rather scanty subsistence by hunting pigs and eating carrion and vermin. The road is fit for elephants and ponies only; and as supplies are not produced on it, only a small party could travel by it.

---

* Abridged from Report by Dr. Campbell, July 1841.

The second route lies for the most part between and equi-distant from the forest and our frontier, say five miles apart from either. In some places, as at the crossing of the Baghmatti, Kumla, and Kosi rivers it is on the frontier. It is travelled easily by elephants and ponies, and very little pioneering would enable horse artillery to pass along it. Hackeries are not useful, except occasionally between large villages, and that only to the west of the Kosi. In no part of the Morung (*i.e.* country to the east of the Kosi) except about Rangeli would hackeries be of use. It would be very difficult to bring guns through the Morung. The country immediately under the hills (there is no continuous outer range east of the Kosi) is quite flat, swamped all the year, and the soil a stiff, tenacious clay, which, when exposed without sward, is not passable; with sward, it is broken into ruts and ravines which render travelling slow and irksome.

The whole of this route, to the Kosi, is peopled, and, with exception to a few spurs from the forest, is cleared and open. Supplies abundant, and cattle swarm in it. All the rivers fordable except the Kosi, which is nowhere fordable at any season.

The route lies by the following stages, distant ten to twelve miles on the average:—Bissaulia; Banurwa; Olyan Patarwa; Burhurwa; cross the Baghmatti; Ingurwa; Gurhara; Dhasali; Jalesar, six miles from Janikpur; Dhanuji; Balaha-Arai; cross the Kumlaji; Thari-Naraha; Sakarpur; Hanumanganj; Bha-

nurwa; cross the Kosi (in six feet of water on the
18th of January); Dewanganj; Kolya; Rangeli;
cross Balan river; Athmonza; Nazarpur; cross the
Konki; Kalikaghar, on the Mechi; Nagal Bandi,
right bank of Mechi; Mechigola, confluence of Mechi
and Siddhi rivers and within the hills. From Bissaulia to the Mechi, say two hundred and fifty miles.

The extreme breadth of the Nipal Terai is not above
thirty miles; its narrowest part, at Bhanurwa on the
Kosi, about twelve miles; its average breadth about
twenty miles.

The Terai, in its breadth, may be divided into four
regions:

1st. *The open Terai* averages ten miles in width,
as far as the Kumla river, and five miles from thence
to the Kosi, beyond which river it does not exist.

2nd. *The outer Cachar*, or outskirts of forest. Always
varying in extent, as after ten years' clearing and
cultivation, it is absorbed into the open Terai. It
averages perhaps five miles all the way to the Kosi
and throughout the Morung.

3rd. *Bhabar, Bhaver*, or *Sal Forest*. Five to ten
miles in width.

4th. *The inner Cachar*, consisting of detached oases
along the foot of the hills between the latter and the
forest.

The Terai, in length, is divided into two provinces
or regions:

1st. *The Morung*, or Terai east of the Kosi. This

district is distinguished by its extreme flatness, stiff clay soil, and horribly pestilent climate.

2nd. The *Terai Proper.* Lying to the west of the Kosi, and marked by a gentle slope to the plains. Varied soil of a black loam, clay, and sand, fit to grow all crops, including sugar-cane, the poppy, and tobacco.

East of Bissaulia the administrative divisions of the Terai are five, from west to east :—1st, Bara and Parsa; 2nd, Rochat; 3rd, Sarlaya Sapturi, on the left bank of the Baghmatti; 4th, Mahturi, on the right bank of the Kosi ; 5th, the Morung, on the left bank of the Kosi, and extending thence to Michi.

The Kosi river is navigable up to Bhanurwa, from which Hanumanganj is fifteen miles distant.

Bhanurwa is a very desirable locality for stationing troops. There is a fine grassy, hard plain for horse artillery and cavalry, with the river for the transport of ordnance and ammunition.

In the Morung, Rangeli is decidedly the safest and most healthy place. Here the river-water is good, and there is a slight elevation of ground. Everywhere else in the Morung the water is bad, and the country a pestilent swamp.

In Rochat is Burhurwa, high and dry on the right bank of the Baghmatti.

In Sarlaya Sapturi is Jalesar.

In Mohturi are both Hanumanganj and Bhanurwa, both well raised above the surrounding country and having a light and fertile soil.

I.   10

The above-mentioned civil and military stations, with reference to salubrity, are greatly superior to the ancient cities of Janikpur and Samraun.

Elephants are fast disappearing to the west of the Kosi, and the Morung is not now able to supply the usual number required by the usage of the darbar, viz. five hundred per annum. The subahs and catchers import largely from the Botanis on the Rangpur and Assam frontiers.

The police arrangements throughout the Terai are excellent in all respects, contrasting favourably with those in our own territory, being more efficient and much less extortionate.

The annual receipts from the Terai (east of Bissaulia) at that time were four lakhs of rupees; but it was confidently expected that when the land measurements and assessments then in progress were completed, the results would give six lakhs.

Many of the middle class, and all the upper class, of people in the Terai—except the Khus officers— have property in our provinces, and at least a moiety of their savings in money is carried across the frontier to our territory, in which their families very generally reside. Accumulated wealth was felt to be a source of danger and uneasiness to the holder from the great liability of its being rapaciously dealt with by the extra-judicial authorities in Nipal.

CHAPTER X.

DESCRIPTION OF THE TOWN AND VALLEY OF NAYAKOT.*

NAYAKOT is the name of a pretty town and district
lying west-north-west seventeen miles from Kathmandu, by the high road to Gorkha. The town is
situated at the northern extremity of the district,
upon a spur descending south-westerly from Mount
Dhaibung or Jibjibia, and at about a mile's distance
from the river Trisul on the west, and the same distance from the river Tadi or Surajmatti on the south
and east.

The town consists of from sixty to one hundred
pucka three-storied houses in the Chinese style of
Kathmandu (chiefly owned by the court and chiefs of
Nipal); of a darbar, called the upper to distinguish
it from the lower on the banks of the Tadi; and of

---

* Condensed from a Report by Mr. Hodgson.

10 *

a temple to Bhairavi; all in the same style. The town consists of a single street, lying in an indentation or crest of the ridge, and is consequently not visible from either side, though the darbar and temple, from being placed higher, are so partially.

Up to the last British war Nayakot was the winter residence of the present dynasty; but as the situation of the town is bleak and uncomfortable at that season, the court and chiefs then usually resided in mansions still standing at the base of the hill towards the Tadi. Like the town residences, these are now much dilapidated owing to the court having been stationary at Kathmandu since 1813.

The town of Nayakot is situated above the level of the Trisul from eight hundred to one thousand feet. On the side towards the Tadi is a fine sal forest, occupying the whole declivity; elsewhere the sal trees, indigenous to the district, are reduced to scrubby brushwood by constant cutting and defoliation. The leaves, being used as plates to eat from, are being constantly carried to Kathmandu for sale.

The ridge on which the town stands is generally of a rounded form, but broken by ruts and ravines, with a soil of a deep red clay. Towards the Trisul on the west, and the Tadi on the south and east, the declivities are precipitous; but towards the junction of these two streams in the south-west the hill falls off more gently, and about a mile and a half below the town spreads into an undulating plain which occupies nearly the whole space between the rivers to the junction at Devi ghat. The plain forms a sort of triangular delta; sides bounded by the rivers, base formed by the ridge. This delta is an elevated plain from one hundred to four hundred feet above the level of the rivers, and it constitutes the chief part of the lowland district of Nayakot. At its north-eastern angle the plain slopes down to the Tadi, on both sides of which the ground is open and level with that river. The whole district of Nayakot is encircled by mountains, forming a distinct valley. The length of the level plain is four miles. The maximum breadth of the entire district or valley is at the base of the triangle and is here four miles. The mean maximum breadth is not above three miles; that of the plateau alone between the two rivers is two miles.

The plateau, in consequence of its elevation, cannot be watered from the Trisul or the Tadi; and as the Nayakot ridge above it, and whence it is derived, yields no efficient springs of water, the plain is dependent exclusively on the rain for its supply of water. Every such plateau or plain in Nipal is called a tar, whereas the low and waterable tracts are called byasi; the latter are generally low and swampy rice-beds on the level of the streams that water them.

These tars are rather more healthy and habitable than the byasis, and are capable of more varied cultivation, but chiefly of trees, since they alone can flourish where they get only rain-water. Hence the predominance of mangoes and other groves over fields and agriculture on the tars of Nayakot. Despite the high temperature of Nayakot, it has no winter or spring crops, the tars being too dry and the byasis too wet for such crops, though they are common in the much colder Valley of Nipal.

While the Valley of Nipal is four thousand seven hundred feet above the sea, that of Nayakot is only two thousand four hundred and fifty feet, whence its heat and its being subject to malarious fever (awal) from March to November.

The Nipalese profess that awal sets in in Nayakot at the same time as it does in the Terai, viz. 15th of March. It probably commences about a month later. The great festival in honour of Devi at Devi ghat does not take place till the middle of April (beginning of Baisakh), and at it thousands of persons from Nipal are always present, and with impunity. The Nipalese account for this by saying that through the intervention of the deity, the awal is "suspended" to all who go to worship her during the time the festival lasts; but that it sets in again as soon as the festival is over. The real fact being that the unhealthy season does not set in until the middle of April, and that the festival has been fixed at the end of the cold or healthy season as a sort of "finish" to it, and simultaneously with the Ashbami and Rammoma and Jambahadeo festivals in the Valley of Nipal. Bhairab, as a form of the Destroyer, is worshipped often under the form of a tiger. They say that the day after the festival closes the goddess lets out the spirit of the savage and destroying monarch of the forests, who, disguised as the "awal" fever, seizes and feeds upon all those whom he finds trespassing upon his domains—the jungles.

The lowlands or byasis are thinly inhabited by a peculiar race of men, who affect to be hill-men and speak Parbattia; but their dark skins, slender forms, oval faces, elevated features, and peculiar barbarous patois, clearly indicate a southern origin. They are exceedingly ignorant and cunning. They certainly do not belong to the Tartaric stock of the mountaineers of Nipal, but either to the ordinary Indo-Germanic stock of the Indian population, or to some of those fragmentary branches which still represent, in various parts of Hindustan, a preceding aboriginal race. These peculiar tribes of Nayakot are Darris, Kumhals or potters, Manjhis, Bramus, and Denwars. The Tharus of the Nipalese Terai, as well as these peculiar tribes of Nayakot and of many other similar low and malarious valleys within the hills, probably all belong to the aboriginal stock of the Indians of Hindustan. They are certainly all closely connected among themselves, and are very different from the Tartar blood of the highland races. Those in the valleys among the hills were probably emigrants from the plains of North Bahar several generations back. Though these hill tribes affect a great distinctness among themselves, and will not usually intermarry among themselves or with any of the races around them, and though they allege that their several languages (dialects) are distinct, yet the differences are but really slight, and probably depend either on the different dates at which the successive emigrations from the plains took place, or on the different parts of the plains from which the ancestors of the respective tribes originally came. They all call themselves Hindus, though they neither believe in the sacred scriptures of the Hindu, nor accept the sacerdotal offices of the Brahmans.

These tribes inhabit with impunity the lowest and hottest valleys in Nipal, just as the Tharus do the Terai of Nipal. The Mundas and Urans, originally emigrants from Chota Nagpur, now reside in the Terai and enjoy the same immunity. Wherever malaria rages from March or April to November beyond the sal forest or within these hill valleys, there these tribes, and these tribes alone, dwell and thrive. Sometimes they collect in small villages, more usually live in scattered cottages built of unhewn stone with a front and overhanging roof of grass or rice-straw.

They follow the vocations of agriculturists, potters, fishermen, and ferrymen, and at all these crafts, and more especially pottery, they are very expert. The Kumhals of Nayakot in particular are renowned for their skill and workmanship in pottery.

While the byasis or lowlands of Nayakot are exclusively occupied by these peculiar tribes, the tars or highlands are occupied by the Niwars, who dwell and build solely in them. The Parbattias seldom venture even so far down as the tars, but usually have their houses on the hills around; and they never suffer themselves to sleep in any part of the lowlands for a single night between April and November.

In neither tars nor byasis do the clusters of cottages ever reach the size of a village; and the dwellings stand for the most part single. The whole district is said to contain seven hundred houses, but this is probably much exaggerated.

The soil of Nayakot contains a greater proportion of clay to silex and calx than the soil of the Valley of Nipal, which latter is derived principally from the debris of granite formation. Hence the reputed fertility and the celebrity of the potteries of Nayakot.

The heights round the valley are not very considerable; they consist, on the north especially, of iron clay of a very deep red tint, and the superficial soil of the tars is for the most part of the same kind, the substratum being usually gravel, whence the dryness of the tars is increased. The soil of the byasis is also clayey, but untinted; and where unmixed with silex or other ingredients, is even more tenacious than the red clay. The pottery clays are exclusively of the red sort. Mica, so common in the Valley of Nipal, is here never met with.

The high temperature of Nayakot admits of the trees—forest and field—as well as of the superior cerealia of North Bahar and the Terai, being cultivated with success, though they cannot be raised in the Valley of Nipal.

Nayakot has also productions of its own—first-rate oranges and pine-apples—which are not found, or only of inferior quality, in the plains of Bahar. The forest trees found in Nayakot and not in Nipal, and identifying it with the Terai and plains, are the sal tree, (*shorea robusta*), burr and peepul (*ficus indica et religiosa*), semel or cotton tree, and many others. The *pinus longifolia* and other mountainous trees are frequently found mixed with them on the declivities around.

The chief of the fruit-trees is the mangoe, of various sorts and great excellence; the tamarind; the bel or jack-fruit; guava; custard apple or sherifa; in fact, most of the ordinary fruit-trees of the plains of India. None of which, however, flourish in the Valley of Nipal. Pears, apples, apricots, plums, plantains, and melons also abound; but no grapes nor peaches. The Nayakot range is very far snperior to that of Nipal.

The agricultural products of Nayakot resemble generally those of Nipal, but whereas there are two annual crops in Nipal there is only one in Nayakot, because of the excess of moisture in the byasis and the total want of artificial irrigation in the tarc. The byasis yield only rice, which is not planted nor reaped at the early seasons of Nipal, but at the late ones of the plains of India.

The rice harvest in Nayakot is not over till the beginning, and often the middle, of December; and then there are no means of drying the fields rapidly enough for a second crop. In Nipal the crops are more than six weeks earlier.

The uk or sugar-cane of Nayakot is superior to that of most parts of India. It is grown on the skirts of the byasis as well as on the declivities of the hills near them.

Of the surface of the tars of Nayakot one-half probably is devoted to gardens and orchards, now much neglected and in sad repair; one-quarter to fields of dry produce; one-eighth to rice or wet produce; and the remaining one-eighth is probably barren.

In the cold months many traders and craftsmen from Nipal visit Nayakot, exchanging grain for rock-salt with the Cis- and Trans-Himalayan Bhotias, dying the homespun clothes of the neighbouring hill tribes with madder supplied by them, or with Indigo from Tirhut. It amounts almost to a little fair from the amount of bargaining and pedlary done there.

The principal rivers in Nayakot are the Tadi and the Trisul. The Tadi (classically termed Suryavatti from its arising at Surya kund, or the sun's fount, which is the most easterly of the twenty-two little lakes of Gosainthan) is thrown off towards the east, as is the Trisul towards the west, from one of the little lakes which lie at the foot of the snowy peaks which rise from the mass of the Gosainthan. The Tadi soon turns to the west and falls into the Trisul, passing in its course below, and forming the southern boundary of the ridge and plateau of Nayakot. Its course may be thirty miles; it is a shallow stream.

Its glen is cultivated nearly throughout; and on its upper course is said not to be malarious. The Trisul is the most easterly of the seven Gandaks of Nipal, and rises from the largest of twenty-two small lakes which occupy the hollows of a series of narrow gorge-like valleys at the foot of the precipitous rocks which run up into the snow peaks of Gosainthan. The largest of these lakes is called Gosain kund, or Nilkhiat kund, and is about half a mile in circuit; and from a rock on its northern side issues, by three principal clefts (hence the name Trisul), the river Trisul or Trisul Gandaki. Its course is westerly to Nayakot, beneath which the Tadi falls into it. It is a deep greenish-blue, and very rapid stream, conducting not only the pilgrim to Gosainthan, but the trader and traveller to Thibet. The valley of the Trisul is narrow and without any byasi on the level of its waters.

At Dhaibung, a considerable village half-way up the ascent of the mountain of the same name, above Nayakot, the Parbattia population begin to yield to the race called Kachari Bhotias, or Cis-Himalayan Bhotias, to distinguish them from the proper or Trans-Himalayan Bhotias.

At Devi ghat, below Nayakot, the Trisul is crossed by a ferry, which is most jealously guarded, and no transport of any sort of goods allowed over it.

During the winter the lakes are thickly frozen over, but the stream of the Trisul continues to run, and the communication between one lake and another is never interrupted, showing that the waters are never frozen right through to the bottom of the lake. The whole district is deeply covered in snow, which melts during the hot weather and rains, so that at the time of the annual pilgrimage—August—in general only the crests of the surrounding hills are covered with snow, though sometimes patches of snow in shady spots may be seen as low as the margins of the lakes.

These lakes lie below the level of perpetual snow, probably at an elevation of twelve thousand to fourteen thousand feet. They have evidently been produced by glacial action. In remote times the series of valleys which surround the base of the highest peaks of Gosainthan must have been filled up by glaciers, which have now entirely disappeared, but whose moraines have dammed up the valleys at all their narrowest parts. In this way a series of deep hollows was formed, which were enclosed between the precipitous sides of the valleys and the moraines at either end by which these valleys were obstructed. These rocky hollows having become filled up with water now form a succession of small lakes, clustered together in groups of four or five, and arranged in tiers one above the other. Each lake is separated from its immediate neighbours by a massive wall of immense boulders heaped confusedly together, over or between which the water from the lake above either falls in cascades or finds its way, by many small and devious streams, into the bosom of the lake below it.

Each lake is situated about fifty or sixty feet above

the level of the lake below it; and it is probable that this terracing of the lakes is dependent on the original slope of the bottom of the valley, before its continuity was destroyed not only by the obstruction of a moraine filling up its outlet, but by the deposition across it, from side to side, of vast masses of boulders at every narrow bend or angle of the gorge in which the glacier was lodged.

Most of these lakes are very deep; their waters are exceedingly cold, and they contain no fish nor aquatic plants. A few small plants and grasses grow on patches of mould near their edges or between the rocks which are strewed around them.

CHAPTER XI.

NOTES OF A ROUTE FROM KATHMANDU THROUGH GORKHA,
WEST TOWARDS KAMAON.

Kathmandu.

Thankot. Here the road leaves the Khalta or Valley of Nipal Proper, and proceeds west to the junction of the Trisulganga and Maheshkhola rivers at a place called

Maheshdobang, ten kos from Kathmandu.

Ghat of Bhangkot, twenty kos from Kathmandu. Here are some stone temples built by Bhim Sen.

City of Gorkha, on the southern or eastern shore of the Dharamdi river. It is situated on the Hunumanbanjang mountain and has a high hill covered with jungle on its north-west. It is twenty-six kos from Kathmandu by the road of Nayakot, and twenty-three kos by this route. It was the original capital of the present dynasty of Nipal. It contains about two thousand houses.

City of Tanahung (Tanhung). One of the petty

chiefdoms conquered by the present dynasty. Thirty-four kos from Kathmandu. Its darbar is in ruins.

City of Pokhra, on Setuganja river. A quondam independent chiefship. The city is large, well inhabited, and contains plenty of supplies and grain of all sorts. Famous for its copper manufactures. There is a large annual fair held here.

City of Satahung. Another quondam chiefdom. Has a darbar.

City of Tansen. A quondam petty chiefdom. It is now the military station of the province of Palpa. A kazi and one thousand five hundred sepoys reside here. There is a new darbar. and a market-place. Cotton cloths in abundance, made by the Gurungs who abound in the district; also a mint, where copper pice pieces are struck. Tansen is sixty-one kos west from Kathmandu.

City of Palpa, sixty-three kos from Kathmandu. Has a darbar and temple of Bhairunath.

Town of Hirdaghat, two kos from Palpa and sixty-five kos from Kathmandu. At the junction of the Kalaganja flowing from the north and the Hirdakhula from the west. Has plenty of supplies.

Butwal, seven kos south of Tansen, in the Terai of Palpa and opposite Gorakpur. Has a large market, where cloths of all sorts and cotton are very cheap. Darbar is in ruins.

Gulmi. Another quondam principality. Has a darbar. It is five kos west from Hirdighat, or seventy kos from Kathmandu.

Village of Nayakot, seventy-seven kos west from Kathmandu.

Magazine of Pentana, eighty-six kos west of Kathmandu. Three hundred and sixty workmen constantly employed here in the manufacture of muskets, under the superintendence of a captain and company of sepoys.

Village of Musinia Bhanjang, ninety-five kos from Kathmandu. Abounds in saltpetre, which is taken from here to Pentana.

Town of Saliana, one hundred and ten kos west of Kathmandu. A quondam chiefship on the Irwala Khola. The town has a darbar and temples, and in the cold weather a sirdar and a company of sepoys reside here. North from Saliana twelve kos, and on the northern side of the Bheriganga river. Crossing that river at the Kohenpani ghat is—

Jajurkot, another small quondam principality. Like all the others, conquered and absorbed by the Gorkha dynasty. It is half a cos from the northern shores of the Bheriganga river. It has the ruins of a darbar, a temple of Devi, and a small Niwar village. It is one hundred and twenty-two kos from Kathmandu.

The road by this route is generally bad; through a mountainous district; over successive ridges, running generally north and south; across or along the intervening valleys, which are watered by streams, though none of the latter appear to be of considerable size. The country is more or less cultivated, and mostly thinly inhabited, with small and distantly scattered villages.

CHAPTER XII.

ROUTE FROM NAYAKOT TO GOSAINTHAN.*

Nayakot.

Along the eastern bank of the Trisul to the confluence of the Betravati or Betruilli stream with the
Trisul eight miles above Nayakot. Betravati rises
in one of the lakes of Gosainthan (to the north and
east of Suraj kund), passes between Jibjibia and
Dhaibung, flows along the southern base of the latter,
to its western extremity, where it falls into the
Trisul. About one hundred yards before uniting
with the Trisul, it is crossed by a wooden suspen-
sion bridge. There is here a small hamlet of three
or four houses.

Ascend the western shoulder of Mount Dhaibung to
village of Dhaibung, situated about two-thirds up the

---

* Compiled from description and notes by Rajmun Sing, Chi-
wallar, August 1854.

mountain on its southern face.* Consists of twenty-eight houses, inhabited by Botias, Niwars, and Parbattias. Over the crest of Dhaibung, descend to the pass between it and Jibjibia; thence to Kabhria or Kafria, two miles from Dhaibung—faces towards north. Village consists of fifteen houses, occupied by Niwars. Near Kabhria the Nipalese were worsted in an action with Chinese.

From Kabhria ascend to Ramchak, about three miles, situated on a hill apparently detached from Jibjibia, and intervening between that mountain and Gosainthan. It is probably a large spur either of Dhaibung or Jibjibia. Hamlet of twelve Botia houses.

About a mile further on, on the same hill, is Garran or Garram, a large Botia village, consisting of thirty-six houses. The Trisul may be seen flowing beneath the hill, along its northern base.

Two miles further on, still on the same hill, is Taria, a Botia village, consisting of fifteen houses.

Near Taria is a large natural cavern capable of covering between two hundred and three hundred persons, formed by an immense rock which overhangs the road. Pilgrims to Gosainthan avail themselves of its shelter as a halting-place. It is called Bhimal-parku by the Niwars, or Bhimal Gupa by the Parbattiahs. The Trisul flows in the valley below it.

---

* At the invasion of Nipal by the Chinese in 1790, the Chinese general Thoong Thang did not descend below the town of Dhaibung, though part of his army did.—*Kirkpatrick.*

11 *

Tradition says that Bhimal, a Niwar Caji, led an
army to invade Thibet. A lama threw this rock
down to crush him and his men. Bhimal, however,
raised his hand, and arresting its downward progress,
left it standing in its present position.

A mile further on is the Botia village of Bakku-
janda, consisting of twelve houses. Thence to Dumchah is about two miles. It is a large Botia village,
consisting of sixty or seventy houses, and contains a
large Buddhist temple built of stone. On the southern
side of its base are three circular slabs, on which are
sculptured, by the Botias, " Om Mani padma om."
On each of the other three sides is a niche containing
a rudely carved figure of a Buddhist deity, apparently
the Buddhist Trinity, Buddha, Dharma, Sangha—one
in each niche. The summit is surmounted by two
circular slabs of stone, roughly carved, and intended
to represent " chattras." *

Three roads meet at Dumchah—one from Nayakot,
one from Gosainthan, and one from the Kerung pass.
In other words, the road from Nayakot here divides,
one branch leading north-east to Gosainthan, the other
north-west to the Kerung pass; on the latter is a
large village named Safrutimria.

From Dumchah there is a slight descent at first
to the bed of the Trisul, thence a very gradual ascent
to Kundi; whence, to the lakes, the ascent is very precipitous and the cold very severe.

---

* Umbrellas.

Four miles from Dumchah is Kundi, a halting-place of merely two Botia houses, with a small Buddhist temple.

Four miles further is Dimchah, a Botia village of eight houses. From Dimchah it is about three miles to the first cluster of the lakes of Gosainthan.

Near Dimchah, between it and Gosainthan, is a small rounded hill called Chandanbari. It was quite covered with numbers of wild flowers of various kinds, forming a natural garden. Snow falls on it during the cold weather, but soon melts again. The superstition of the people, of course, attributes the growth of these flowers to the cherishing care of the deity of the district.

Near Chandanbari, a little above it by the road-side, is a small uncarved stone, about a foot high, which is worshipped as Ganesha, and the spot is called Lauri-Vinnaik—from Lauri, a stick—in consequence of its being the practice for all travellers to deposit their sticks, if they have any, at the shrine of the deity, whose severe anger will be incurred if any one should proceed beyond this spot towards the sacred lakes with a stick in his hand. It appears to be a practice similar to the common one of depositing a stone or pebble on the cairn at the top of any stiff pass.

The man from whose account the above itinerary was made says that during no time of his journey, neither during the ascent nor during his two days' stay at the lakes, did he experience the slightest inconvenience or oppression in his breathing, pains in his head, dizziness, &c. The only peculiarity he observed was that after ascending from Kundi his sense of taste was impaired; his appetite was very good, but he could hardly distinguish the taste of one thing from another. Even a bottle of Exshaw's brandy and some cheroots, with which I furnished him, were no exception, as he says they seemed to have lost all their flavour as long as he was above Kundi.

CHAPTER XIII.

ORIGIN AND CLASSIFICATION OF THE MILITARY TRIBES
OF NIPAL.—TABULAR VIEW OF THE TRIBES.*

1st. *Brahmans.*

2nd. *Khus,* of which there are twelve subdivisions :
1st, Thapa; 2nd, Bishnyat; 3rd, Bhandari; 4th,
Karki; 5th, Khangka; 6th, Adhikari; 7th, Bisht;
8th, Kunwar; 9th, Baniah; 10th, Dani; 11th, Gharti;
12th, Khattri.

The *Ektharya* are insulated tribes, ranking with
Khus.

The *Thakuri* are the royal lineages, ranking with
Khus.

3rd. *Magars,* of which there are three subdivisions :
1st, Rana; 2nd, Thapa; 3rd, Alaya.

4th. *Gurungs,* of which there are no subdivisions.
The Brahmans of Nipal are much less generally ad-

---

* Condensed from a paper by Mr. Brian Hodgson, dated
October 1832.

dicted to arms than the Brahmans of the plains; they
do not, therefore, properly belong to the present subject.   They are now introduced as necessary to eluci-
date the lineage and connections of the military tribes,
and especially of the Khus.

The proper martial classes of Nipal are the Khus,
the Magars, and the Gurungs.

The great aboriginal stock of the inhabitants of the
mountains of Nipal, east of the river Kali, is Mon-
golian.

From the twelfth century downwards the tide of
Musulman conquest continued to drive multitudes of
the Brahmans of the plains of Hindustan into the
neighbouring hills, which now compose the western
territories of the kingdom of Nipal.   There the Brahmans soon located themselves.   They found the
natives illiterate and almost without a creed, proud,
and fierce.   To confirm the influence derived from
their own learning, they determined to convert these
Parbattiahs to Hinduism.

Khus.—To the earliest and most distinguished of
their converts they communicated (in defiance of the
principles of the Hindu faith) the rank and honours
of the Kshatriya order.   The same rank was also communicated to the offspring of Brahman intercourse
with the hill women.   From these two roots (the converted Khus, and the illegitimate offspring of a Plain
Brahman with a Khus woman) sprang the now numerous and powerful tribe of the Khus, originally the
name of a small class of creedless barbarians, now the

title of the Kshatriya or military order of the kingdom of Nipal. The offspring of the original Khus females by the Brahmans received, with the honours and rank of the second order of Hinduism (Kshatriya), the patronymic title of the first order (Brahman).

To the present day (despite all the opposition of the Brahmans to a custom so opposed to the principles of their creed) the proud Khus race insist that their children by Brahman fathers shall be ranked as Kshatriyas, but wear the sacred thread, and assume the patronymic of Brahman. The original Khus, thus favoured, naturally became entirely devoted to the Brahmanical system. They agreed to put away their old gods, and take the new ones; to have Brahmans for gurus, and not to kill the cow. For the rest they made, and still make, but little of the ceremonial law in whatever respects food and sexual relations. Their active habits and vigorous characters could not brook the restraints of the ritual law; moreover, they had the example of licentious Brahmans to excuse their neglect. The few prejudices of the Khus are useful rather than otherwise, inasmuch as they favour sobriety and cleanliness.

Almost all the officers of the army are of the Khus tribe. Magars and Gurungs combined compose less than one-half of the privates and non-commissioned officers. The Khus is generally slighter, more active, and less fleshy than either the Magar or the Gurung; more arrogant, passionately fond of arms; averse to all labour in arts, but will enter into agricultural and pastoral pursuits.

The progress of Mohammadanism in Hindustan daily drove fresh refugees to the Nipalese mountains. The Khus tribes availed themselves of the superior knowledge of the strangers to subdue the neighbouring aboriginal tribes. They were almost uniformly successful; and in such a career, continued for ages, they gradually merged the greater part of their own habits, ideas, and language (but not physiognomy) in those of the Hindus. The Khus language became, and still is, a corrupt dialect of Hindi, retaining not many traces of primitive barbarism.

Ekthariah.—The Ekthariah are the descendants, more or less pure, not of the Brahmans by a Khus female, but of Rajputs and other Kshatriyas of the plains, who either sought refuge in Nipal from the Musulman, or voluntarily sought military service as adventurers. Not having the same inducements as the Brahmans had to degrade their proud race by union with Parbattiah females, they mixed much less with the Khus than the Brahmans had done. Hence, to this day, they claim a vague superiority over the Khus, although in all essentials the two races have long been confounded.

Those among the Kshatriyas of the plains who were more lax in their alliances with Khus females were permitted to give their children the patronymic title only, but not the rank, of Kshatriya. But their children, again, if they married for two generations into the Khus, became pure Khus, and at the same time re-acquired all the privileges and rank, though they no longer retained the name, of Kshatriya. While in Nipal they were Khus, not Kshatriya; but if they revisited the plains, they bore the name and were entitled to every privilege attached to Kshatriya birth in Hindustan. The Ekthariah is the third and less fruitful root of the Khus race.

Thakuris.—The Thakuris, similar in extraction, differ only from the Ekthariahs by the circumstance of their lineage being royal. At some former period, and in some unimportant state or other, their progenitors were princes. The present royal family are of the Sahi dynasty.

The Kirats are natives of the Kiranti district, a tract to the east, towards Sikkim. Till 1847 they were looked down upon as being an inferior race, and were not admitted into the army. In 1847 they were enlisted for the first time as sepoys by Jang Bahadur. There is now one regiment of the *campon* (term confined to the *regular* army) almost entirely composed of them, and several are scattered among other corps. They rank considerably below Gurungs.

Limbu is the name of another eastern tribe who are also now enlisted as sepoys; they are low caste, like Kirats. They are remarkably good sportsmen; the district they inhabit (Limbuana?) lying near snow, where provisions are scarce, they hunt for the pot.*

---

* Limbuanah,—the country of the Limbus,—is the tract lying between Sikkim and the Arun river, below the snows. It formerly

The Lepchas are, properly, the aborigines of Sikkim; but a few are scattered through the Kiranti country.

Magar.—The Magar and Gurung military tribes supply a large number of the soldiers of the Nipal army.

Gurung.—From lending themselves less early and heartily to Brahmanical influences, they have retained to a much greater extent than the Khus tribe their national peculiarities of language, physiognomy, and—in a less degree—of habits. In stature the Gurungs are generally larger and more powerful than either the Magar or the Khus.

Gurungs and Magars, being excluded from political employ and military commands, have less community of interest and sympathy with government than have the Khus; but they are still very loyal, and, like all Parbattiahs, very national in their feelings. In the Gurung and Magar corps the officers (up to captains) are all Gurungs and Magars.

The language of the Magar differs from that of the Gurung only as remote dialects of one great tongue, the type of which is the language of Tibet. Their physiognomies have peculiarities proper to each, but with the general Calmuk caste and character in both. The Gurungs are less generally and more recently redeemed from Lamaism and primitive

---

belonged to Sikkim, but it was early conquered and permanently annexed by the Gorkhas.

impurity than the Magars, and are considered much below them in point of caste. Gurungs eat buffalo meat and village pigs' meat also. Magars eat neither the one nor the other. But though both Magars and Gurungs still retain their own vernacular tongues, Tartar faces, and careless manners, yet from constant intercourse with, and military service under, the predominant Khus, they have acquired the Khus language—but not to the oblivion of their own—and adopted, with, however, several reservations, the Khus habits and sentiments.

As they have submitted themselves to the ceremonial law of purity and to Brahman supremacy, they have been adopted as Hindus; but they have been denied the sacred thread, and take rank as a doubtful order below the Kshatriya—not Vaisya nor Sudra, but a something superior to both of the latter grades.

The offspring of a Khus male and a Magar or Gurung mother is a titular Khus, but a real Magar or Gurung; the descendants fall into the rank of their mothers, retaining only the patronymic, as in other cases above mentioned.

Gorkha.—The original seat of the Khus is ordinarily said to be Gorkha, because it was thence immediately that they issued, ninety years ago, under Prithi Narayan, on their conquering excursions into Nipal. But the Khus race was, long previously to the age of Prithi Narayan, extensively spread over the whole of the Chaubissia; and they are now found in every

part of the existing kingdom of Nipal. The Khus
are rather more devoted to the house of Gorkha, as
well as more under Brahmanical influence, than the
Magars or Gurungs. On both accounts they are less
desirable as soldiers for the British service; although,
from having a good deal of lowland blood in their
veins, the Khus race would probably bear the heat of
the plains better than the Magars or Gurungs.

The original seat of the Magars is most of the central and lower parts of the mountains between the
Jingruk (Rapti of Gorakpur) and the Marsayangdi
(or Marichangdi of our maps) rivers.*

The original seat of the Gurungs is in the line of
country parallel to that occupied by the Magars, and
to the north of it and extending to the snow in that
direction.

Modern events have spread both Magars and Gurungs over most parts of the modern kingdom of
Nipal.

The Magars and Gurungs are Hindus only because
it is the fashion. The Hinduism of the Khus is not
very strict. These highland soldiers,† of all three
races, who despatch their meal in half an hour and

---

* "The Bora-Mungraunthor Satahung, Payang, Bhiskot, Dhor,
Garahung, Risung, Ghirung, Gulmi, Argha, Khachi, Musikot, and
Isma."—*Hodgson.*

† After the Nipal war Ochterlony expressed an opinion (con-
fidentially to Lord Hastings), "that the Company's sepoys could
never be brought to resist the shock of these energetic mountaineers *in their own ground.*

satisfy the ceremonial law by merely washing their hands and faces and taking off their head-dress before cooking, laugh at the strictness of the Hindustani sepoy, who must bathe from head to foot and make puja ere they can begin to dress their dinner, must eat it nearly naked in the coldest weather, and cannot be in marching trim again in less than three hours. In war the Gorkha sepoy carries several days' provisions on his back; the Hindustani would consider such an act degrading.

In Nipal all service, but especially all military service, is by annual tenure, and all tenure of lands attached only to actual service*; and the usage is to change a considerable number of the men annually in order to have a larger available body of trained men scattered over the country than the State can afford to pay at once. A man off the roll of employ is termed Dakhriah; one in employ is Jaghriah.

Prior to the reign of Ran Bahadur, who died in

---

* An exception to this rule, is in the case of the so-called Rajah of Mustang, a Bhotia, who holds a small tract in perpetuity around Muktinath; it is, however, rather a farm than a jagir.

Even the Raj Guru holds his appointment subject to annual renewal. He is appointed by the King, and may at any time be removed for misconduct, political intrigue, &c. As a general rule, or except in case of revolution, where his party may be displaced, the Guru holds his office for life; and if he has given general satisfaction, the probability is that his son or nearest relative will succeed him; but there is no necessity for this, as the office is not hereditary. Should a Guru be displaced, he at once loses his sacred character, and becomes a mere Brahman pandit.

1805, the lands of the State were assigned in jaigir to a class of chiefs called Omran, whose followers, called Omeria, constituted the feudal array and sole military force of the country. This system was abolished before the chiefs could ground any territorial connection upon it. The whole military force now directly belongs to, and is in the pay of, the State; and this has been the case since the beginning of the present century. Before that time the recent origin of the kingdom and vigorous central administration prevented the jaigirs from becoming hereditary. Permanent assignments of land to the Church were numerous, but small, before the same era; but Ran Bahadur swept much of its revenues into the exchequer, and Bhim Sen still more afterwards.

CHAPTER XIV.

DIVISIONS OF CASTE AMONG THE NIWÂRS.

THE grand division of the Niwars is into—

1st. The *Sheo-margi* Niwars, who are worshippers of Shiva, and are, in fact, Brahmanical Hindus ; and

2nd. The *Buddha-margi* Niwars, who are worshippers of Buddha.

Of the whole Niwar population one-third is probably purely Hindu in its religion, the remaining two-thirds being Buddhist.

The Sheo-margi Niwars consist of the following divisions or classes :—

1st. *Upadea*, priests, Brahmans of the highest class, and admitted into the Talleju temples.

2nd. *Lawarju*, also Brahmans and priests, but inferior to Upadea.

3rd. *Bhaju*, Brahmans who give spiritual, but *never* medical, advice in cases of sickness.

4th. *Thakuju* or *Mallah*, Kshatriyas of the original

royal or Rajah caste. Some of them are sepoys in the Gorkha army; but they do not enter into trade, nor private service.

5th. *Nikhu*, Kshatriyas, painters of certain religious subjects. They paint the figure, eyes, &c. on the image of Machendra and on the wheels of his car; also the figures inside the temples of Talleju; but they do not do ordinary painters' work. The Nikhu officiate at the Machendragatra; they bring the figure of the god out of his temple at the beginning of Baisakh, and carry it to the large tree, where they wash it with their own hands. They cover the god up in clothing for eight days; on the ninth they put him in the sun, paint him, robe him, and put him to rights for the grand festival; and having done so, their work is over, and the god is made over to the Banhras, who take charge of him throughout the festival exclusively. At the close, when the god is unclothed and his shirt shown to the people, only the Banhras officiate as priests and touch the god; but men of the eleventh Sheo-margi caste, Sheristas, are on the car to manage the secular part of the *tamasha*.* But the Banhras unrobe the god, and they exhibit the shirt. They also receive the fees on that occasion.

6th. *Josi*, Vaisyas, neither Brahmans nor priests; but their business is to expound the Shastras.

7th. *Achar*, Vaisyas, priests of Talleju temples of Kathmandu and Bhatgaon, but not Brahmans.

---

* *Tamasha*—a show or spectacle.—(ED.)

8th. *Bhanni*, Vaisyas, cooks for the gods of the Talleju temples.

9th. *Gaoku Achar*, Vaisyas, priests for small temples only. They superintend at such temples the rites connected with deaths, but have nothing to do with actual funeral ceremonies.

10th. *Sheashu*, Chatriyas.*

11th. *Sherista*, Chatriyas.

Both supply sepoys to the army. They intermarry and eat together.

12th. *Makhi*, Sudras, ordinary cooks and table attendants.

13th. *Lakhipar*, Sudras, ordinary cooks and table attendants, but of inferior standing; rather assistants to the former. The two are like our Khitmatgar and Masalchi. Both are domestic servants, and all the above classes of Hindus will eat from their hands.

14th. *Bagho Shashu*, Sudras, domestic servants of all ordinary work, but not cooks.

The above fourteen divisions are genuine worshippers of Shiva in the Hindu style. They never worship Buddha in any form, nor visit his temples for religious purposes. They are distinct classes, and will not eat together, nor intermarry.

The above classes may be grouped into the four regular Hindu castes :—

Brahmans, first, second, and third.

Kshatriyas, fourth, fifth, tenth, and eleventh.

Vaisyas, sixth, seventh, eighth, and ninth.

---

* Same as Kshatriyas.

Sudras, twelfth, thirteenth, and fourteenth.

The Buddha-margi, or Buddhist Niwars, are divisible into three principal classes :—

1st. Orthodox Bandyas, or "Banhras," whose heads are closely shorn.

2nd. Orthodox Buddhists, but not Banhras, who wear a top-knot of hair upon their crowns, and are collectively called "Udas."

3rd. Inferior or heterodox Buddhists, who combine Hinduism with Buddhism; who- are Sheo-margi as well as Buddha-margi; who are Buddhists by name, but are more or less of Hindus in reality.

Each of the above three orders consists of a certain number of classes or divisions, each of which represents and inherits a certain trade or profession. Many of these hereditary occupations are not sufficiently important to afford entire support or subsistence to the members of the craft. In such cases the members of these crafts practise other avocations of a general character, such as agriculture, tailoring, &c.; but the member of one craft never interferes with, or encroaches upon, the technical duties and rights of another. Thus a carpenter will not do the work of a stone-mason, nor a brick-layer that of a painter. But any man may be an agriculturist, though there are certain classes whose especial hereditary duty is the attending to the crops.* Any man may

---

* Any man may be a *Banya*; there is no distinct *caste* of Banyas.

be a tailor, as there is no hereditary class of tailors;
or any man may do cooly's work, carry burdens, or
make himself generally useful as a means of gaining
his daily bread. But whatever his present occupation
may be, every Niwar, whether Sheo-margi or Buddha-
margi, belongs to some hereditary craft or profession,
though circumstances may prevent his devoting himself to it exclusively.

The orthodox Bandyas, or Banhras, are divided
into the following nine classes, the duties of which
are strictly hereditary :—

1st. *Gubharju.* To this class all priests of the
highest order, called the "Vajra acharya," belong.
But Gubharjus are not limited to priestly duties;
some of them are Pandits. The present Residency
Pandit is a Gubharju; his grandfather, Amirla Nanda,
a great friend of Mr. Hodgson's, was a Vajra acharya,
and officiated as such on suitable occasions.* Some
Gubharjus, who are poor or uneducated, attend to

---

* The hereditary calling of the Gubhal or Gubarju is that of
priest. The Vajra Acharya, like all other professions, is hereditary; but a Vajra acharya by *birth*, need not exercise *priestly* duties,
unless qualified to do so; he may, as the pandit in the office does,
devote himself to some other calling. Every Vajra acharya is a
Gubharju; but only a few Gubharjus are Vajra acharyas. The
Gubharjus apparently hold the same relation to other Banhras
which Brahmans do to Hindus. Among the Banhras and Udas
the Vajra acharya alone does all duties of a priest; but among
the Jaffus and superior Buddhists, a Hindu Punhonir is called in
to co-operate with the Vajra acharya.

agriculture; some who are poor become Bhikshus or inferior priests; and some take to other avocations. My tailor is a Gubharju.

2nd. *Barrhaju.*

3rd. *Bikhu.*

4th. *Bhikshu.**

5th. *Nebhar.*

These four are gold and silver smiths, but they only make ornaments.

6th. *Nibharbharhi,* workers in brass and iron. They make metal images of the gods, also cooking utensils, "kalai"† our dishes, &c.

7th. *Tankarmi,* make guns and cannons in iron, brass, or other metal.

8th. *Gangsabharhi.*

9th. *Chiwarbharhi.*

These two are carpenters and workers in wood of all sorts; also plasterers, white-washers, &c.

The above nine classes of Banhras will eat together and intermarry among each other, but not with those below them.

---

* The *hereditary* calling of a Bhikshu is that of a gold or silver smith; but many of them exercise priestly duties of an *inferior* kind; all superior priests are Vajra acharyas; all *inferior* ones are Bhikshus. A Vajra acharya from poverty or want of learning may sink to become a Bhikshu; but a Bhikshu, however wealthy or learned, cannot become a Vajra acharya. In figures of Buddha, inferior attendants upon him are often represented; they are called Bhikshus.

† That is, line them with tin.—(ED.)

The orthodox Buddhists, who are not Banhras, are called collectively Udas; they wear top-knots of hair on their crowns, and are divided into the following seven classes:—

1st. *Udas*, Mahajans and foreign merchants, who deal chiefly with Tibet and Bhutan.

The Udas Niwars are distinctly inferior as a class to the Banhras. A Banhra may let his hair grow, and become one of the Udas; but a Udas Niwar can never rise and become a Banhra. In the same way, a Udas Niwar may sink and become a Jaffu; but a Jaffu cannot become an Udas.

The Udas Niwars, till of late years, were the most wealthy and influential class in the country; of late years their wealth has diminished, and with it their importance.

The Jaffu, or agricultural Niwars, are by far the most numerous class; they probably constitute half the Niwar population.

At the present day the " Sarmis," or oil extractors, though not a very numerous, are by far the most wealthy class of Niwars.

2nd. *Kassar*, workers in metallic alloys.

3rd. *Loharkarmi*, stone-masons. They make images of the gods, and temples, chaityas, &c., as well as work in stone for private houses.

4th. *Sikarmi*, carpenters.

5th. *Thambat*, makers of vessels and general workers in brass, copper, and zinc.

6th. *Awar*, tile-makers. They not only make tiles, but they put them on to the roofs of houses.

7th. *Maddikarmi*, bakers.

The above seven classes will eat together and inter-marry; they will eat from the hands of a Banhra, he being, as a Banhra, their superior. But a Banhra will not eat from the hands of any of them. Of course, therefore, there can be no intermarriage be-tween these six classes and the Banhras.

These seven classes of Udas Niwars are orthodox Buddhists, but are not Banhras. They wear top-knots of hair on their crowns, but are in no way Sheo-margi. They never frequent or worship at Hindu temples, though they may privately, or in the course of their Buddhist devotions in their own houses, do puja to some of those deities who are common objects of worship to Hindus and Buddhists, as Ganesha, Devi, &c.

The inferior or heterodox Buddhists, who openly worship at Hindu temples and are thus Sheo-margi as well as Buddha-margi, consist of the following classes :—

1st. *Mu*, men who cultivate the aromatic herb, mussa, which is sold in large quantities; it is used as an offering to the gods, and is also much worn in the hair. This class have nothing to do with other flowers, nor vegetables, &c.

2nd. *Danghu*, land-surveyors and measurers.

3rd. *Kumhar*, makers of clay vessels of all sorts, potters.

4th. *Karbujha.* Their hereditary duty is as musicians who play a particular instrument at funerals, not at any festivities; but they are mostly employed in agriculture.

5th. *Jaffu* or *Kissini.*

6th. *Boni.*

Cultivators of the fields.

These six classes are all more or less connected with agriculture and land, and are collectively called Jaffu, as the seven preceding classes are collectively called Udas; in each case the collective name being taken for the whole from the one class who greatly predominates among them.

The six classes of Jaffu Niwars rank next below the Udas, and decidedly above all those whose names follow them in the list. All these classes eat together and marry among each other.

7th. *Chittrakar*, painters of all sorts; house painters as well as picture and portrait painters.

8th. *Bhat*, dyers of red colours to all sorts of hair or woollen cloths, but not to linen.

9th. *Chippah*, dyers of blue colour to any and every kind of texture.

10th. *Kaua* or *Nekarmi*, workers in iron of all sorts, blacksmiths; will make horse-shoes, tulwars, knives, or anything.

11th. *Nau*, barbers and barber-surgeons.

12th. *Sarmi*, extractors of oil from mustard or any vegetables.

The Sarmis are the most wealthy class at the present day; they have encroached upon the Udas, and made their money as Mahajans or merchants, and as Banyas. Any man may be a Banya. There are Banyas of any and all castes.

13th. *Tippah*, cultivators of vegetables.

14th. *Pulpul*, men who carry lanterns and lights on the occasion of funerals.

15th. *Kaussa*, inoculators for small-pox.

16th. *Konar*, carpenters who make the chirka and other machines with which the women make thread; they do not do general carpentering, nor will general carpenters make these machines.

17th. *Garhtho*, gardeners.

18th. *Katthar*, wound dressers.

19th. *Tatti*, workers in cotton wool (rui) for clothing for the dead, and for night-caps for infants' heads when their hair is first cut off.

20th. *Balhaiji*, men who make the wheels for the car of Machendra; they occasionally do a little other carpentering.

21st. *Yungwar*, men who make the car of Machendra.

22nd. *Ballah*.

23rd. *Lamu*.

Palki-bearers for the royal family and for some of the wealthy sirdars.

24th. *Dalli*, a class of sepoys.

25th. *Pihi*, makers of wickerwork baskets, dhokahs,* karmus, and wicker chattahs† such as the poor use in the rain when working in the fields.

26th. *Gaowah.*

27th. *Nanda-Gaowah.*

Cowherds, eat together and intermarry.

28th. *Ballahmi*, wood-cutters; bring wood for house use.

29th. *Gaukau*, men who drag the car at Machendra and Indra and Bhairab jatras.

30th. *Nalli*, men who paint the eyes of the golden figure of Bhairab on the Machendra car.

The men who dance, wear masks, do the buffoonery in fact, at the Indra jatra and other Niwar festivals, are of any and all castes; there is no rule for them. The majority are Jaffu. Those who live in the vihars round the temples, and attend and take care of the god and his property, are Banhras.

There is no class or caste of Baids, or doctors; any one possessing the necessary knowledge may be a doctor.

The above thirty classes of heterodox Buddhists, though of inferior status to the Banhras and other orthodox Buddhists, are yet all "caste" men, and from their hands any Hindu will, or may, drink water.

The following eight classes of mixed Buddha-margi

---

* Measures holding ten handfuls of corn.—(Ed.)
† Umbrellas.—(Ed.)

and Sheo-margi Niwars are " out-castes," *i.e.* Hindus
will not take water from them :—

31st. *Nai* or *Kassais*, butchers, killers and sellers of
buffaloes' meat.

32nd. *Joghi*, musicians at Niwar festivals.

33rd. *Dhunt*, musicians at Niwar festivals.

34th. *Dhauwi*, wood-cutters and makers of charcoal.

35. *Kullu*, workers in leather.

36th. *Puriya*, fish-catchers, executioners, and dog-
killers.

37th. *Chamukallak*, sweepers.

38th. *Sanghar*, washermen.

By the above classification the Niwars would appear
to be divided into sixty-eight distinct hereditary
classes :—

Sheo-margi Niwars . . .	14 classes.
Bandya or Banhra Niwars . .	9 ,,
Orthodox Buddhists, but not	
Banhras, called collectively Udas	7 ,,
Heterodox Buddhists, or mixed	
Sheo-margi and Buddha-margi	38 ,,
Total	68 classes.

CHAPTER XV.

CATHOLIC MISSION IN NIPAL.[*]

THE Capuchins had an establishment in the valley, at Patan; the only remaining trace of their presence is the part of the Polyglot inscription attributable to them, and which still exists. They came originally from Pekin to Lassa, where they had large establishments and a good library. Some years ago I was enabled to pick up the fragments of this library at Lassa, and lately I presented it to the Pope. No such or other trace of them was discovered by me in Nipal. The Chinese Emperor drove them from Pekin, and then from Lassa, seizing and confiscating their all, and expelling them across the snows. The Niwar dynasty of Patan received them kindly and gave them lands. But before they could make any great progress in con-

---

[*] Extract from a letter by Mr. Hodgson to Mr. Erskine, Sept. 1850.

version, came the Gorkhas, who expelled them from the
country.   They retired to the plains, and were afforded
an asylum by the Rajah of Bettiah, and in his lands,
at and about the village of Churi, they still dwell with
their Niwar flock, which has increased, but not
greatly, and only by fresh births at Churi, and not by
any additional incomers from the valley, whence probably not above one hundred to two hundred souls
proceeded with the original emigrant fathers.   In
the " Journal of the Royal Asiatic Society " for 1848
are the translations by Mr. Hodgson of the " grants
of land," by virtue of which the mission was established at Patan.   The original deeds are inscribed on
copper, and are or were in the possession of the Roman
Catholic bishop at Patan.   They are in the Niwari
language, interlarded with a good deal of Sanskrit.
" Jaya Rajya Prakas Malla Deva," Prince of Nipal,
was the grantee.

CHAPTER XVI.

LEOPARDS.—DOGS.—BUFFALOES.

LEOPARDS abound in the jungles in all the hills surrounding the valley. They often come down into the
villages on the edges of the valley, and sometimes
even into the centre of the valley, and commit great
depredations. They occasionally attack men, oftener
children, but most usually confine their attacks to
cattle, sheep, goats, &c. In 1852, Jang had a number
of deer of different breeds in an inclosure, with high
walls, of some thirty or forty acres. This inclosure is
about two hundred or three hundred yards only from
the Hospital and Residency compound. A leopard, in
the autumn of 1852, having found out this preserve,
used to come down about every second night and kill
and eat one or more deer. These leopards are very
vicious, often killing apparently for the mere excitement of it. One night this leopard killed three
deer, of which he ate the half of one and merely

sucked the blood from the throats of the others.   On
his way back to the Nagarjun mountain, where he had
taken up his abode, and to which we tracked him, he
fell in with a Brahmany Bull, asleep probably on the
ground.   The leopard, although his hunger had been
sated by the deer, killed the bull too, and sucked the
blood from his throat.   Probably he was thirsty, and
wished for a draught of something toothy !   I accompanied Jang one morning on foot in following the
track of this brute.   He had a number of attendants
with him and some shikaries.   It was wonderful to see
how the latter followed the track by his footsteps,
where it was often quite imperceptible, not only to me,
but even to Jung.   We tracked him nearly half up
the mountain, when the jungle became so thick that we
were obliged to give up the pursuit.

On our way I had incidentally informed Jang that
I had not yet had breakfast, and was very hungry.
He said nothing, but, without informing me, instantly
sent off an express to Thappatalli for breakfast to be
sent to meet him.   On our way back we met the carriage coming at full gallop; it stopped at once; out
got a jemadar, and produced, to my surprise, an excellent still warm breakfast.   Jang and his companions
squatted down on the road-side, and directed me to do
the same, about two or three yards from them.   Out
came fowls, stewed, curried, &c.; goat's meat, grilled,
stewed; cutlets of pork; pilaued pheasant; eggs in
different forms; some very nice crisp sort of cracknell;
chapatis of different kinds; with some fruits, &c.

On this we all made a most hearty meal, Jang always helping me first with his own hands; no knives, forks, or spoons, or plates had been brought, so I used the knife and fork which Nature had given me, and ate my food off a plate made of leaves of the sal tree sewn together. After breakfast I distributed cheroots, of which the Nipalese are very fond, especially when they do not have to pay for them. I returned home.

Two or three days after, this identical leopard was caught in a trap* which had been set for him in the course of his "run" on the Nagarjun mountain. He was taken to Thappatalli, and in the afternoon of the same day I went down to see him killed. Jang proposed turning him out into a "bear-pit," constructed after the model of the pits in our English Zoological Gardens, in which were seven or eight bears. The trap was accordingly placed on the parapet surrounding the edge of the pit, and which was about fifteen feet in diameter. An old bear clambered to the top of the pole to watch the proceedings, and we stood round the parapet expecting to see the beast fall or

---

* Their traps for wild beasts are very ingeniously constructed. It is a long box, like a mouse-trap with a small chamber at the end, in which a live goat is tied. This chamber is separated from the principal one by a hanging door, supported by a string, connected with the principal door of the trap. When the beast enters, and puts his foot on a little bit of stick to which the strings are tied, both doors fall at the same moment. He is caught, and the goat is saved, being separated from him in a different chamber.

spring into the pit among the bears. The door of the trap was raised, when in a moment, with a horrid and peculiar noise, between a roar and a growl, the leopard made a tremendous bound out of the trap, right across the pit, just clearing the old bear on the pole, touched the opposite parapet with his feet, close by two men who were standing there, and sprung down into the garden. Finding himself once again free, he crouched down on a little bit of lawn about twenty yards off, and began to reconnoitre; looking up coolly at us, and evidently waiting to see our intentions. On our making no demonstrations of hostility, he sneaked off into a thick hedge, about eight feet high, close behind which was the wall of the garden. This was about 3 P.M. Jang, who thoroughly knows the habits of these beasts, said he would remain there perdu till night without straying, so we might safely leave him for an hour or two, while we went to see a boar-fight, and he could send for his dogs. In the course of an hour or two we returned, and, as he had foretold, found our friend still in the same place. We could not see him, as the hedge was too thick, but the rustling told us his whereabouts. Jang, who was very inveterate against this particular leopard, in consequence of the number of his deer which he had killed, determined to try and have a cut at him with his talwar. Telling me to keep close to him, and rather behind, we went down to the gravel walk, in front of the hedge where the brute was concealed. Jang stood about ten yards from the hedge, with his talwar raised; I close behind him. Captain

Sutaram threw a number of stones into the hedge. Disturbed and irritated, out rushed the beast with a roar, straight at where we were standing. The great majority of the spectators made rather a hasty retreat. Jang stood like a rock ; up went the talwar, forward came the leopard ; another instant, and I thought it was all up with him. He seemed, however, daunted by Jang's steady bearing, and seeing the glittering talwar commence its descent, he suddenly made a backward spring, when he was only about a yard from Jang, and disappeared again in the hedge.

Jang now sent for the dogs. About twenty Nipal hunting-dogs were brought, but were at once set aside as useless. He then sent for his imported Highland deer-hounds, "Pearl" and "Diamond," with their three young ones, the latter being twenty months old. The dogs were brought down to the gravel walk, taken up to the edge of the hedge, where the brute was, and then all together loosed with an encouraging "hist." Then was seen the superiority of the pluck and blood and breeding of the British dog. Without a sound, no barking, yelping, or even growling, and without one second's hesitation, in they all went with a rush. There was a tremendous scuffle, some fierce growling from the leopard, and the shaking of the bushes told us what a scrimmage was going on ; but the dogs never gave tongue. We could see nothing, from the thickness of the hedge. In about half a minute they emerged, dragging the leopard with them on to the gravel walk. The two old dogs had him firmly, one

13 *

by the throat, the other by the side of the head; the three others were fixed on his shoulders and neck. They were all throttling him; he struggled hard, but could do nothing, except scratch somewhat with his claws. The dogs shook him repeatedly till he was apparently dead, when they were taken away. However, by throwing some water over him, he revived a little again, and then all the Nipal shikari dogs were loosed on him, about twenty in number; the majority, however, were afraid to touch him even then, helpless as he was; a few shook him and bit him about the head. The life appearing at last out of him, he was suspended by his neck against a post, with his belly to the post, the body hanging loose, steadied only by its weight. With a talwar, a Korassan blade, Jang then with one blow, about the centre of the back, cut the body in two; the lower half being prevented from dropping to the ground only by a small portion of the loose skin of the belly which remained uncut. The Nipal dogs were then brought up and blooded; they devoured the entrails, liver, &c., with great avidity, poor beasts, as if they were half-starved.

On another occasion, when I was at Thappatalli, a large leopard was loosed from a trap on a small lawn where Jang, myself, and a few others were standing. Jang and his attendants were armed with talwars or kookeries.* With a stifled roar the beast rushed towards an open walk close by, at which a sepoy was standing

---

* Kookery (or kukri), the short sword or knife used by the Ghorkas, whether in hunting or in war.—ED.

with his kookery ready in his right hand and his turban wrapped round his left arm, which he used as a shield. The beast raised himself on his hind legs, and endeavoured to strike down the man with his fore-paws, but at the moment of contact the man caught him a blow with his kookery which cut his jaw in half and his head open, and as he staggered back he caught him another backhander over the other side of the head, which cut through his eye into the skull The beast fell to the ground, roaring horribly. Jang rushed in, and with his talwar cut his body open, so that the liver and entrails protruded (breaking his talwar by the force of the blow), and after a blow or two more the brute was dead. A few days afterwards I met a common wood-cutter on the road bringing in on his back the skin of a large leopard, stuffed with straw, but cut about a good deal on the head, otherwise uninjured It appeared that the leopard had attacked the man while alone in the jungle cutting wood ; the man repulsed and finally killed the brute with blows of his kookery, sustaining no injury himself. He was bringing in the skin as evidence to enable him to claim the five rupees which is always given by the Nipal Government as a reward to anyone who kills a leopard in the jungles. The man did not seem to think he had performed any remarkable feat.

Jang is very fond of getting up "buffalo fights."

---

* If any sepoy, or Government servant, sees or hears of a leopard or other wild beast in or about the valley, and fails to report it to the minister, he is fined *five rupees.*

A large well-fed bull buffalo is kept in a paddock; another bull is then driven into the same paddock. The two rivals approach each other cautiously, occasionally stopping and pawing the ground; after a short time they close, but without any rush. Forehead to forehead they stand, and lock their horns together. Then they begin to get excited; their tales lash their sides, and they push away, each trying to gore his opponent's head and neck with his horns. Sometimes they get down on their knees, and if one's head slips, so as to unlock their horns, one or both generally get severely gored on the neck or shoulders; but as long as their horns remain locked it is a mere pushing match and no damage is done. They continue in this way sometimes for half-an-hour, neither one giving way. At length one feels himself overmatched, and suddenly giving way, bolts off as hard as he can go, the other pursuing. If the victorious one can come up with the beaten one, he gores him and endeavours to upset him from behind. He rarely succeeds, however, as both are two much winded to run either far or fast; and fear makes the beaten one run faster than the other.

At this time, while in retreat from a contest, the buffalo is a very dangerous animal to meet; he will gore anybody who stands in his way. During the fight, while horns are interlocked, they seem so absorbed in the excitement of the fight as to be unaware of the approach of anyone or of anything going on around them. In one case, I saw a sepoy ap-

proach two who were fighting (either of whom would
have attacked him had he been disengaged), and with
a kookery hack away for five minutes at a log of wood
which had been secured to the fore leg of one of the
buffaloes, to prevent his doing harm, and which now
fettered his movements in the fight.   The man after
some trouble cut through it and took it off from the
chain.   Neither buffalo took the slightest notice of
him, nor of one of Jang's English dogs who had
come up and stood barking and yelling at them within
a yard or two of their heads.

At Thappatalli I saw a young cow buffalo, about
two years old, with horns not more than a foot long,
turned into a pit in which was a full-grown though
rather young tiger, who had never had so large an
animal given him before.   This was the same tiger
who was brought up into the room, led by one man
holding him by a chain, to see Lord Grosvenor and
party when they visited Thappatalli.

The tiger flew at the buffalo and seized her by the
head, bringing her down on her knees.   With a violent
effort the buffalo threw him off.   The tiger returned
to the charge, but the buffalo planted so well-delivered
a blow with her horns in the tiger's belly that it
threw him some yards across the pit against the wall.
The tiger on this retreated to his den, a sort of cavern,
about three feet high and four feet deep, constructed
to protect him from the weather, &c.   In this he
crouched down, and would not come out again.   The
buffalo by this time was so excited and infuriated,

that she actually went down on her knees at the mouth of the den, and endeavoured to get hold of the tiger with her teeth and drag him out. The tiger howled and roared, but would not come out; so the buffalo was eventually shot in the pit. In the jungles, a tiger will never attack a herd of wild buffaloes, and very rarely a single one unless he can spring on him unawares.

CHAPTER XVII.

WILD ELEPHANTS.

In December 1851 I accompanied for a few days the camp of the Maharajah and Jang Bahadur on a shooting excursion in the Terai. The rendezvous was at Hetowara, where we all arrived on the morning of the 19th. In the afternoon the King, Jang, myself, and some of his brothers made a circuit of a few miles, on elephants through the jungles, to see if we could pick up any game.

In the course of an hour or two, Jang came upon fresh tracks of elephants, and prepared for a *dour** after them. Three or four staunch fast elephants were selected, their howdahs and trappings removed on to others, so that they were quite free from any gear which could embarrass them in passing rapidly through the tree jungle. Besides his mahaut each elephant had one other man on his back. On this occasion there were only four or five elephants, Jang, Captain Sutaram, and three or four others accompanying them. The

---

* Dour, or daur, a chase.—Ed.

riders wear almost as little clothing as the elephants, and take off their turbans, shoes, kummurbunds, &c., so as to be quite free to use their limbs. Each mahaut was provided with a set of ropes, to act as lassos to secure the wild elephants if they came up with them. Jang and his party started off in pursuit; the King, myself, and the bulk of the party returning to camp. On our way back Ranudat Sing shot a large male sambar deer, which we had some difficulty in hoisting up on to an elephant's back.

Shortly before sunset, as I was sitting outside my tent smoking a cheroot with General Ranudat Sing, Jang returned to camp, bringing with him in triumph a fine female elephant, which he had caught after we left him. He had come upon a small herd of them, but only succeeded in separating and securing this one. The lasso having been well secured round her throat, one end of the long rope was fastened to one large tame elephant, who went before, leading the way, while the other was, in the same way, fastened to another large tame elephant (Jang's own, on which he was seated), who followed behind in order to administer a push or prod with his tusks as a reminder in case the newly captured one jibbed or objected to go on.

These two tame elephants were very fine ones, thoroughly broken in to their work, and had been both engaged in the capture of the new one. It was very curious to see the skilful way in which they guided their prize safely through the camp, close to my tent, despite all her resistance, without swerving from the line, or coming in contact with a single tent-peg.

The new one, much frightened, tried once or twice on entering the camp to throw herself down, so as to prevent her further progress. Immediately Jang's elephant, behind, touched her up in the quarter with his tusks, not fiercely so as to do any harm, but with sufficient energy to show what she would get in case of further resistance. She jumped up, and tried to bolt off forward or to one side. The leading elephant's rope kept her steady, and prevented her swerving. Jang waited a minute or so outside my tent to get a cheroot. The leading and the following elephants, by tightening their respective ropes, kept the new one fixed in one spot, as she could neither advance nor recede. The tame ones went through their parts with the greatest docility and gravity, perfectly understanding their respective duties. After a minute's delay, on they went through the camp to the ground where all the tame elephants were picketed under a large group of trees, about two hundred in number. The two tame elephants guided the new one with the greatest skill through the trees, ropes, &c., till they brought her up to a large stake about fifteen feet high and firmly fixed in the ground, to which she was to be secured. The leading elephant led her straight up to it; and when her neck, round which the rope was fastened, came up to the post, the two tame ones making a turn with their respective ropes, she was

fairly secured from moving away. The tame ones
immediately (Jang continuing on the back of his
elephant, with his " once " white kid gloves and
patent leather boots still on) closed on her, one
standing on each side, and leaning rather against
her. Her head being fixed, this kept her quite steady.
The mahauts then firmly secured the ropes in knots
around her neck, so that there was no danger of her
slipping them during the night. They now had to
secure her feet; no easy matter, as she kept kicking
and struggling most violently. However, the tame
elephants kept up the pressure on her sides, and with
their trunks played with her trunk and head so skilfully to divert her attention from her front feet, and
prevent her seeing what was going on, that two men
succeeded in crawling under the tame ones' bellies
(who kept their own feet steady so as not to hurt
them), and fastening a figure-of-eight knot firmly
round her two front legs just above the feet.

They now had to put a noose round one of her hind
legs to keep her steady and prevent her slewing her
body round too much. She plunged so violently at
first, and afterwards, apparently knowing what they
were about, kept her hind feet so firmly on the
ground, that this was a matter of difficulty. However, at last, by putting a rope round the other foot,
and pulling it, at the same time knocking it with a
stick, they induced her to raise her foot and make
the attempt to slip off the rope; immediately they
threw the noose over her raised foot. However, she

managed to push it off with the other several times before it was securely fixed. She was now firmly bound head and foot. The tame ones were withdrawn, and she was alone for the first minute since her capture. It was wonderful to see the prodigious efforts she made to loose herself; but the ropes were too strong, and the post too firmly fixed. The rope round her neck prevented her rolling or throwing herself on the ground, which she tried to do, and which, had she succeeded in doing, she would probably have strangled herself. After a little—when it was seen that the ropes to her neck and fore feet were sufficient—the noose to her hind feet was let go. She renewed her struggles, crying most piteously all the while: she kicked most tremendously, and actually repeatedly raised her hind foot right up to her neck, scratching most violently at the rope round her throat to get it off. In these attempts she frequently struck her own ear, so high did she lift her foot. She was now left for the night. No food was to be given to her for three or four days, as the continued hunger would wear her strength and her spirit too, so as to make her more tameable. In the course of three or four days, when she became less violent, they would give her a little food, and then move her about, secured by ropes, in company with tame elephants. In about ten days or a fortnight she would be sufficiently tamed to cease all resistance, to let a mahaut ride her, and only to require teaching to make her obedient and tractable.

When an elephant is to be broken for howdah work, his education, of course, is more protracted, as he requires to be so perfectly obedient.

There was a very large elephant caught by Jang in the Terai, which he had brought up to Nipal and broken in at Thappatalli. After the brute had recovered his footsoreness from the journey, and the wounds round his neck and feet, caused by the tightness of the ropes cutting through the skin during his early struggles, his education commenced. Two tame elephants, standing side by side his neck and feet, were firmly secured by ropes; then a network of rope was put all over his head, trunk, and body, and a crowd of boys and men clambered up these ropes and stood and sat upon him, some on his back, some on his neck, head, trunk, everywhere in fact where—with the assistance of ropes and mutual support—they could get a footing. Numbers more stood all round him, patting and coaxing him. There must have been at least twenty men standing on him at one time. These all kept pounding on him with their bare feet; at the same time a band played and with drums, &c. made the most discordant noises. Guns, too, were constantly fired off before him, and afterwards from off his back, to accustom him to hear or see the discharge without flinching.

At first he was much frightened, but was quite helpless, so firmly was he bound. Gradually he became more accustomed to it; then nicely made cakes, &c. were given to him. This state of things was kept up with relays of men and boys for several days and nights, the elephant never being allowed to sleep nor to rest. The pounding on his skin with their feet must, without bruising him, have greatly fatigued him and tended to reduce his powers of resistance. After a few days, as he became more docile, the ropes were loosened and gradually removed, the numbers of men on him reduced, food more plentifully given him; then his trunk being secured, they kept playing with clothes, &c. on or about his head, made men continually climb up and down by his trunk, petting and feeding him all the time, so as to accustom him to the practice of men climbing about his head and neck. This system went on, its severity gradually relaxing, for two or three weeks, when he was so docile that he would allow his mahaut to stand by and play with him, to mount him when he liked, and dismount by his trunk; and would let Jang, who superintended the operations in person, feed him with cakes. This was about two months after his capture. He had now to be taught to go out on the roads quietly with his mahout, and to be accustomed to the different objects he might meet on the roads. For the first few days, for the sake of security to prevent his bolting in case of getting frightened, he had two elephants with him with leading ropes to his neck. However, in a few days he went so quietly that the ropes were dispensed with; and I met him frequently taking his airing, sometimes with Jang on his back, without any kind of restriction.

His education was now all but completed as far as docility and safety were concerned. He would kneel down, rise up, &c. at the word of command; stop, turn, &c. when in motion. They only now had to teach him to carry the howdah, when, about four months after his capture, he was taken ill, refused his food, lingered evidently in great pain for a few days, and then died. Jang, myself, and the " elephant doctor " tried different remedies, which he made no resistance to our doing, but with no effect.

The next morning there was a post-mortem examination, which I was requested to superintend. The poor brute had died of internal obstruction and inflammation. It was a curious sight to see. An elephant is so large and heavy that it would be quite impossible to drag away his body for burial. It has, therefore, to be divided into portions, and taken away piecemeal. In this case his head was taken off and cleaned, as Jang wished to keep the skull. His internals were all taken out very neatly, washed, and laid out for my inspection. Jang examined them closely, and seemed thoroughly to understand the cause of his death. This over, the body was cut into numberless bits and taken away; some of them were buried, others thrown into the river.

Jang seemed quite to be able to recognise the different appearances of the healthy and the diseased parts, so as to be able to distinguish one from the other. He is very much interested in anatomy, though of course his knowledge is chiefly theoretical, as his religion would not allow him to dissect. On one occasion, when one of his servants had injured his skull from a fall, Jang explained to me his view of the nature of the internal injury. To do so he sketched, with a pencil on a bit of paper, a map of the course and distribution of the arteries of the brain and base of the skull, pointing out which went to the ears, which to the eyes, nose, &c. Of course it was not quite so correct anatomically as to secure his "passing" at the College of Surgeons, but it was correct in the main, and showed that he had a very fairly clear idea of the parts he was demonstrating, and of the injuries to which, from their position, they were most liable.

December 19*th*.—We spent the night at Hetowara, our rest only disturbed by the bellowing and trumpetings of the elephants, and especially the distressing cries of the new captive. The next morning (20th) we were ready to start at daybreak, the King, Jang, and myself heading the party, with about one hundred and fifty other elephants following, carrying, some of them, sirdars, &c., and many of them merely carrying their mahauts. Jang proposed that he would shoot at any male deer we should meet, while I was to take the females, as he objected to shooting the latter. The cortége followed the course of the Rapti river westward for about a mile, when we came to the point where the Kara Naddi stream falls into the Rapti; crossing the Kara Naddi, we struck off towards south into the jungle in quest of game. The jungle here consists of rather stunted sal trees, with semel or cotton trees. The trees being all very close together and each struggling towards the light, their trunks have run up to a considerable height before they give off their boughs, which over-head form a very dense canopy of leaves, and are an excellent protection from the sun.* The grass, which in the rains grows luxuriantly and to a great height, had been burnt at the commencement of the cold weather; the ground, therefore, was blackish in colour and open, many of the trunks seared, charred, and some quite burnt and dead. Here and there a trunk, uprooted or broken by storm, lying across the road, gave a very gloomy character to the land-scape; but, from the absence of grass, the elephants were able to go on quickly and without any difficulty or danger of falling into holes or inequalities. The absence generally of lower or horizontal boughs re-moved all necessity for care for our own heads or howdahs. The mahaut, however, always had his kukery ready to strike off any projecting bough or creeper which came in the way, the elephants them-

---

* " The vaulted arches beneath are filled with thousands of high unbroken columns, which sustain one vast and trembling canopy of leaves." . . . "A pleasing gloom and an imposing silence have their interminable reign below, an outer and different atmo-sphere seeming to rest on the cloud of foliage; while the light plays on the varying surface of the tops, a sombre hue covers the earth."—Cooper's " Description of American Forests."

selves also exhibiting wonderful skill in removing all obstacles out of their own path. We formed a long and tolerably regular line, which marched steadily on in hopes of driving any game before it. The King's elephant was in the centre, Jang's on one flank, mine on the other. We proceeded some miles, however, without seeing a single head of game. The jungle gradually changed, became more open, grassy, and the trees better grown and branched. Silence was throughout strictly enjoined by Jang. Presently Jang sighted a female sambar deer in advance of the line. Bringing up his howdah close to mine, rifle in hand, he jumped into my howdah, and without a word, but by motion of his hand, signalling the line to halt, he pointed out to the mahaut the deer's whereabouts, as I could not see her. So silent was the party, and so carefully did my elephant advance, that we came within forty yards of a fine deer grazing, without her seeing us, in the midst of some long grass. Jang handed me the rifle, and I took a steady pot at the shoulder, but did not make a very good shot, as I ought to have killed her on the spot. However, she fell wounded and struggling furiously. The dogs were sent ior; there was a few minutes' delay, during which her struggles ceased, and all was still. We thought her dead, as we could not see her from the length of the grass. However, the moment the dogs arrived, up she jumped and went off, though not very fast. The dogs followed close, each with his own man or keeper on foot. We soon lost sight of them

14 *

owing to the length of the grass and the thickness of the jungle; but for some time we could hear the shouts of the men and the barking of the dogs. This deer was shot through the chest, and managed to keep ahead of the dogs all the day. She ran towards Hetowara by a circuit of some miles, the men and dogs all on her track, which they never lost through the thickest jungle. Towards sunset she became quite exhausted, and the dogs coming up, she was despatched and skinned, and the meat sent off to our camp, where it arrived about midnight, and was rather acceptable to all, as our supplies were always difficult to obtain.

The track or spoor is very unmistakable; the grass is beaten down and flattened by the large feet, the separate footsteps being often distinct; the bushes, &c., and often large boughs broken off, mark their line of march. The skill in tracking is shown in distinguishing the fresh from the older marks, and in some cases singling out, when there are many, the freshest of all, and following it alone to the exclusion of the rest. At this tracking Jang is a great adept, and as we went along frequently pointed out the marks of elephants, which he knew at a glance were old, though they appeared fresh to me, but which, had he followed, would only have led him a wild-goose chase.

We saw glimpses of two or three other deer bounding in the distance through the long grass, but we did not get another shot. About noon Jang came upon the track of wild elephants; he and a party immediately started off in pursuit. They never came up with them, however, and did not return to camp at Dardara till after dark.

The King and myself, finding it was a "no-day," left Jang and the rest of the party, and started for camp. For three or four miles we went through the tree-jungle, occasionally crossing the deep and dry bed of a nalla, where it was astonishing to see how cleverly the elephants picked their way up and down the steep banks, often overgrown with jungle. At length we came down again on the left bank of the Rapti river, along which the road from Hetowara to Dardara goes. It is a mere footpath, which follows closely the course of that river, sometimes on one side, sometimes on the other. Here we fell in with the stream of coolies carrying the baggage, tents, supplies, &c. of the camp, broken here and there by parties of sepoys of the two regiments (Rifle and Light) which were in attendance on the King and Jang. Marching in this way, no order is attempted to be kept. They are present for morning and evening call, and those on duty never leave sight of their charge, whether it be one of Jang's horses, his dogs, his luggage, or his wife's palki. But those off duty straggle on, stopping to eat, drink, or smoke when inclined, and only anxious to get to camp in time to prepare their evening meal and their quarters for the night.

The grass jungle and reeds on either side of the path were so impenetrably thick and high that those on foot, almost the whole way, had to go in single file, occasioning much delay in their arrival in camp, and causing much and often amusing confusion as the King's elephant which led, closely followed by mine, came upon a long line of sepoys, servants, coolies, &c. who had to get out of the road as best they could, often in a very higgledy-piggledy manner, pushing each other into, and often tumbling over each other in, the long grass. This reedy grass was so high that it frequently, as the elephant pushed through it, met on either side over the top of the howdah. Frequently, when the King's elephant was not ten or twelve yards from mine, I could hear his voice calling to me, but could not see the least portion of either his elephant or his howdah, a sea of this dense grass intervening between us. Here and there the grass had been either burnt, or, from the stony character of the soil, had not grown. From these open patches we could see something of the surrounding scenery, which was very picturesque. The Rapti was close to us; a broad but mostly shallow stream, with rough stony bed, its water brilliantly clear. On the opposite or right side of the Rapti were ranges of hills all densely covered with almost impenetrable tree-jungle, and mostly sloping down to the side of the stream. Here and there we could see up a vista or valley between two such hills, down the centre of which, or winding round successive spurs thrown off from the hills on its sides, came a small stream or feeder to the Rapti. Such streams, though very slight in the cold weather, are in the rains often tumultuous and violent torrents, and quite impassable either for man or beast.

We crossed and recrossed the Rapti three or four times, in some of the fords the water coming up nearly to the elephants' bellies; and at about eight miles from Hetowara came upon a little temporary village, called Dardara, consisting of about twenty huts formed of grass and bamboo, in which reside a few of the natives of the Terai, and others who are in attendance on the crowds of cattle which come in thousands from all parts of India to pasture in the Terai.

We passed Dardara and encamped, about one mile beyond it, on an open spot on the left bank of the river. The tents and traps were late in coming up. The sepoys in camp, immediately they arrived, set to work at building, first for the big-wigs, myself included, and afterwards for themselves, small temporary huts, which they quickly constructed of strong sticks and stakes stuck into the ground, and then boughs, with leaves on them, interwoven upon and between them. They made them generally three-sided, with roof, and open only on one side. Of course these would not protect against heavy rains, but they answer capitally against the cold and the dew. A range of them, in about half an hour, were constructed on my piece of ground, in which I put my servants, &c.

21st December.—Before daybreak the camp was awake and preparing to start. On joining the rendezvous in front of Jang's tent, I found an immense fire, round which Jang and his brethren were standing, the King on an elephant being also present.

About a mile from our encamping-ground we crossed the river, and, quitting the valley of the Rapti, directed our course through some low ground, covered with tremendous grass-jungle for three or four miles, when we came down on another stream, the Manhauri, which, rising among the hills to the north, follows a long and winding course, and at last falls into the Rapti near Chitaun. The stream is a considerable one; in some places its channel is upwards of one hundred yards wide; in others, where the channel is narrowed by rocks or adjacent hills, the stream is strong and the volume of water considerable. Like all these mountain streams, its bed is rocky and the water brilliantly clear; immense boulders lie about in all directions, indicating the power of the torrent when swollen by the rains. The hills on either side are richly covered with thick jungle, and there was no trace visible of any attempt at cultivation; all was wild, grand, and very picturesque.

We followed up the course of this stream for five or six miles, fording it frequently; occasionally, where the river made an abrupt bend, cutting across the little promontories, so as to save distance, but never leaving the bed of the river for any time. We saw no game of any sort save a few wild ducks. The ground was so rough and stony that our progress was but slow. About noon we arrived at the ground

where it was proposed we should halt for three or
four days in order to catch the elephants of which
intelligence had been brought to Jang that they were
in the immediate neighbourhood. The river here,
after bending abruptly round the base of a small but
almost precipitously conical rocky hill about one hundred feet high, emerged by a narrow channel through
a sort of gorge, on one side of which the rock was
quite precipitous, to the water's edge; on the other
was the aforesaid little steep hill, its sides sloping
very steeply down to the river. Across this gorge or
pass, which was here about forty yards wide, a very
high and strong stockade had been constructed of
stones and rocks as a foundation, from either side of
which sprang stakes, some twenty feet high, which
were inclined at an angle towards each other so as to
meet and cross at the tops, enclosing a triangular
space inside, where they were fastened by rope. These
again were crossed in all directions by bamboos,
placed horizontally and firmly secured, strong stakes
in many places being driven into the ground as extra
security, with their points sticking out like a *chevaux
de frise*. The inside of this stockade was hollow and
could hold a number of men, who, armed with muskets and protected by the woodwork and bamboo,
could make a formidable resistance in such a gorge
to the passage either of men or elephants. The
rocks which formed its foundation, and the stakes
driven in between them, allowed the waters to pass
without difficulty at this time of the year; but in the

rains the whole structure, which had been only just made, would rapidly be swept away by the swollen waters of the torrent. A doorway of wood, large enough to let pass through it a mounted elephant, was formed in the centre; but having bamboos placed crossways before and behind it, it did not catch the eye, nor appear a weak point. In fact, part of the stockade required to be removed to open the door, the object of which was to allow the tame elephants, or the wild ones after they were caught and secured, to be led through it into our camp. The ground was a very bad one for encamping upon, being confined and stony. However, the sepoys were set to work, and they soon cleared away the loose rocks, stones, &c., levelled the ground where practicable, and pitched our tents; the ground, being the dry bed of the river, was too hard to admit of tent-pegs being used, so the ropes were all secured to heavy stones, which did just as well.

All our tents were pitched close to the stockade. The sepoys then set to work to cut boughs and sticks from the jungle for their own quarters, and soon, on the opposite side of the river, a little colony of huts arose on a piece of open ground. They constructed, too, of stones, a very fair temporary bridge connecting the two camps on the opposite sides of the river, so that we could walk dry-footed from one camp to the other.

The rest of the day was spent in moving about the camp, smoking and talking with Bam Bahadur and Ranudat Sing, both of whom, towards evening, became musical, and, sending for their English flutes, played me " God save the Queen," " Rule Britannia," &c. They had learnt a little from Mr. Ventnon, a Frenchman who was employed for some time by the darbar as bandmaster, and having practised a good deal since, and having good ears naturally, they now played very fairly; at least, understandably, as I was able to make out and distinguish the tunes. I retired to bed early as it was bitterly cold at night, and the cold wind whistled along the bed of the river most unmercifully. Jang, who had gone out to reconnoitre for the elephants, did not return to camp till near midnight. He was off again at daybreak, having heard of a large " must "[*] male elephant, whom he was determined either to catch or to kill for the sake of his horns. He is most indefatigable in pursuit of his game. All day long, and night too if necessary, he will follow a track over the worst ground, often on foot, and where he is obliged to fast the greater part of the time, or take merely any fruit, &c. which may be procurable.

22nd December.—Early in the morning all the tame elephants, with beaters, &c. were taken away some miles up the valley of the Manhauri to come up, if possible, with the wild ones and drive them towards the stockade at our camp, where it was proposed to catch them.

After breakfast we all went up to the top of the

---

[*] *Must* (or more correctly *mast*) means here "mad with sexual longing."—(ED.)

little conical hill on one side of the stockade, from which we commanded an exceedingly good view of the surrounding country; and in perfect safety ourselves, we should be able to see all that went on below, in consequence of the precipitous sides of the hill, which were scarcely practicable for a man, quite impracticable for an elephant to climb. Bam here explained to me the nature of the campaign. For about eight miles from where we were the Manhauri river flowed through a narrow valley, bounded on either side with high, often nearly precipitous, hills, densely wooded, and covered with jungle from top to bottom. Here and there, as the river flowed round a shoulder of a hill, the valley widened for two or three hundred yards; but generally the hills came down almost to the water's edge. The only good approaches into or exits from this valley were at the two ends, either where the river entered it, eight miles from our camp, or where it quitted it through the narrow gorge now blocked up by the stockade. There were a few narrow passes here and there on the sides, either between adjoining mountains or at the top over the shoulders of them; but the jungle in their neighbourhood was so thick, and the approaches so steep, that no elephant, unless driven to them, would attempt to quit the valley by such bad roads, but would naturally keep near the river at the bottom of the valley where they could move rapidly and freely, rather than venture up the sides of mountains so steep and thickly wooded that their footing would become insecure and their progress consequently very slow.

The stockade at our camp having been completed about six weeks before, and made so strong that no elephant could force it, the valley was converted into a *cul de sac*. The other end was open, and through it a herd of elephants,—consisting of a large male, with several females and some young ones—who for some time had been known to be in the neighbourhood, had been cautiously watched, and insensibly guided by men well up to the work, rather than driven, into the valley. Once in it, a strong stockade had been rapidly thrown up across its mouth, and a number of sepoys and others stationed there constantly to frighten by their muskets, &c. the elephants from making any attempt to force it. The herd was now enclosed in a valley eight miles long, with either end stockaded to prevent their escape. Strong guards were stationed at each stockade, and also at each of the little passes before alluded to, at which it was possible, but not probable, the elephants might try to escape. In case of any elephants approaching any of these points the sepoys would discharge their muskets, and the others would shout, strike stones together, and by their noise endeavour to frighten them back.

As elephants are, generally speaking, very timid animals, and as they had plenty of room to range in, through a thickly wooded valley of eight miles long, there was not much danger of their trying to force the passes, unless they were molested and frightened so as to become desperate; and strict orders had been given that no molestation should be offered to them. Accordingly we found on our arrival that these orders had been so strictly obeyed, and the passes, &c. so strictly watched, that the whole herd, believed to consist of about twelve, exclusive of young ones, were in the valley, though a good deal scattered about among the jungle, as their supply of the particular food they liked was pretty well exhausted from their having been shut up (in prison, as Bam called it) in a confined valley for some weeks. The elephants must have been on short commons for some time. This, of course, would make them less strong and courageous, and so render them more easy to secure. This is all part of the system.

The object now was, by means of tame elephants, beaters, &c., to collect the herd together, and drive them down to the end of the valley where our camp was. Here, driven into a corner, with the road of exit in front shut up by the stockade, on either side steep and almost impracticable mountains, well occupied too by crowds of sepoys, &c., and in their rear the tame elephants and beaters, they would be completely hemmed in, and so be secured alive without difficulty. The two regiments in camp were used as beaters, and splendidly they did their work. It is part of the agreement with every sepoy, on being enlisted, that he is to be ready at any time to assist in operations in the sporting field.

The little round hill from which we were to see the spectacle commanded an admirable view of the ground where the scrimmage of the capture was to take place. The river flowed round two sides of its base, the third side looked up the valley and commanded a view for about half a mile, when the river disappeared round a shoulder of one of the hills. In its rear our little hill was connected by a narrow neck or isthmus with a large steep mountain which lay behind us, and formed one of the boundaries of the valley. From this isthmus a steep, narrow footpath led down to our camp, and was the only road of approach either for man or beast to the summit of our little hill. The half mile of the valley which was open to our view, and down which the elephants were to be driven towards the stockade, was about two hundred to three hundred yards in width, on either side flanked by the mountains covered with very thick jungle, and having the river winding through its centre, between sandy and rocky banks, for the most part very shallow and fordable. In one or two places, where it made a sudden turn either round or beneath precipitous rock, the river was very deep. Just opposite where we were, and about forty yards before it reached the stockade, it flowed beneath a precipitous face of the hill, whose base it had partly undermined, and was here deep enough for an elephant to swim with his whole body beneath the water.

This day (the 22nd) was spent idly waiting for the approach of the elephants. Two or three false alarms

were given ; the elephants were so scattered that the
beaters were unable to collect them. We smoked,
laughed, played chess, cards, flute, &c. till sunset,
when, instead of wild elephants, I was delighted by
the arrival of two tame ones bringing Law and Clif-
ford, who had come on from Sigauli to see the sport.

About 9 P.M. Jang returned to camp pretty well
knocked up. He had come to close quarters at last
with a remarkably fine " must " tusker. He had
been on his track nearly all day, and at length had
sent several balls into his head and shoulders, but
without apparently much effect. He did not part
company with him till after dark, and intended returning to the fight early next morning.

December 23rd.—Early in the morning, after having
had a cheroot and seeing a " nautch," Jang started.
We spent the morning on the top of the little hill,
talking and smoking with Bam, his brothers, and
other sirdars. The King came up for an hour or so,
as he had done the preceding day; but his presence
did not add much to the liveliness of the party.*

---

* Bam and his brothers appeared to treat the king most unceremoniously, as if they considered him a mere nonentity. They
went on talking, laughing, and smoking, just as freely before him
as when he was not there. The other Sirdars (Hendah Thappa,
&c.) treated him with much marked respect. He was much delighted with my spectacles and eye-glass, especially the former,
which I lent him, and which he wore throughout the afternoon.
From the extraordinary prominence, and convexity of his eyes, I
have no doubt he is very short-sighted, and therefore found my
concave glasses materially assist his vision.

He was very affable to us, and Law tried to make him understand the distinguishing characteristics of Walers* and Arabs. The King listened, but I do not think he understood half, or was interested in any of the conversation.

As we were getting rather tired of waiting, we heard the distant rattle of musketry up the valley, the echo reverberating from side to side. There was an instant exclamation of delight, as this firing showed the elephants were approaching. It proceeded from parties of sepoys stationed at various points in the jungle wherever there was a path which seemed likely to afford a line of retreat or escape to elephants. They were accompanied by numbers of villagers and others with sticks and stones, which they rattled so as to increase the noise whenever the elephants came near. The sepoys were ordered always to reserve their fire till the elephant was close on them, then to fire blank cartridge in a volley in his face; at the same time the stones and sticks were rattled and knocked together so as to add to the noise. This was always sufficient; and the elephant retreated, generally much faster than he had come. At every turn, on either side, whenever they attempted to quit the valley and get into the jungle, a volley of musketry met them and frightened them back, at the same time that a crowd of tame elephants, with an army of beaters, &c., were driving

---

* Anglo-Indian for horses from New South Wales.—(ED.)

I   15 them on from behind. Thus their only course was forward, along the course of the valley towards our stockade. As they came nearer and nearer the reports of musketry became more frequent; sometimes on one side, sometimes on another. Then all was silent for some time, when musketry was heard again, but unfortunately in the distance; the elephants had evidently doubled back. The excitement now became very great. Presently the reports were again heard coming nearer and nearer, and more frequent; still nothing was seen. At last, after one very near report, a cloud of white smoke rising from the jungle about a mile from us showed us the exact whereabouts of the herd; they had charged in that spot and been met by a volley. Another report and another in rapid succession, each accompanied, or rather preceded, by a cloud of white smoke. Then silence for a few minutes. Suddenly a succession of rapid discharges of musketry on the opposite side of the valley, but still among the jungle, showed that the elephants were trying to force their way in that direction. They were, however, so steadily met by the sepoys, who never flinched, that they were always driven back. Still nothing, save the clouds of white smoke rising from different spots on the hill-sides, could be seen. Presently the discharges became more frequent and much nearer, and at last a white column of smoke was seen to emerge from the trees, only about half a mile from us, close to the point where the valley opened out to our view. We knew that the herd must be at that point. As the beaters came on behind them, we could now distinguish the distant voices and shouting of the men; discharge rapidly succeeded discharge. Suddenly all was silence again, and we shortly heard the firing again, but at some distance; the elephants had evidently made good a charge and broken through the line of beaters. Presently, however, the smoke, the rapid firing, and the shout of the beaters showed us again that the herd was approaching, and ere long, at the edge of the jungle, half hidden by the bushes, we descried the head and neck of an elephant peering round to see if the ground were clear for her to emerge into the open. Apparently satisfied by seeing no one in front, and hearing the firing, &c. behind, she came out, followed by a young one; then another female with her young one; then two or three more, following each other at short intervals, each one always stopping a little to reconnoitre before she left the protection of the jungle. On they came in single file at a good trot across the open ground on the side of the stream, which latter they forded two or three times, the young ones cantering on by their mothers' sides. They passed close under the hill where we all were, evidently not aware of our presence, as we kept strict silence. On seeing the stockade stopping their further progress, they were at fault. Collected together, apparently to deliberate, and then following the largest, they turned and tried to enter the woods on the hill opposite to us by a pathway which led

15 *

into the jungle. They were, however, all of a sudden, on nearing it, assailed with such a discharge of musketry from men concealed there that they again recoiled into the open ground; they then turned, with a view of returning again to the jungle they had first quitted; but at this moment from it emerged a large party of tame elephants, with two large "must" ones accompanying them. In all directions the firing continued, closing gradually in on them, so as to confuse and frighten them still more. In a minute the tame elephants, each with two mahauts on it, were mixed up in a mass with the wild ones, firing and shouting going on all the time. The hustling and pushing were tremendous, and it was impossible to make out the exact mode of throwing the lasso, or, in fact, often to distinguish the tame from the wild ones. All of a sudden a wild one burst from the crowd. We thought it had escaped, but were delighted at seeing that the lasso was fixed round her neck, and two large elephants were in close attendance upon her; they were evidently letting her tire herself by running and pulling against the ropes, as an angler lets a large fish play and run off with the line before he attempts to land him.

Out came presently another wild one, similarly accompanied, from the confused mass, in which elephants wild and tame—mahauts hopping about like mad monkeys on their backs and vociferating violently as they were hurling ropes and picking them up again—were all blended together in the centre; while in a sort of outer ring were the two large "must" elephants standing as still as possible, stationed at points to cut off all retreat into the jungle in case a wild one should succeed in detaching herself from the mob. This elephantine mass kept swaying backwards and forwards till they came close on the edge of the river, where, overhung by precipitous rock, it was very deep. In rushed the wild ones closely pursued and accompanied by the tame ones, as well as by their own young ones. The water was soon over their heads, but still the scrimmaging went on; the mahauts clung, like leeches, with wonderful tenacity to their elephants, as the water deepened each mahaut raising himself into a standing position on the elephant's back; so that as the elephant swam along you could see the tip of his trunk only above the water, and about a yard behind it the black head and shoulders of the mahaut, all of whom, partly by treading, partly by swimming, managed to keep to their own elephants.

There must have been altogether about twenty elephants in the water together, all pushing, wallowing, fighting, trumpeting, rolling like a party of hippopotami having a frolic, and the little mahauts popping up and down here and there among them, busy in taking advantage of the confusion to secure the ropes round the wild ones' necks. After a few minutes in the water, the wild ones, probably finding themselves fatigued by the struggle, made a rush towards the shore, hoping to gain the jungle again. But it was too late. During the melée the mahauts had managed to secure the lasso round the neck of every one of the wild elephants, seven in all; so that there was no chance of escape. However, the knot in the lasso of one of them had unfortunately in some way got wrong and become a mere noose or running knot. As the elephant plunged violently on reaching the shore, the mahauts, unaware of this, gave her her head, with a view of letting her run a little and so tire herself out. She suddenly stopped, staggered for a moment, and falling heavily forward, rolled over on her side quite dead. The noose had evidently suddenly tightened during her struggles, and she was strangled. Seeing what had happened, the mahauts instantly cut the rope; but it was too late, she was quite dead. It was a great pity, as she was the finest elephant of the batch. She had a young one with her, a few months old, and about as large as a small heifer. This young one, despite the confusion and noise around it, would not abandon its mother; but, uttering moans and whines, kept trying to coax her to rise, lifting up her trunk, stroking her about the head, pushing her gently, and whenever any of the tame elephants were brought up to the spot the little thing charged them with the greatest fury. It was curious to see the quiet way in which its charges were received by the tame ones, who, with their trunks, gently put the youngster aside, taking no more notice of her than a mastiff or a bloodhound would of a lap-dog's puppy.

While the above scrimmage was going on in the

water, one of the captives, a female, was being led off by two large tame male elephants. The sight of the others fighting in the water appeared to excite greatly one of the tame ones. He became unmanageable, and charged with the greatest fury on his tame colleague, who did not seem to understand what he was after. Despite the efforts of the mahauts, they began hustling and pushing. Meantime the captured one, who was secured by a rope to each of these tame ones, taking advantage of the confusion, endeavoured to bolt, and in doing so drew tight the ropes; the unmanageable and larger of the male elephants at the same moment charging on his colleague, embarrassed somewhat by this tightening of the rope, fairly knocked him over, and he fell heavily on his side. One of his mahauts managed to scramble off, the other was thrown some distance over his head; fortunately neither was hurt. The victor then furiously charged the vanquished while lying on the ground, trampling and kneeling on him and trying to gore him with his tusks; the captive elephant meantime pulling away with all her might in her endeavours to escape. Fortunately there were lots of sepoys about, who immediately formed round and kept up a continued fire to try and distract his attention; but all to no purpose. However, the mahaut, who kept his seat on him all the time, rapidly taking off the little clothing he had wrapped round his person, very cleverly managed to throw it over his eyes and so blind him for the time; the others immediately cut the rope connecting him with his colleague and the captive, and he was, by dint of coaxing and beating about the head, led off, still blindfolded, through the stockade to his own ground in camp, where he was secured apart from the others, as he was evidently becoming "must." When he was gone, his colleague, who had been sadly mauled, managed with difficulty to rise, his mahaut getting on him again, still secured by a rope to the captive.

But matters were now changed. After the pommelling he had, he was quite knocked up, and was no longer capable of leading off his captive in triumph. The captive accordingly trotted off towards the jungle, dragging him after her. Two others, however, were despatched after them, who, without much trouble, fairly secured again the fugitive captive and led her off to camp, relieving the other, who came back very slowly, being evidently a good deal hurt. He died a few days afterwards from the effects of the pounding he had received; probably he had some internal fracture or severe injury.

The captives were now all led off to camp, and secured firmly to posts prepared for them. Including the one which had been strangled, they had secured seven elephants, all females; of these, one managed to twist the rope fastening her to the post in such a way during the night that she was strangled, and was found dead in a kneeling position next morning; so that they had only five live wild elephants as the result of the day's sport.

Jang returned to camp in the course of the evening and told us that, after a hard running sort of fight all day with the large "must" elephant, in which an immense number of balls had been sent into his body, they had at last brought him on to his knees, and despatched him by a volley into his head. He was a very fine animal, but too fierce to capture alive. They sent the next morning and cut out his tusks, which were very fine and perfect ones.

During the night we were several times waked by the piteous cries of the captured elephants, but especially by those of the little young one, who still kept guard by her mother's corpse, which was lying not more than one hundred yards from our tents. The cry of an elephant in distress is particularly mournful and expressive. During the night Jang had the young one secured and brought into camp, where she was tied up at a distance from our tents.

The following morning (24th December), after breakfast, another elephant was reported to be in the neighbouring jungle, having escaped or got separated from the herd yesterday. The same system was observed of driving her, by volley-firing and crowds of beaters, out of the wood. Being alone, she was very shy, and there was considerable delay in getting her out of the wood just opposite to where we were seated. Jang went in on foot with the other beaters. Presently she was driven to the edge, and on emerging with a loud bellow, two large tame elephants who were there stationed with ropes to secure her were so frightened that they turned round and fled as fast as they could, and at a tremendous pace the wild one, trunk erect, loudly bellowing, charged after them. It was the only really good charge I saw, and continued for about two hundred yards across and along the open ground, when the wild one gave up the pursuit and turned into some thick jungle. She was, after some hours' beating, driven out of this and captured without any accident. We did not see the capture, as after her escape into the second wood we quitted camp to return towards Sigauli.

Jang lent us elephants, which took us that afternoon to Derdera, where we slept; and on the 25th marched to Hetowara, where we slept, and ate our Christmas dinner. Thence we went, by regular marches, on to Sigauli.

The King and Jung remained two days longer, during which they caught two or three more elephants; their camp then proceeded westwards to Chitaun (at the junction of the Manhauri with the Rapti) in quest of rhinoceroses.

The road back from camp to Hetowara was by the same route as that by which I had come; but the whole camp, &c. having marched over it, the jungle, grass, &c. was so beaten down, that there was no difficulty now in getting along, nor did we run any risk of losing our road in the jungle (which we might easily have done in coming), our track being very clear wherever our elephants had marched.

CHAPTER XVIII.

RHINOCEROS-HUNTING.

THE great beat for rhinoceroses is along the valley of the Rapti river, in the neighbourhood of Chitaun, a largish village or small town situated at or near the confluence of the Rapti and the Manhauri rivers. There are large tracts of level country here, covered with dense high grass jungle; in this the rhinoceros lives, constructing runs or burrows in the grass, along which he moves, the grass meeting over his head, so that he is not seen by one out of the run, although he may be very near.

Jang was very successful this year; they killed several, and wounded a large number of rhinoceroses. Generally the elephants are afraid of them, and were it not that the long grass screens the rhinoceros from the elephant's eye, there are very few would stand the charge. The elephants are stationed in different "runs" along which the rhinoceros is ex-

pected; when he gets very near, if he sees his way
blocked up, he makes a peculiar grunt like a boar
and charges straight ahead. The elephant almost invariably bolts when he hears this grunt; the great
thing is to get a good shot at the brute's head as he
comes slowly along his run, before he utters the grunt
and before he commences his charge.

Bam Bahadur shot one, at Chitaun, just at this
moment, the ball entering through one eye and smash-
ing his brain; so that the brute rolled over dead with
only one ball in him. The skull and skin were sent
up to Nipal, and are now at Thappatalli. Out of the
skin, after being cleaned and cured, they make capital
water-buckets; these are immensely strong, never
break, and are impervious to water. Out of the
horns they manufacture various articles: from the
spreading base they make richly carved cups or
urgas, which are susceptible of high finish and polish;
from the thinner upright part they make handles for
kookeries.

Midway between the eye and the ear is a good and
almost certainly fatal spot to hit if you get a side shot
at his head; but as he is usually coming down towards
the elephant at the time of firing, you generally fire
straight at his front, and then you ought to aim at
the spot just between the eyes. Random shots about
his head and body may ultimately prove fatal from
internal injury or hæmorrhage, but make no obvious
impression at the time.

Of the rhinoceroses shot on this excursion very few

were killed outright; they escaped into the jungle severely wounded and died, some of them almost immediately, others not for two or three weeks. Their bodies were found by men sent to look after them, and their skulls and skins sent up to Nipal.

Though the rhinoceroses abound in greater numbers in the western Terai, especially about Chitaun, the horns of those found in the eastern Terai and those which are imported from Chittagong are much the longer, finer in texture, and better coloured, having little or no white in them, and, from being harder, take a finer polish. The Chittagong rhinoceros has two horns, a long one (two feet or more in length) in front, a short one (a few inches only) immediately behind it. The horn of the male rhinoceros is larger and rougher at the base, but is not generally so long as that of the female. The male uses his horn much more than the female in fighting, rubbing against trees, &c., and generally manages to break or wear the end off so as to shorten it.

CHAPTER XIX.

AN EXECUTION.

Saturday, 26th March, 1853.—A sepoy, a Khatri, having committed a murder under aggravated circumstances, was sentenced to have his head cut off; this day was fixed, about ten days after the crime. Executions always take place either on Tuesdays or Saturdays, as unlucky days. The place always used on these occasions is a small level piece of ground on the right bank of a small stream which falls into the Bishnmatti at the ghat on the road to Sambhunath. The stream making an abrupt bend at this point, there is a small level ground left between its banks and a steep hill, round which it is winding, and over which the road passes. The sides of this hill form an amphitheatre, and afford a capital site for viewing the "tamasha" beneath.

The officiating minister having heard from Kusbur that I was anxious to be present at the execution,

with great courtesy and consideration for my con-
venience rather than the prisoner's feelings, sent to
say that at whatever hour I liked the man's head
should be taken off, and that it should not be done
till.I arrived on the ground !

The afternoon—two hours before sunset—being
fixed, I was at the place of execution punctually at
the appointed time, 4 P.M. Some mistake, however, as
to the hour occurring, I had to wait nearly two hours.
A few, perhaps a dozen, people were waiting also. The
majority of the passers-by, however, of whom there
were many, did not seem to think it worth the trouble
of waiting for. Just about sunset a crowd in the
distance indicated the approach of the prisoner, whom
they were accompanying. The man had left the
prison at 4 P.M. and been conducted on foot, with
his arms pinioned behind by a cord, all through the
principal thoroughfares of the city, a crier proclaim-
ing the nature of his crime and of his punishment.
This had collected about three hundred persons, who
came with him. The crowd took their seats on the
ground around overlooking the place; the officer of
adaulat came with a general's salaam to me and
apologis?d for having kept me (not the prisoner)
waiting so long. The prisoner walked to the appointed spot, surrounded by about twenty men of
Paurya caste (low caste, who always perform the duty
of executioners—a grade above Mihtars). They selected a smooth spot, a few yards from the stream,
for him to kneel upon, the ground being covered

with the bones of previous criminals who had been executed in the same place. The man seemed indifferent to all about him. He had a sulky, scowling look, but said nothing. Except a rag round his loins, all his clothes had been removed. He was directed to kneel, which he accordingly did; his arms were firmly tied behind his back, his hair gathered up into a knot and tied at the top of his head. Two or three of the executioner-men examined his position and moved his head about, according to their respective fancies, evidently looking at it in a professional light, and calculating at what particular angle, or in what spot they would, were it their duty, make their blow, so as best to exhibit their skill. The man seemed to take their manipulations with great nonchalance.

All was now ready, and I expected the poor devil would be at once put out of his misery and suspense. But a rather important omission had occurred; " what is everybody's business is," proverbially, " nobody's," and among the twenty or more executioners present not one had brought with him a kookery or sword with which to take off the man's head! None of the spectators were willing to lend their kookeries. After a little delay, two or three were pressed from the crowd; then followed a discussion as to whether they were sharp enough. One was selected, and the executioner said he could, with a little sharpening, " make it do " (*i.e.* hack off the head in three or four blows); and he forthwith began to sharpen it on a stone, every now and then trying the edge on his finger, and talking and laughing all the time.

All this time the condemned was kneeling, pinioned, close by, hearing, of course, all that passed. Meantime the crowd began to get impatient, not at the brutal indifference to the prisoner's feelings manifested in these preparations, &c. before him, but from fear that it would soon be too dark for them to see the spectacle clearly. The kookery having been sharpened as far as that was possible (being a very bad one), was submitted to the sort of sheriff of the adaulat who was superintending the proceedings. Acting, I fancy, under orders of the general, who had probably told him to take care that, as a European officer would be present as spectator, everything should be done in a correct way, the sheriff condemned the kookery as unfit for service. A further delay occurred, greatly to the disgust of the spectators, who kept calling out to them to make haste, " or it would be dark." At last one of the Gorkha sepoys in attendance upon me volunteered his " talwar," amid loud applause for this disinterested offer. The talwar was handed to the executioner, who, feeling its edge in the most artistic style, pronounced it a first-rate one; and with an air of pride, like a child with a new toy, at using so superior an instrument, he went to the side of the poor wretch, who was still kneeling bound, and had been so for at least a quarter of an hour, which had been wasted in getting the instrument ready.* A cord, two or three yards long, was then fastened to that already binding his arms above the elbows behind his back; this was held firmly by two men, to support the body and prevent the man losing his balance in leaning forward. This being secured, the man still kneeling, his body was brought somewhat forward, supported by this rope from behind; his head was adjusted in a convenient position so as to render the neck straight, the edge of the talwar was lightly laid for a moment on the neck for the executioner to take

---

* I have often seen very much more care, in the preliminaries, taken on occasion of a buffalo's head being cut off by one blow with a *kora*, by a general or Sirdar, as a display before a crowd of their skill and strength, than was shown on this occasion as to removing a man's head.

So careless are the authorities on the matter of arranging that the executioner should always be provided with a good weapon, that it is always left to chance,—the executioners being left to bring their own instruments. Sometimes, in consequence, either from the badness of the blade, or the want of skill in the performer (generally from the former cause), the condemned is hacked fearfully before his head comes off—three, four, or more blows occasionally being struck. When the Pandees were executed, on the restoration to power of Martabar Singh, some of them brought with them their own kookeries (good ones and sharp), to ensure the operation being skilfully performed. On that occasion they (the Pandees) were attended by many attached followers. A curious ceremony was performed with some of them : a follower held the head of the condemned steady between his hands at the moment of decapitation, they having a belief that when an innocent man suffers death unjustly in this way, any friend who holds his head for him at the moment of death ensures for himself eternal salvation in the future world.

his aim, the talwar raised in the air, and descending like lightning, the man's head was instantaneously severed from his body; at the same moment the cord supporting the body was let go from behind, and the headless corpse fell heavily forward, falling upon its own head, in a tremendous jet of blood from the neck. Two or three convulsive twitches there were of the extremities, and also of the eyelids and brows, when the eyes assumed a ghastly upward-turned squint, and all was over.

The surgical part of the operation was certainly beautifully performed; but the delay, want of consideration to the man's feelings, and utter indifference of the spectators, were disgusting. There were about three hundred or four hundred spectators; but, curiously, among them I did not see one single woman.

The moment the head was severed there was a cry of "Wah! wah!" of applause from the spectators at the skill shown by the executioner, who turned round with the air of a hero, evidently proud of the exploit. The sword was cleaned and returned to the sepoy, who refused to part with it, as he said he had inherited it from his father, who had used it much in the late war with the English. It was a very good blade, and very sharp. No one touched or went near the corpse, which, according to custom, was left on the ground as food for jackals, vultures, dogs, &c.*

---

* The body is not allowed to be burned or buried; it is very quickly eaten by the jackals, &c.; the bones alone, many of them

The crowd immediately dispersed, evidently well pleased with the *tamasha*.

Since Jang's return from England executions have become comparatively rare. Capital punishments are now confined to cases of murder and culpable homicide. He has greatly mitigated the severity of the criminal code; and has altogether done away with "mutilation" as a punishment. The only case of mutilation of which I have heard since Jang's return occurred in 1852, and was richly deserved. A man went about the country giving out that Jang was intending to sacrifice one hundred and fifty infants as a propitiation to the deities, and that he (the prisoner) was commissioned by Jang to select the victims. Of course this produced a great sensation in the rural districts through which the man went, and mothers hastened to offer him large sums as bribes for him to pass their children and take others. The man was arrested, a grand parade assembled on the Tunakhal, the culprit's offence explained to the troops, and his tongue (the offending organ) cut out before them. He was then, minus his tongue, led away through all the districts where he had previously been, as a warning to show the people not only the falsity of his previous statements, but the consequences of so gross and wicked a lie against the powers that be.

---

gnawed and broken, remaining strewed about. The ground is almost white from them, and the place a regular Golgotha.

" Capital " punishment is never carried into effect against a Brahman. He has his head shaved, is made to eat pork, offal, drink wine, and, his caste having thus been taken from him, he is taken to the frontiers and expelled the country. Women also are never executed ; they are imprisoned, branded, caste taken, sold as slaves, or expelled the country, or benosed, but never executed. The cutting off the nose is not, however, generally done by Government ; but is a private punishment, usually summarily performed by the injured husband on detecting a wife's infidelity ; he takes off her nose with a kookery, and then turns her out of his house.

Kah Sing, havildar of the Residency guard, showed me one day the kookery with which he had cut down a man who had seduced his wife. He was at the time using it to cut and pare some radishes, which he was eating with great gusto. I asked him, " And what did you do to the woman ? " " Oh," says he, " I cut off her nose and turned her out of doors ; I gave her five rupees to prevent her from starving." He had kept possession, as in such cases the fathers always do, of the children. The woman loses caste, children, rank, home, nose, and all.

CHAPTER XX.

PROFESSIONAL VISITS TO JANG BAHADUR.

November, 1852.—Jang asked me to see professionally a " lady of rank " who was staying at his house. He at first made some mystery as to who she was, but afterwards told me that she was own sister to the present Maharajah. She was eighteen years old, and married to the Rajah of Jumlah. She had been confined eight months before, at her husband's home, and had never since been well. She had gradually been emaciating, had a terrible cough, with constant expectoration, besides some internal disease. Her husband had brought her to Kathmandu as a *dernier ressort* for advice.

Jang told me that all the Nipal doctors had given up her case as hopeless; but he wished me to see her. If, on seeing her, I was of opinion that I could cure her, I might undertake the treatment of the case; and if I succeeded, I should receive fifteen thousand rupees (one thousand five hundred pounds) as a fee. But that if I thought I could not cure her, he advised me to have nothing to do with the case; as, in the event of her death after my attending her, I should get the credit of having killed her.

He led me through several small rooms in the private apartments at Thappatalli to a small apartment, or rather passage with one window, in which the lady was. Her bed or mattrass was on the floor, and she herself, and the bed also, covered with a number of rich and handsome shawls. She made no objection to my seeing or speaking to her. She sat up in bed, and answered the few questions I put to her willingly, showed me her tongue, and held out her arm for me to feel her pulse. She bared her arm to the shoulder, and her feet to the ankles, to show me how emaciated she had become. Poor girl, her case was evidently hopeless, as she was in the later stages of consumption, besides other local affections. She was striking in her appearance, and singularly like her brother the King. Her skin looked very sallow and rather dark, but Jang says, when she was in good health, that she was remarkably fair for a native. I made a salaam to her, and retired; and explained to Jang that as I thought her case hopeless, I would have nothing to do with it. He said I was quite right,* and then

---

* She died about four months afterwards.

hurried me into his garden to see a wild boar fight with some Nipal hunting-dogs.

A wild boar, which had been caught in the jungles several months before, and since kept in a paddock and fattened up till he was quite unwieldy, was turned into the gardens. About a dozen Nipal dogs (Buansi) trained for hog-hunting, were turned out, and soon took up the scent, giving tongue loudly. They followed on his track for about one hundred yards, when sighting piggy, they all collected, barking and snarling, around him, piggy standing at bay, and none of them daring to attack him. Jang, his brothers, myself, with a number of others, running up, piggy turned tail. This was a signal for an immediate attack from the dogs, who, however, all flew at him from behind, seizing him by the hind leg, quarter, or tail, anywhere in fact out of reach of his tushes; very different from English dogs, who would have gone straight at his head and neck. The moment piggy felt their teeth, he faced about; off went the dogs in all directions; off went piggy again; again the dogs were at him from behind. This went on, a sort of running fight, for some time, piggy frequently facing about and setting his pursuers at bay, but only once getting hold of one of them, whom he shook most viciously, till the pig was so worried and winded that he lay down in a bush and could make no further resistance. The dogs were then pulled off, and a bullet sent through piggy's heart. Next day a large piece of his loin, covered with a layer of fat nearly two inches thick, was sent to me. I had it dressed, and its flavour was most delicious, the flesh white in colour, and tender.

The hills round the valley abound in these wild pigs. They are caught, when young, in numbers, brought into Kathmandu, and then fattened on the cleanest food. Their flesh is very delicious, and the Nipalese, of all ranks and castes, are exceedingly fond of it. Of course they would never eat pork from a common village pig. In fact, they will not eat the flesh of any pigs born in captivity, even though sire and dam are genuine wild ones.

November, 1851.—I was summoned in haste by Jang Bahadur to go to his brother Bam Bahadur's house, in order to attend Bam's youngest wife, who had that morning been confined of a live child, but the mother was considered in a dangerous state.

On arriving at the house I found Jung, Bam, and two of the other brothers. They explained to me the nature of the case, and asked me to explain to them what I should do if admitted to see her. The Raj Guru who then came in stated that there was not the slightest objection, as a •matter of caste, to my seeing her if she herself had no scruples. Jang then went up to see the ladies, and arrange for my going up too. His mother and several of the female members of his family were there. He explained to them my opinion that medical interference was necessary, and that if she did not receive some assistance she would certainly die. The patient, however, said she felt sure that she should die if nothing were done; but she did not fear death, and would much sooner die than allow me to see and treat her,* as, should she do so, all other women would point at and taunt her with having allowed me, a European man, to see or have anything to do with her. She was supported strongly in these views by her mother-in-law and the other ladies. All Jang's persuasions failed, and on his pressing the matter he got well abused by the ladies for his pains.

He returned and told us the result of his visit, adding, " What can you expect from such a set of fools ? when you attempt to reason with them, they answer you with abuse."

Nipalese ladies do not seem to differ widely from their sisters in other parts of the world, and Jang seems to have met with the usual fate of sensible men who endeavour to oppose by argument or reason the prejudices of women.

Bam and the Raj Guru then went up to see if they could do anything, but they were no more successful than Jang had been. Bam apologised for the unnecessary trouble he had given me, and presented me with a fee of one hundred rupees.†

---

* She died eight days afterwards.

† This was an unusual piece of courtesy and liberality. As a general rule, they never give a fee, either to me, or to their own native doctors, unless the case treated turns out successfully. Thus, I may vaccinate a child twenty times, but I get no fee unless

In cases of this sort, of course, Jang cannot force or oblige his wives or females to submit. Any violence done to their prejudices would create a storm of odium, &c. against him and me too. His attempts, however, have been successful, in several cases, in preventing satti. This very day, when I was at Bam's, Jang's own sister's husband (son of Kaji Delhi Sing) had died of a lingering illness. The widow was very anxious to perform satti. Jang sent the guru to her to dissuade her. After considerable discussion she yielded, and consented that her husband's corpse should be burnt alone.

Since that time Jang has uniformly set himself against satti; he cannot prohibit it, but he does everything to discourage it. In October 1852, when the "Barra Captain Sahib" (Jang's most intimate and attached friend), who had been with him from infancy, and accompanied him to England) died of dropsy, Jang, by his efforts and persuasions, succeeded in preventing either of his widows from performing satti. He says, and probably truly, that when the common people get accustomed to see that men of rank die and their bodies are burnt without satti, they will, of their own accord, gradually give up such an inhuman and unreasonable practice. There is already a considerable diminution in the number

---

it "takes." They will not pay for mere "medical attendance" unless that attendance is followed by decided *advantage* to themselves.

of sattis; they do occasionally take place, but very rarely.

Jang has great faith in European surgical skill, and is, indeed, very fond of surgery, at which he often does a little himself. I remember his excising a small fatty tumour from a man's neck very successfully; and in any cases of slight injuries among his followers he generally doctors them himself. He has a sort of laboratory in his garden where he prepares constantly a large quantity of a particular sort of medicine, in which he has great faith.* Its composition is a profound secret; he says it contains the precious metals, even diamonds and pearls. He considers it very valuable, and, I suspect, drives a profitable trade by selling it in small quantities to his brethren and family and others when sick. As a compliment to him, and to please him, they will willingly take it, and pay well for it too, whatever faith they may have in its real efficacy.

I have seen it applied in some cases, where certainly it did no harm, though I do not think it did much good. I remember a couple of sepoys getting a good deal mauled about the face, neck, and arms by a bear whom Jang was in pursuit of, and they came to the rescue. The wounds were not serious, though very

---

* In medical cases, Jang says his own country doctors understand their treatment better than Europeans do. When he himself is indisposed he never consults me medically, but does invariably in everything surgical.

painful, skin-deep. Jang said, as they were slight, he could cure them with his own medicine.

I have often found it exceedingly convenient to be able to borrow some of his instruments when our hospital was deficient in them.

Jang has great faith in vaccination, and has had all his children, most of his brothers', and those of the royal family vaccinated. I received five hundred rupees for vaccinating his eldest boy in 1850, when he was in England.

In 1851, shortly after the detection of the conspiracy against him and the removal to Allahabad of the State prisoners, he took me to the house of the " Mihla " Sahib (the King's brother, and one of the prisoners) to vaccinate his little girl, the King's niece. As Jang was suspicious that there might be some treachery against him in this the house of his enemy, he took a brace of Purdey's pistols, loaded, with him, concealed in his dress, and a talwar under a loose robe, which he wrapped round him. When the child was brought in, Jang had our chairs brought to the table, and rather surprised me by drawing out his pistols, putting them on full cock and laying one down on the table before me, another before himself. He did not say a word, but gave me a look which I understood fully. It was the first time I ever vaccinated a patient, and a princess too, under protection of a cocked pistol. When it was over, putting the pistols in his belt, and wrapping his robe round him, he retired for a few minutes into the private apartments of the child's mother, just to pay his respects. Fortunately, nothing untoward occurred to him; and we left the house without having any "scene." I received two hundred rupees as a fee. Jang occasionally amused himself by vaccinating patients, but rarely succeeded with them.

In August 1854 Jang asked me to prescribe for one of his wives, daughter of the ex-Raja of Coorg, who was very ill. I declined doing so, unless I saw the patient. He then allowed me to see her. Her apartments are low, narrow, passage rooms, and she was lying on a mattrass-bed on the floor, with a slave-girl using a hand-punkah over her. Her hair was unconfined, and loose over her shoulders.

On the second visit I opened a large abscess on her right side, much to Jang's delight and the astonishment of his own two native doctors, who were present. On her being a little faint, I told them to give her a little water; while she drank it, I had to stand up in the sill of an open window, looking into the Court, so that my feet might not touch the drugget, or any part of the furniture directly or indirectly connected with her bed, although two minutes before there was no objection to my feeling her pulse, &c. &c., examining and lancing her side—a regular case of swallowing the camel and straining at the gnat.

This, however, is a common practice even among themselves; when a lady is sitting on a couch or a sofa, any male relations who may be admitted to see her and talk to her, must keep at such a distance that they do not touch the carpet on which her seat is placed; of course they may not sit on the same couch. The elder brother, as a general rule, is not allowed to see the faces of his younger brothers' wives; but the younger brothers may see the faces of the wives of all those brothers who are older than themselves. Before an elder brother, the wife of his junior, if in the room, keeps her face veiled as a mark of respect. This rule is pretty strictly observed among people of rank and position.

CHAPTER XXI.

EARLY HISTORY OF NIPAL.

THE kingdom of Nipal, until towards the close of the eighteenth century, was of very limited extent. It consisted of three small principalities, whose united jurisdiction extended over the Valley of Nipal Proper, as well as over the adjacent lands, as far eastward as the Dudh Khosi River (beyond which was the independent country of the Kirantis) and westward to the Trisalganga river which formed the boundary between the territories of Nipal and those of the Gorkhas. The Gosain Than mountain shut them in towards the north,* while the Medina Mall forest (south of

---

* The northern boundary, in the time of the Niwar dynasty, extended up to the passes. of Kerang and Kuti. On the Chinese invasion in 1792, the Chinese took from the Gorkhas a considerable tract of land to the south side of those passes, and these districts, inhabited by Tibetans, have continued subject to China up to the present day. The Nipalese boundary, therefore, at present does not extend to the snow, but stops short of it (a little on the north side of Mount Dhaibung).

Chitlung) formed their southern boundary and separated them from the hill country of the Rajah of Makwanpur. This secluded region was inhabited by a race of Hindus called Niwars. They were a quiet, industrious, and unwarlike people; but, when circumstances required, they proved themselves, on various occasions, not to be wanting in courage or determination.

The dynasty which ruled over this country was one of great antiquity, having occupied the throne of Nipal, without interruption, since the commencement of the fourteenth century.

The traditions of the Niwars represent that the first dynasty established in the country was that of Naimani, which lasted for four hundred and ninety-one years, at the end of which time Bhal Singh, a Rajput, of the posterity of Mehip Gopal, at the head of an army, invaded and subdued Nipal. He and his sons reigned for one hundred and eleven years. The Mehip Gopal dynasty was put an end to by Yellang Kirant, who conquered the country at the head of an army of Kirantis.

The Kirant dynasty continued, under twenty-seven kings, for about eight hundred years, when they were in their turn dispossessed of the kingdom of Nipal by Nevesit, a Chattri of the Suraj Bansi race, and whose family name was Barmah. In the reign of the thirty-third king of this race, one of the descendants of the original Naimani or Gapti family conquered Nipal, and established a dynasty which lasted for one hundred and seventy-five years, when the country was again invaded and subdued by one of the Chattri of the posterity of Nevesit, who expelled the Gaptis, and re-established the Chattri dynasty of the Barmahs, which lasted, under forty-five kings, for upwards of two thousand years.

The last but three of these kings left three sons, who reigned successively after their father, but they all died without leaving any male issue. One of them, however, left a daughter named Satti Naik Devi, who was crowned Queen of Nipal. She married Haris Chandar Deo, Rajah of Benares, by whom she had an only child, a daughter, named Raj Lachmi, who succeeded to the throne on the death of her mother. She was deposed by a kinsman, named Jai Dab, who had only reigned a few days when Harh Singh Deo, or Hari Singha Deva, Rajah of Simraun Garh, capital of Mathila, or North Bahar, or Tirhut, and of the posterity of the Suraj-Bansi princes of Oudh, having been driven from his kingdom by the Mussulmans of Delhi, and his capital destroyed, took refuge in Nipal, conquered it, and put an end to the dynasty of the Barmahs. This occurred AD. 1322.

Harh Sing Deo had no difficulty in conquering Nipal, and the crown continued in his family until the extinction of the Niwar dynasty of Simraun Chattris through the final conquest of Nipal by Prithi Narayan in 1769

Harh Singh Deo's ancestors are believed to have acquired, some generations back, and to have maintained a footing in Nipal, by the possession of some territory. This would account for the facility with which, when he and his followers had been compelled to abandon the Terai and his capital, Simraun, he speedily reduced the whole of Nipal to subjection to his authority.

The seventh successor of Harh Singh Deo, was Jai Ekshah Mal, who died about A.D. 1568. He much enlarged the city of Bhatgaon, in which was his principal seat of residence.* At his death he left three sons and one daughter, among whom he distributed his dominions as follows:—

To Rai Mal, the eldest, he gave the principality of Bhatgaon†; which at this period was bounded on the

---

* Jai Ekshah Mal completely subdued the rival Rajahs of Patan and Kathmandu, and annexed their territories to his own.

From this date the three principalities, though they remained distinct, and were ruled over by separate kings, yet continued all to be governed by princes of the same family, the Simraun Chattris. None of the Niwar kings, therefore, could from this date have been Buddhists, though they undoubtedly were very tolerant to their Buddhist subjects, and very liberal in their support of Buddhist temples and institutions.

† The territories of the King of Bhatgaon extended chiefly towards the east, where the Dudh-Kosi separated his kingdom from the country of the Kirantis. Within the valley his possessions were the smallest; but beyond the valley they were the most extensive of any of the three kings.

The successors of Rai Mal on the throne of Bhatgaon were: Bhu Bhin Mal; Besson Mal, who took Banepa from the house of Ran Mal; Triloke Mal, from whom the house of Rattan or Ratni Mal of Kathmandu took Banepa, Changhu Narayan, Sanku, and Kuti; Jaggat Johi Mal; Jai Jeta Metro Mal; Bhopat Indra Mal; Ranjit Mal.

west by the Baghmatti, on the east by the Kosi river, on the north by Kuti, and on the south by the forest of Medina Mal.

To Ran Mal, the second son, he gave the territory and valley of Banepa, lying to the east of the Valley of Nipal, and bounded on the north by Sangahchuk, on the south by the forest of Medina Mal, on the west by Sangah, and on the east by the Dudh Kosi.

To Ratni, or Rattan Mal, the third son, he left the principality of Kathmandu ; bounded on the east by the Baghmatti, on the west by the Trisulgunga, on the north by the mountain of Gosain Than and by the Kerang Pass, and on the south by the northern boundary of Patan.

To his daughter he gave the principality of Patan* (the refractory Rajah of which city had been subdued by Jai Ekshah Mal). Its limits were to the south the forest of Medina Mal, to the west the mountains of Lamadanda, to the north the southern line of Kathmandu, and to the east the Baghmatti.

During the two hundred years which elapsed from this division of the kingdom into three principalities, till its conquest and reunion by Prithi Narayan in 1769, although the power of the respective branches

---

* The territories of Patan were the most extensive within the valley, as they also included Kirtipur and Thankot, besides Chitlong, Pherfig, and Sisapani. Kirtipur at one time was the seat of an independent prince, but it was afterwards included within the possessions of the King of Patan.

was constantly fluctuating, yet ascendency for the most part appears to have been maintained by the elder one, that of Bhatgaon.

Ranjit Mal (who reigned forty years) succeeded his father Bhopat Indra Mal as King of Bhatgaon, and was the last of the Niwar .kings who reigned over Nipal.

But little authentic or important is known of the events which occurred during the respective reigns of these Niwar kings. The principal facts recorded concerning any of them chiefly refer to the building of temples, darbars, powas, &c. Jait Mal, father of Jai Ekshah Mal, established weights and measures, and considerably enlarged the city of Bhatgaon. Bhopat Indra Mal also added largely to Bhatgaon and to Thimi.

The want of information is not confined to our knowledge of the kingdom of Nipal alone, but applies still more strongly to all the other numerous states which at that time extended through the whole length of the Himalayas, from Bhotan to the Satlaj.

In the middle of the eighteenth century, when the British under Lord Clive were with difficulty establishing a firm footing in Bengal, that portion of the Himalayas which is now consolidated into the compact kingdom of Nipal was broken up into a number of petty principalities and small independent states, which, though constantly warring among themselves, had little or no connection with the plains of Hindustan. The vast tract of forest, and of marshy malarious land which skirts, almost uninterruptedly, the southern face of the Himalayas, from Assam in the far east almost to the Satlaj in the north-west, formed an insuperable bar to any regular intercourse between the nations of the plains and those of the hills.

Thus isolated from connection with Hindustan, the hill Rajahs and their subjects became, as it were, " a peculiar people." Absorbed in their own internal affairs—at one time warring with neighbouring chiefs, at another occupied in pastoral pursuits, or in hunting expeditions within their own territories—they knew little and cared less about the political changes and revolutions which were occurring in Bengal. Inhabiting a cool and bracing climate, they were physically far superior to the languid and enervated Bengalees. The virgin purity of their native soil had never been sullied by the foot of the foreign invader ; they were the only Hindu states which had not been degraded by Mohammadan conquest. Morally, therefore, as well as physically, they looked, and they still look, upon themselves as superior to any of the Hindus in the plains. These feelings induced a proud independence and energy of character, almost unknown in other parts of India. These mountaineers, one and all, were Hindus on principle and by descent ; but they refused to be hampered by all the bigotry and prejudices of-Brahmanical law. While they retained the substance, they rejected much of the shadow of Hinduism, and openly disregarded many observances which were and are considered as essential by the more orthodox professors of that religion in the plains. Such conduct naturally gave great offence. The Hindu of the Himalayas began to be looked on by the Hindu of the plains very much in the same light that the Protestant is looked upon by the Roman Catholic. As the orthodox Roman Catholic calls the Protestant a "heretic," so the orthodox Brahman of Benares calls his brother Hindu of Nipal a "Pariah." These various differences in religion, in customs, in occupations, and in language engendered great bitterness of feeling between the races of the plains, and the races of the hills. The bigoted Hindus of Bengal held very little intercourse with the proud independent mountaineers whom they regarded as "aliens in religion, aliens in language, and aliens in blood." The hill tribes throughout the Himalayas—the natives of Sikkim, of Kiranti, of Nipal, of Gorkha, of Palpa, of Doti, of Kamaon, of Garhwal, and of Sarmur—saw their Hindu countrymen of the plains one after another subdued by a handful of British soldiery; but, undisturbed in the seclusion of their own mountain fastnesses, they were indifferent spectators to the struggles which were going on, and never directly or indirectly interfered or offered to assist in stemming the tide of European conquest. This neutrality on their part with respect to the general politics of India was the result, not of any system of policy, but of their feeling that they were so shut out by natural and, as they considered, impenetrable, barriers from the rest of the world, that they felt no interest in the momentous struggle which was revolutionizing Hindustan.

The people of the plains regarded the hill tribes in the same manner. They felt no interest in their movements. They looked on the sturdy mountaineers as formidable in their own hills, but as not dangerous elsewhere. The vast forests and the malarious tarai beyond which they lived would, they knew, prevent the hillmen from making incursions, beyond mere border forays, into the plains. They knew that the vast mountain regions extending from the Brahmaputra to the Satlaj were as inhospitable as they were extensive; that the towns were but few, the population poor, but yet such as were to be dreaded when fighting in defence of their hearths and homes; in fact, they were fully aware that there was nothing in the whole tract to tempt their cupidity, to gratify their love of plunder, or to repay them for the dangers and hardships of mountain warfare.

The natives of the plains, therefore, although they could not altogether ignore the existence of the hill tribes, yet looked on them politically as *hors de combat.* The indifference which the hillmen displayed towards the politics of Hindustan was, therefore, abundantly returned by the natives of the plains, who felt utterly unconcerned in the fierce contests which were constantly occurring, especially towards the middle and close of the eighteenth century, between rival hill Rajahs of whose names even they were ignorant, or between petty principalities of whose existence they were hardly aware.

It is in a great measure owing to this feeling of indifference that we now know so little of the separate and individual states of which this vast mountain republic, extending over territory upwards of eight hundred miles in length, was composed. The names even of many of them are forgotten; the origin of the state of Gorkha, the most warlike and powerful among them, is little better than conjectural; and of the Niwar kingdom of Nipal itself—the most important, the most populous, and the most highly civilized of them all, and the only one which had any regular intercourse with the plains—we cannot say we know with certainty anything of its annals, or of its people, until towards the close of the eighteenth century, when, the British power being firmly established in Bengal, the last prince of the Niwar dynasty, in his last efforts against Gorkha aggressions, appealed to our arms for aid in expelling the Gorkha invader from the Valley of Nipal.

The circumstances which led to this appeal are curious and interesting. It is from this date (1767) that our political relations with Nipal commence.* For

---

* The first political transaction between the British and the Nipalese after the Gorkha conquest was the following one :—The hill country of the Rajah of Makwanpur having come into the possession of the Nipalese by right of conquest in 1772, they claimed also the Makwanpur lowlands in the Terai, for which the Makwanpur Rajah had been accustomed to pay to the British, as

some years previous the British had carried on a rather extensive trade with the Niwars, but no Treaties, or political connections with the country or people, had been formed. The British had always looked on the reigning Rajah of Kathmandu as necessarily ruler of Nipal, although the contemporary Rajahs of Bhatgaon and Patan held territory equal to and sometimes exceeding that of the former prince. The slight intercourse which had existed between the British and the Niwars had been purely of a commercial character, and no occasion had offered, nor indeed had been desired, for contracting political obligations between the two Governments. The invasion of the Valley of Nipal by Prithi Narayan at the head of a Gorkha army, led to our taking a more decided interest in the affairs of that country.

From the published account of Father Guiseppe, who was in the valley at the period of the invasion and was an eye-witness of many of the scenes which he describes, it appears that the Sardars of Patan had placed on the throne Gainprejas, a man of courage as well as great influence through the country. He was

---

tribute, one elephant annually. The Nipalese agreed to do the same, and actually paid us an elephant annually as tribute until 1801, when we relinquished it in the Treaty of Commerce and Alliance. Thus, within three years of the conquest of Nipal, Gorkha shrewdness and desire for gain induced them to pocket their pride, and enabled them to acquire a large tract of cultivated land on the easy condition of paying one elephant a year into the Company's commissariat.

afterwards deposed, and, after some years of conten-
tion, they made an offer of the throne to Prithi Narayan,
King of Gorkha. Prithi Narayan deputed his youngest
brother, Dalmadan Sah, to govern the kingdom of
Patan for him. Dalmadan Sah,* once established on
the throne, refused to acknowledge the authority of
his brother, and he was supported by the people and
Sardars for some time in carrying on war against him.

After a time Dalmadan Sah in his turn was deposed, and Taiz Ner Sing, a poor man, but of the
royal blood, was placed upon the throne by the Sardars
and people of Patan.

Meantime Ranjit Mal, King of Bhatgaon, became engaged in war with the kings both of Patan and Kathmandu; and applied for assistance to Prithi Narayan,
who readily afforded it, hoping by this means to
recover the throne of Patan, which had already some
years before been voluntarily offered to him by the

---

* This Dalmadan Sah left one son, whose eye-sight was destroyed by Ran Bahadur (Swami as he was called after his abdication) in order to disqualify him from the throne, and prevent
him from ever gaining it. On Ran Bahadur's death without a
legitimate heir (and both his children were illegitimate) the
crown would have reverted to this lad, by name Kula Chandra
Sah, as the legitimate heir to the throne, being own nephew to
Prithi Narayan. Ran Bahadur destroyed his eye-sight when a
child by pouring the milky juice of the cactus into his eyes.

February, 1854.—Kula Chandra Sah is now alive, very old, and
stone blind. I met him at Thappatalli, where he had gone to pay
his respects to Jang Bahadur. He has been, in his day, a mischievous intriguer against the Thappas, he himself having always
been a warm ally of the Pandis.

nobles of that principality, and from which his own
brother Dalmadan Sah had been deposed and driven
into exile. Ranjit Mal, however, soon discovered
that his new ally, taking advantage of the dissensions
which existed among the kings and nobles of the
different principalities, was intriguing to possess himself, supported as he was by an army of Gorkhas, of the
whole country of Nipal. The King of Bhatgaon, therefore, came to friendly terms with the sovereigns of
Patan and Kathmandu, and the three princes united
their arms to defend their own possessions and to endeavour to expel Prithi Narayan and his army from the
country. Prithi Narayan succeeded in securing in his
interest many of the mountain chiefs, especially those
connected with or feudatory to the principality of
Patan, by promises to keep them in possession of their
jagiers and largely to augment their authority and importance. By their assistance chiefly he gained possession of all the mountains which surround the Valley
of Nipal, and built numerous small forts upon their
summits, in which his troops were stationed, and from
which they were able to command all the approaches to
the valley. Then collecting his forces, he entered the
valley and laid siege to the city of Kirtipur, anticipating little or no opposition. Kirtipur is situated in
the south-west quarter of the valley, and stands alone
upon and around the level crest of a hill, about two
or three hundred feet above the surrounding plain.
It was strengthened on all sides by a wall which encircled the whole town, having in it a few gates which

were strongly fortified * ; while within were several buildings which acted as fortresses, especially in the upper part of the town, around and supporting the durbar, which was situated at the highest point of the hill. Considering the rude materials with which war was then carried on, Kirtipur may be said to have been a very strong, if not an impregnable, post of defence. At this time Kirtipur was subject to the King of Patan, and to him the inhabitants naturally looked for support; but none being afforded to them, they applied for assistance to Gainprejas, the deposed king of Patan. He promptly marched with an army to their relief, fought a pitched battle with the forces of the King of Gorkha, and gained a complete victory. A brother of the King of Gorkha was killed on the field of battle, and Prithi Narayan himself narrowly escaped with his life by fleeing to the mountains.

The people of Kirtipur then elected Gainprejas as their king. Having failed in this attack, Prithi Narayan attempted to starve the country into submission by causing a famine. With this object he posted troops at all the passes of the mountains, to prevent any provisions being supplied to the inhabitants of the

---

* The ruins of these forts still exist on several hills. On " Deochoak " there are four, the branches of which are very distinct. On the low range of hill connecting Nagarjun with Kukanni there are three or four others. On the east side of the valley, on the hill of Changu Narayan, there are rather extensive remains of fortified forts, which were probably occupied by the Gorkhas during their operations against Bhatgaon.

valley. Every man, woman, or child detected or suspected of violating the orders he issued on this subject, was hanged immediately, and Father Guiseppe saw the bodies of many such offenders hanging on the trees by the road-side.

Not gaining his object by these means, he had recourse to the assistance of that ever-intriguing class, the Brahmans, and by their means fomented dissensions among the leading nobles of Nipal, and attached many of them to his party by holding forth liberal and enticing promises. When he thought he had a party sufficiently strong he again advanced with his army to Kirtipur, and laid siege to it on the north-west quarter, that he might avoid exposing his army between the two cities of Patan and Kathmandu. After the siege had lasted several months, Prithi Narayan sent a message demanding the regency of the town. An insulting and exasperating answer was returned to him, fastened to an arrow. Enraged at their still holding out, he ordered an immediate attempt to storm the town on every side; but the bravery of the inhabitants defeated all the efforts of the Gorkhas, who, after losing a large number of their men, retreated, and, raising the siege a second time, withdrew their army to the hills. A brother of the King of Gorkha, named Suru Partab, was wounded by an arrow during the attempt to storm the town, but was afterwards cured of his wound by a member of Father Guiseppe's mission.

After some months, Prithi Narayan, collecting all his

forces, sent them for the third time to besiege Kirtipur. The inhabitants defended themselves with their usual bravery for six or seven months; at the end of which time the three kings of Nipal assembled with their forces at Kathmandu, and determined to march a body of troops to the relief of Kirtipur. At this critical time a noble of Patan, a personal enemy of Gainprejas, went over to the Gorkhas, and treacherously led their army into the lower part of the town. The gallant inhabitants might, and would, still have defended themselves, having many fortresses and strongholds in the upper part of the town to which they could retreat if necessary. But the wily Gorkha proclaimed a general amnesty, and the inhabitants, greatly exhausted by the length of the siege, surrendered themselves prisoners upon the faith of it. The Gorkhas immediately seized all the gates and fortresses within the town; and two days afterwards, by order of Prithi Narayan, some of the principal inhabitants were put to death, and the noses and lips of every one, even of the infants who were not actually found in the arms of their mothers, were cut off; none escaping except the few who could play on wind instruments, and who might be of use, therefore, as musicians in the army of the conqueror. Gainprejas himself, with a few followers, escaped to Patan. The name of the town was ordered to be changed into Naskatapur, or the City of Cut Noses.

Immediately after these brutal orders had been most fully executed, Prithi Narayan marched his army against Patan, and laid siege to the town on its western side. After several engagements, in which much blood was shed on both sides, the courage of the townsmen began to fail, the Gorkhas having threatened that, unless they surrendered within five days, they should not only have their noses cut off, but also their right hands,—a barbarity which, no doubt, would have been practised without compunction.

Just as the men of Patan were on the point of surrendering, the siege was one night suddenly raised, and the Gorkha army led off towards the plains, in consequence of Prithi Narayan having become aware of the unexpected appearance in the Terai of a body of British troops, under Captain Kinloch, who were marching to the assistance of the King of Nipal.

It appears that in the beginning of 1767, during the third and last siege of Kirtipur, the Niwar Rajah had appealed to the British for aid against the King of Gorkha. Anxious to maintain the advantageous trade, by which gold and many other valuable commodities were imported from Tibet and Nipal into Bengal, the British Government despatched Captain Kinloch, with a small force, to the assistance of the Niwar Rajah. Although we do not know the amount or value of this trade with Nipal and Tibet, it must have been considerable to have warranted a direct interference on our part, to the extent of arms, for its protection.

Captain Kinloch reached the foot of the Nipal hills in the middle of the rains of 1767, after suffering

TEMPLE OF SAKYA SINGHA, AT PATAN.

much from sickness and want of provisions, he was obliged to return from before the fort of Harihar-pur, in the district of Makwanpur, beyond which point he was unable to penetrate. Though the result of this expedition was most unfortunate, as far as the prestige of the British name at the time was concerned, yet it had the good effect of creating a successful diversion, which drew off the Gorkha army from before Patan, and so postponed the fall of that city for nearly a year.

Finding that Kinloch's force had retreated, the Gorkha army returned to Nipal, and ascertaining that Gainprejas, who had applied to the British for aid, had left Patan and was in Kathmandu, they at once proceeded to the latter city and laid siege to it. By means of the intriguing Brahmans, the Gorkhas succeeded in cajoling Gainprejas and his followers by false promises and assertions, and one night in September 1768, during the celebration of the Niwar festival of "Indra Jatra," they introduced secretly a large body of troops into the city. Gainprejas, with three hundred of his best troops, with difficulty escaped to Patan on the same night. Having thus gained possession of Kathmandu, Prithi Narayan again laid siege to Patan. Knowing that he had no chance of reducing the city by fair means, he again had recourse to the agency of the Brahmans. The King of Patan (Tez Ner Sing) and Gainprejas did all in their power to keep up the courage of their troops, and of the townsmen; but finding that their nobles and

I. 18

followers, fearful of Prithi Narayan's vengeance and cajoled by the false promises of the Brahmans, were inclined to surrender, the two gallant princes retired to Bhatgaon; and Patan, without a struggle, was surrendered to the Gorkhas. A general plunder of the city followed, the nobles were all massacred, and every kind of brutality practised on the wretched inhabitants.

Amidst these scenes of cruelty it is gratifying to be able to record that, through the interest of one of the sons of Prithi Narayan, Father Guiseppe and the Catholic mission were allowed to retire with all the Christians into the possessions of the English. They settled at Puri, about six miles from Bettia, and at that village the little colony of Roman Catholic Christians has remained until the present day. At the commencement of 1769 Prithi Narayan acquired possession of the city of Bhatgaon, by means of the same treachery and intrigue which had previously gained for him Kathmandu and Patan. Gainprejas, with a few followers, in a gallant attempt to escape, was wounded in the foot, and died a few days afterwards. Ranjit Mal, being very old and infirm, was treated with kindness and respect and obtained permission to retire to Benares, where he soon afterwards died. Tez Ner Sing, the King of Patan, appears to have rendered himself in some way personally obnoxious to Prithi Narayan; he was certainly confined in irons until his death, if he was not actually put to death by order of the conqueror. The mother of Gainprejas, who was blind from old age, was allowed to retire to Benares;

but before she started she was deprived of all her jewels. Jai Prakash, Rajah of Kathmandu, was imprisoned after the fall of his capital; and he did not long survive the loss of his liberty and of his throne.

The fall of the three capitals, Kathmandu, Patan, and Bhatgaon, was at once followed by the submission to the conqueror of the whole country of Nipal. Prithi Narayan was a cowardly, cunning, and inhuman prince, and on gaining the throne of Nipal he perpetrated the greatest atrocities, and massacred almost every person of distinction connected with the late Niwar dynasty. On the conquest of the valley, he dropped the title, though he retained the crown of Gorkha, and he assumed, and his descendants have ever since borne, the simple title of King of Nipal. The conquest of the valley, from the first siege of Kirtipur in 1765, till the fall of Bhatgaon in the commencement of 1769, occupied four years. We are quite ignorant of the details connected with the several sieges and engagements, nor are we in any single case informed of the numbers of troops engaged, either on the Niwar or the Gorkha side. No one can deny to the Niwars, especially to the men of Kirtipur, the credit of having displayed the most heroic bravery in defence of their capital; while the Gorkhas have earned eternal disgrace by the savage barbarity with which they signalized all their triumphs. It is said that the Gorkha army which accompanied Prithi Narayan to Nipal, was very weak in numbers, that the men were ill-accoutred, ill-armed, and undisciplined,

and that their chief had not the means either · of
recruiting their numbers or rendering them more
efficient. This is assigned as a reason by the Gorkhas for the length of time it took them to reduce the
valley to submission. It may very probably be true
that their army was, in every way, in a most inefficient
state, but this fact does not detract from the gallant
patriotic spirit shown by the Niwars, under the high-
spirited and heroic Gainprejas, but only makes it still
more evident that, had it not been for the unfortunate
failure of Kinloch's expedition, the timely assistance
of the British would have maintained the Niwar
dynasty on the throne of Nipal.

CHAPTER XXII.

THE GORKHAS IN NIPAL.

PREVIOUS to their invasion of Nipal, very little is known of the Gorkhas as a nation, or of the dynasty which ruled over them. Their royal family claims to be lineally descended from the Rajput princes of Udaipur. It is stated that on the Mohammadan invasion of Rajputana in the twelfth century, when several branches of the reigning family of that country, preferring exile to slavery, dispersed themselves over Hindustan, one branch, from which the present dynasty of Nipal is descended, migrated towards the Himalayas, and settled themselves and their followers in the lower range of hills, constituting the country of Palpa. From Palpa they advanced into the adjacent hills, and ultimately gained possession of the kingdom of Gorkha, over the whole of which country they firmly established their authority, and from its capital city they derived their national name of Gorkhali. Not

contented with the original limits of the hill state of
Gorkha, they gradually encroached upon the lands of
the neighbouring Rajahs, until, in the course of some
generations, they had rendered subject to their sway
the greater part of the country watered by the seven
mountain streams which unite, near the plains, to form
the river Gandak. This region is known, in their
own language as the "Sapt Gandaki," or country of
the seven Gandaks. The most eastern of these seven
rivers is the Trisulganga, and it formed the boundary
between the kingdoms of Gorkha and Nipal. For
some six generations the Gorkhas appear to have
occupied themselves chiefly in consolidating their
power and arranging the internal government of their
newly acquired territories. When, however, Prithi Narayan, son and successor of Ner Bhopal Sah, ascended
the throne, the national feeling was again directed
towards foreign conquest. This ambitious prince
invaded, subdued, and annexed to the Gorkha crown
the whole of the dominions of the three kings of
Nipal. The two countries of Gorkha and Nipal
were united into one kingdom, under one name,
and ruled over by one prince; and from that date
(1769) to the present time no attempt has ever been
made by the Niwars, or any other party, to dispute
the authority, or to disturb the uninterrupted succession, of the Gorkhali dynasty to the throne of Nipal.

Having established his power in Nipal, Prithi
Narayan crossed the Dudh Kosi river, the eastern
boundary of his new dominions, over-ran with his

army the countries of the Kirantis and of the Limbus, annexed them to his own, and extended the frontier of Nipal to the Michi river, which separated it from Sikkim.

Prithi Narayan did not long enjoy his newly acquired honours. This active and energetic prince died in 1771, leaving two sons, the elder of whom, Singh Partab, ascended the throne on his father's death. Soon becoming jealous of his younger brother, Bahadur Sah, he imprisoned him, and it was not without considerable difficulty that Gusraj Misr (the Royal Guru) obtained his release on condition of his going into exile. Singh Partab added to the conquests of his father some districts lying to the south-west of Nipal (Tannahung, Someshwar, Upadrong, and others). He died in 1775, leaving one legitimate son Ran Bahadur Sah, who succeeded to the throne, being at the time an infant in arms. He left also an illegitimate son, by a Niwar woman, named Sher Bahadur. On Singh Partab's death, his brother Sah Bahadur returned at once to Kathmandu from his exile at Bettiah, placed his infant nephew on the throne, and himself assumed the government of the country as Regent. Constant quarrels, however, took place between him and the child's mother. He was after a time imprisoned, and then driven into exile for the second time. The infant king's mother, Rani Rajendra Lakshmi, a woman of remarkable energy and talent, then assumed the reins of government. During her regency she introduced many improvements into the army, and subdued and annexed several petty states, among them Palpa and Kashki, all lying to the westward of Gorkha.

On her death Bahadur Sah returned to Nipal, re-assumed the Regency, and exercised unlimited power. While Regent, he either absolutely annexed, or rendered tributary to Nipal, all the estates lying between Kashki and Sirinagar, including the territories of the Chaubisia and of the Baisia Rajahs, or the dominions of forty-six petty princes, all of whom were Rajputs and were previously tributary to the Rajah of Jumla. The Chaubisia principalities lay immediately to the west of Gorkha; and the Baisia states are still further west, lying between Chaubisia and Doti. The allegiance of all these different chiefs was secured either by hostages retained at Kathmandu, or by marriages contracted between them and the reigning family of Nipal. Ran Bahadur, the young king, still a minor, was married to a daughter of the Gulmi Rajah.

On the conquest of the Valley of Nipal, the British Government had acknowledged the King of Gorkha as Sovereign of Nipal, and, as such, had restored to him the lands which had been seized by Captain Kinloch in the Terai of Bettiah in 1767. With the exception of this recognition there is no trace of any connection between the British and Nipal Governments from the period of the Gorkha conquest until the administration of Lord Cornwallis, when a treaty of commerce was made by Mr. Duncan, then Resident at Benares, between Nipal and the Company, dated March 1792.

This treaty was a purely commercial one, and regulated the duties on imports and exports between the territories of the Company and those of Nipal.* The articles of this treaty were not fairly carried out by the Nipal Government, and the treaty became a dead letter. At the time when this treaty was negotiated, Nipal was threatened with invasion by the forces of the Emperor of China. The hope of securing our

---

* The principle of this treaty was that a duty of two and a half per cent. *ad valorem* should be reciprocally levied by either Government on all articles of trade transported from the dominions of one State into or through the dominions of the other.

In November 1834, various discussions having taken place between the two Governments concerning their commercial relations, the British Government determined to set the matter of the Treaty of 1792 at rest, and they officially referred it to the Darbar, stating that they attached no importance to the question, and would leave the Darbar to settle the validity or not of the past commercial treaties, the Darbar being at liberty to consult its own ideas as to what was best for its own interests. The Darbar formally and officially deny the existence of the Treaty of 1792, or that it is binding on either party; but express a wish to make a new engagement *de novo*. In March 1835 the Darbar accordingly proposed a draft of a new commercial treaty, having for its object the levy, once for all, at one time and in one place, of an *ad valorem* duty of four per cent. by both Governments, and at the same time formally rescinding past treaties of 1792 and 1801, and substituting the new one for them.

The Governor-General, in reply, wished to encourage Nipalese commerce and exempt it from all duty by establishing entire free trade between the two countries. The Darbar, suspicious of our having ulterior objects in thus foregoing all present advantages of taxation, reject the proposal, abandon their own new treaty, and formally and officially fall back on the *status quo ante.*

neutrality, if not our actual assistance, was the real motive for their apparent willingness to form a treaty with us.

For many years previous to 1792 the Nipalese had encroached on the territories beyond the Himalaya, and into the plains of eastern Thibet. The Llama of Digarchi, spiritual father to the Emperor of China, applied to the Chinese for assistance, but his application was unattended to. The Nipalese, becoming emboldened by the apparent indifference of the Chinese, advanced by the Kuti pass to Digarchi, and plundered the sacred temples of that town. The Emperor of China then despatched an army of seventy thousand men, in order to inflict signal punishment on "the robber," as he styled the King of Nipal. This army advanced steadily, and, easily overcoming any resistance the Gorkhas attempted to make, reached Nayakot, only twenty miles from Kathmandu, in September 1792. The Nipal Darbar, in despair, submitted to make a hasty and degrading treaty, the exact terms of which are not known to us, with the Chinese authorities. On the approach of the Chinese army the Nipalese applied to Lord Cornwallis for assistance by our arms.* This Lord Cornwallis (15th September

---

* The Chinese came by the Kerang pass. The Chinese general, Thung Than, did not descend below the town of Dhaibung or mountain of that name; but part of his army came to the valley of the Trisulganga. There was an obstinate action at Khatria between the Chinese and the Nipalese, a day's march from Dhaibung. The Nipalese were beaten.

1792) declined to afford, on account of the peace then existing between the British and Chinese, and the danger to our trade with Canton which would ensue should that peace be interrupted. He, however, offered, as soon as the Tarai opened, to send a British envoy to mediate a peace between China and Nipal. Meantime the Nipalese had succumbed to the Chinese, and the Imperial army had been withdrawn beyond the Himalayas.

As several subjects of discussion, however, between the British and Nipal Governments, still remained unadjusted, Major Kirkpatrick, the appointed envoy, though the ostensible object of his mission was now over, was allowed to proceed to Kathmandu, where he arrived on the 1st of March 1793, being the first Englishman who had ever visited Nipal.

The chief objects he had orders to carry out were of a commercial nature; he was to try and induce the Nipalese to act up to the Treaty of 1792, for the encouragement of trade and traders, especially the woollen trade with Tibet, through Nipal; and as a means of protecting such trade, as well as improving the friendship between the two nations, he was

---

At Rassoa, midway between Dhaibung and the Kerang pass, is a stream with a bridge over it: and the Nipalese disputed the passage of the bridge with the Chinese for three days.

There was an obstinate action immediately below the Deorali (Gosainthan Mount). The Nipalese were driven back to Dhunchu; thence to Khabora.

to urge on them the establishment of a resident British officer at the Court of Nipal. Unable to effect any of these objects,—the semblance even of coinciding with our views not being kept up by the Darbar, now that the exigency which had induced them to apply to us was passed,—Kirkpatrick returned to Bengal; and so terminated our first mission to the Gorkha Court.

The Government of Nipal remained in the hands of Bahadur Sah as Regent until 1795, when his nephew Ran Bahadur, who during his minority was purposely kept in a state of profligacy and ignorance, suspecting a design on the part of his uncle to keep him in perpetual pupilage, if not actually to usurp the crown, suddenly threw him into prison, and in prison he died a few days afterwards, it is supposed by his nephew's hand. Ran Bahadur ascended the throne, and assumed the management of the State, at the age of twenty, in 1795. He had two wives. His first and senior, the Maharani, was a daughter of the Gulmi Rajah. She was a virtuous and high-minded princess, but unfortunately was childless. She was soon neglected by the King, and her bed deserted. His second wife was the daughter not of a Rajput, but of a Parbattiah Chatri, and she bore him one son only, Ranudat Sah, who was the legitimate heir to the throne.* In addition

---

* His legitimacy is questionable, in consequence of his mother not being a Rajput, and the royal family can marry only Rajputs. In this view, both Ran Bahadur's children—Ranudat Sah, as well as Garwan Jodh Bahram Sah—were illegitimate; and it was in

to these two Ranis, Ran Bahadur had an amour with a girl, the daughter of a Brahman, but to whom he was not, and by the laws of caste could not be, married ; by her he had a son in 1795, necessarily illegitimate, but whom he afterwards adopted as his heir, in exclusion of his legitimate son by his junior wife.

Ran Bahadur remained on the throne, ruling with great tyranny and guilty often of the most violent and atrocious acts, until 1800, when, as he was decidedly insane, he was compelled to abdicate, by his all-powerful and able minister Damudar Pandi, backed by the whole of the priesthood, who were bitterly hostile to the King, in consequence of various outrages which he had perpetrated against their sacred body and religion, on the occasion of his Brahman paramour having poisoned herself, after recovering from an attack of smallpox, when she found that she had lost her beauty, and with it her influence over the King.*   Having adopted his illegitimate son, Garwan

---

consequence of fearing that, after his death, both of them might be set aside in favour of Dalmadan Sah's child (who, as Prithi Narayan's own nephew, was unquestionably the legitimate heir to the throne), that Ran Bahadur destroyed the eye-sight of this young child by pouring the milky juice of the cactus into his eyes.

* On this occasion Ran Bahadur vented his rage on the temples and images of Devi, or Parvati, in several parts of the valley. Some small temples to the goddess in the neighbourhood of Sambhunath, one or two near, but not in, Pashpatinath, and the large temple to Devi, known as Talleju, adjoining the darbar in

Jodh Bikram Sah, Ran Bahadur abdicated in his favour
and retired to Benares. The bastard prince, then aged
between four and five, was placed on the throne, and
all ranks swore allegiance to him. To reconcile the
younger Rani to the supersession of her own son,
Ranudat Sah, who was considered by many to be the
only legitimate heir to the throne, she herself was
appointed Regent, and her child, the young prince,
aged six, was nominated Chauntra, or head adviser
to the Crown. Chauntra Sher Bahadur Sah (illegitimate son of Partab Singh, by a Niwar woman, and
consequently half-brother to Ran Bahadur) was also
appointed guardian and Regent for this juvenile
minister (the Rani and Sher Bahadur being joint-
Regents). Damudar Pandi and Bim Sah Chauntra were
the leading ministers. The Maharani, or senior, but
childless, Rani, accompanied Ran Bahadur to Benares
and remained with him there for some time, but she
was so insulted and maltreated by him that she soon
became anxious to return to Nipal, not only to escape

Kathmandu, were desecrated and defiled by him in every conceiv-
able way. The shrines were covered with human excrement and
all sorts of filth, and worship in these temples forbidden. No
one dared oppose the violence of the King, and the shrines and
temples remained defiled and unworshipped till after his abdication, when they were purified and reopened for general worship.

The story about his battering down the temples at Pashpati
with artillery, &c., as given by Smith, is mere fiction. The temple
at Pashpatinath is devoted to Siva; the King's fury was wreaked
solely upon those in honour of Devi.

from the tyranny of her husband, but that she might establish her lawful right of being Regent for the young Rajah, in place of the younger Rani who had usurped that office. The ex-Rajah in retiring was accompanied by young Bhim Sen, who at that time occupied almost a menial appointment about the royal person, and several chiefs and followers of the Thappa party. The Rajah was very well treated by the British Government, who appointed Captain Knox as his Political Agent, and advanced considerable sums of money at different times to defray the expenses of himself and his attendants.

The presence of the ex-Rajah in our territories made the Nipalese once more willing to enter into terms of alliance with the British Government. They were apprehensive that, without the restraint of a treaty on our part, we might seize the first occasion to employ our power in reinstating Rajah Ran Bahadur on the throne. A " Treaty of Commerce and Alliance " was accordingly formed in 1801, and by the terms of it the Darbar agreed to receive a permanent British Resident at Kathmandu. In this treaty, as in that of 1792, political considerations were made subordinate to those of commerce. The chief points insisted on were—first, the encouragement and protection of the trade through Nipal, between India and Tibet ; secondly, the repayment by the Darbar of the sums of money which the British Government had advanced to Ran Bahadur, when at Benares ; and thirdly, an arrangement for the settlement of boundary disputes, and the surrender of Dacoits, Thugs, and other fugitives whom we were unable to secure in consequence of their having hitherto always found an asylum in the territories of Nipal. In accordance with this treaty Captain Knox was appointed as British Resident at the Court of Nipal. Considerable delay occurred between the time of Knox's leaving Patna and his arrival at Nipal, in consequence of the constant quarrels and jealousies which arose among the deputies who were sent to meet him and escort him to the capital. At last, through the efforts of Damúdar Pandi, these obstacles were removed, and Captain Knox arrived at Kathmandu in April 1802. He was accompanied by Dr. Buchanan Hamilton and two other officers.

Lachman Sah, son of Bim Sah Chauntria, and Karbir Pandi, son of Damudar Pandi, with a third Sardar, a son of a Nipal chief, were sent to Patna, to remain there as hostages for the proper treatment of the British mission, and as pledges of the sincerity of the Nipalese Government. While at Patna all their expenses were defrayed by the British Government, and they were treated with every mark of respect and consideration. At the time when Knox was despatched to Nipal by Lord Wellesley, the Nipalese had not completed the conquest of Kamaon or the more westerly hills; the possessions of Nipal then were very nearly the same as they are now, except that at present she holds Doti, which at that time was an independent state. Knox was accredited to the junior Rani as

Regent, and on his arrival, Damudar Pandi was the First Minister of State. He was a man of talent, firmness, and moderation; these qualities, added to the reputation of personal courage and gallantry as a soldier, gave him great influence, not only over the Rani, but in the councils of the State. His colleagues—Bim Sah Chauntria, who was Governor of Kamaon in the war of 1814–15, and Gujraj Misr—were able and moderate men. These three ministers were all openly in favour of the British alliance; yet their characters for honesty stood so high that they were never suspected, even · by the Nipalese, of any political corruption. Captain Knox wished to take all three ministers into the pay of the British; but they set too high a value on their own, as well as their country's, independence to be induced to consent to the proposal.

For some months after his arrival, all Knox's efforts to obtain the signing of the treaty were unsuccessful. He was treated with courtesy, but not with confidence or cordiality, by the Darbar, who showed itself on that, as it always has on every other, occasion to be averse to actual treaties, or intimate connections with the British, looking on such relations as the first step to the loss of national independence. At last, however, news arrived that the senior Maharani had left the ex-king at Benares, and was actually on the frontier. This brought matters to a crisis; for, as the Maharani was known to have a strong party, among the Thappas, in her favour at the capital, the Regent Rani was fearful that the British might espouse her cause if any slight were shown to Captain Knox; she, therefore, at length formally received and ratified the treaty of alliance which Knox had brought to Nipal.

The Regent Rani was also apprehensive that the return of the Maharani would lead to the restoration of Ran Bahadur, as the Maharani would naturally do all in her power to recommend herself to the favour of the ex-Rajah, in hopes of bearing him a son, who should succeed to the throne, and displace the bastard Garwan Jodh Bikram Sah, who then occupied it.

In November 1802 the Maharani crossed the frontier, and was reported to be *en route* for Kathmandu. An armed force was sent against her, who made prisoners of all her male attendants, but allowed the Queen herself to escape, with her female escort, to the plains.

Having ascertained that the feelings of the soldiery generally were in her favour, the Maharani, in February 1803, again crossed the frontier, and advanced towards the capital. The troops sent to oppose her progress everywhere espoused her cause. She entered the valley in triumph; and as she approached Kathmandu, the Regent Rani, in alarm, fled to Pashpatinath, taking the young Rajah with her. The junior Rani was deposed, and the young Prince brought back and placed on the throne under the charge of the Maharani as Regent. Damudar Pandi was continued in full power as sole Minister, and the Pandi party generally were installed in office.* The deposed Rani, after executing a deed of formal surrender of her late office as Regent, was, through the mildness of the Maharani's temper, allowed a full pardon and exemption for all past transactions. This revolution is remarkable as having been the only one recorded in Nipalese history which was unattended with any bloodshed.

Although the new Regent at first made friendly professions, yet it was well known that she was thoroughly averse to the British alliance; and Damudar Pandi, who was in favour of acting up to the recent treaty, and was opposed to the restoration of Ran Bahadur, was daily losing his influence over the Maharani. About this time Umar Singh Thappa (the Hero of Malaun) was taken into the Cabinet. Under these circumstances, finding that all his efforts to induce the Nipalese Government to fulfil the terms of the treaty of alliance were unavailing, and that the Darbar was gradually resuming its former unfriendly tone, and manifesting more and more clearly its strong repugnance to his continuance as Resident at Kathmandu, Captain Knox and party withdrew from Nipal and returned to the British provinces in March 1803.

---

* In Knox's time, as now, the chiefs were possessors of authority derived directly from the Rajah, and continued to them at his discretion; they were not then, nor are they now, hereditary holders of tracts of country, with annexed powers of government therein, on condition of feudal service to the State.

Thus ended the second British mission to the Court of Nipal. In January 1804 Lord Wellesley addressed a letter to the Rajah of Nipal, in which, after adverting to the fact that the Nipalese hostages at Benares "had been treated with every degree of respect and attention, and entertained at the public expense, while the British Resident at Kathmandu had been repeatedly treated with indignity by the members of the Nipal Government, and was ultimately compelled, by their misconduct and violation of public faith, to abandon their capital and enter within the Company's territories," he formally renounced and dissolved the alliance between the two States. At the same time he expressed himself as anxious to remain on terms of "amity and peace," but added that, as the alliance was dissolved between the two Governments, he had no reason for keeping the ex-Rajah of Nipal, against his own will, within our territories; and he should, therefore, now yield to the constant wishes of Ran Bahadur to return to Kathmandu by giving him leave to quit Benares.

This dissolution of the alliance, involving an abrogation of the old commercial treaty, left us, with the Nipalese, in the same negative state that we occupied previous to 1792.*

---

* Although the two treaties of 1792 and 1801 were thus formally abrogated, yet the operation of the treaty of 1792 practically has continued ever since, only it has been strictly unilateral, or observed only by the British. Nipal goods have been, and still

Ran Bahadur immediately availed himself of his liberty, and returned to Nipal, where he was well received by his faithful wife, the Regent Maharani. On his approach to the capital he was met by Damudar Pandi, at the head of a large body of troops, who had come out apparently with the intention of opposing his advance. Bim Sen Thappa, who was with the King, and exercised much influence over him, urged his master to seize that favourable opportunity to at once overthrow the Pandi, and secure the allegiance of the troops who were with him. Ran Bahadur, well knowing the loyalty of the Gorkha soldiery, advanced fearlessly to meet them, and tossing his cap into the air, exclaimed, "Now, my brave Gorkhas, who's for the Sah, and who for the Pandi?" The appeal was successful. The soldiers crowded round the King with acclamations and cries of devo-

---

are, charged only two and a half per cent. *ad valorem* duty by us; whilst our merchandise.has been, and is, subject in Nipal, under various forms one way or the other, to treble and quadruple of the treaty rates. In all other respects but rate of customs duty, as observed by us only, both treaties after 1804 became a dead letter. The Nipalese profess only to levy two and a half per cent. on British goods; but tolls are not levied in one lump, nor at one time; they are collected piecemeal, and repeatedly in different places and under different forms. The merchant has no means of ascertaining the actual authority for these various charges, nor of calculating beforehand their percentage pressure on his profits. In this way the duties levied in Nipal on British articles of trade are swollen easily to from seven to ten per cent. instead of remaining at two and a half per cent.

tion; Damudar Pandi and his son, abandoned by their own troops, were seized, put in irons, and carried to the rear of the royal procession, which advanced, without further opposition, to Kathmandu; and Ran Bahadur entered his capital in triumph at the head of the very troops who had been sent to oppose him.

Damudar Pandi, his son, and a large number of the Pandi party were beheaded at the instigation, it is generally believed, of young Bhim Sen Thappa, who was appointed sole Minister,* who was at that time described by Hamilton as "being as vigorous, ambitious, and unprincipled as his savage master." Ran Bahadur, finding that the oath of fidelity to his infant, though illegitimate, son, Garwan Jodh Bikram Sah, was considered by the soldiery as still binding upon them, contented himself with the title of Regent, and under that name assumed the government of the country, though, in reality, he exercised the full powers of royalty until his death.

During his Regency he was guilty of many acts of tyranny, and his violent conduct soon drove a number

---

* The conclusion of a Lal Mohur from Ran Bahadur to Bhim Sen, on appointing him Minister, is in these terms:—" If I violate this solemn pledge, may one hundred and twenty grades of my ancestral relations be turned into filth-born insects of hell by the wrath of all the gods and goddesses. If, on the contrary, I keep this pledge, may the gods, in reward, give so many of my ancestors a place in heaven."

of chiefs, who were fearful lest their past connection
with the Pandis might bring them to ruin now that
Thappa influence was predominant at Court, into a
conspiracy with Sher Bahadur (illegitimate half-
brother of Ran Bahadur) for the purpose of again
getting rid of him.

Ran Bahadur, having learnt of the existence of the
plot, by the advice of Bhim Sen suddenly sent for
Sher Bahadur, and suggested to him to quit the
capital and join the army then engaged in the conquest of the western hills.   Sher Bahadur, having
given an insulting reply, was ordered for immediate
execution; instantly drawing his sword, he mortally
wounded the Regent, but was the next instant himself cut down by Bal Nur Singh Konwar, a Thappa
chief, who, for that act of gallantry in defence of his
Sovereign, was permitted ever after to wear his shield
in Court in the Rajah's presence.*

General Bhim Sen Thappa immediately obtained
possession of the person of the young Rajah, then
only ten years old, and had him proclaimed King,

---

* This Bal Nur Sing Konwa was the father of General Jang Bahadur. For this act of loyalty he was made a Kaji, and the
title and rank of Kaji made hereditary in his family. Jang himself, in accordance with this privilege, became a Kaji on his
father's death about 1840. Bal Nur Sing was wounded severely
in the left shoulder at the siege of Kot Kangra, where his father
was killed. Jang has in his possession the broken talwar (broken
by the violence of the blow) with which his father almost cut
Sher Bahadur's body in two.

with the Maharani as Regent, and himself as Premier.
He forced the junior Rani, who had opposed his
claims to Premiership, and always leaned towards the
Pandis, to perform satti with her husband's (Ran
Bahadur's) corpse ; and under pretext of their having
been concerned in Sher Bahadur's conspiracy, caused
a large number of chiefs and sardars, opposed to him
and his party, to be put to death. Bhim Sen continued as sole Minister of Nipal from this date until
1837.* The Maharani Tripur Sundari, who was his
firm ally, and is believed to have been bound to him
by more tender ties than those of politics, lived until
1832, and maintained her influence in the Court and
in the country undiminished until her death. She
was a legitimate, but left-handed, wife of Ran Bahadur, having been the daughter of a Thappa jemadar
of the troops at the capital. Her death, in 1832, was
the first material blow to the power of Bhim Sen.

---

* The Nipal chiefs might, and may, quarrel among themselves
for the possession of official dignities under the Crown, but there
is not an instance on record of a Gorkha chief setting himself in
open defiance of the Crown for the purpose of establishing independent authority. Nor is there an instance of a Nipal chief
taking bribes from, or selling himself for money to, the British
or any other foreign State.

In 1801 Captain Knox wished to take Damudar Pandi and some
of his colleagues into our pay; but they would not listen to the
proposal. In 1816, as before in 1801, our Government offered
pensions to certain Nipalese sirdars, but the Darbar had foresight
enough to reject the offer.

After the dissolution of the alliance in 1804, until 1812, the British intercourse with Nipal was of a desultory and unsatisfactory character. It consisted almost entirely of fruitless attempts to induce the Darbar to assist our border officers in the suppression of Dacoity and robbery in the Terai, and of unavailing remonstrances against the aggressions of the Nipalese on our frontier throughout its entire length. These aggressions appear to have been part of a regular system of determined, but stealthy, encroachment upon our territories, which had commenced in 1787, and was continued, without intermission, until 1814, when it became the immediate cause of the Nipal War.

After the death of Ran Bahadur, General Umar Singh Thappa, at the head of a Gorkha army, advanced through the western hills, conquered and annexed Kamaon and Garhwal, and established the authority of the Nipalese over the western hill states, almost to the banks of the Satlaj.

*　　　*　　　*　　　*　　　*

CHAPTER XXIII.

AFTER THE NIPAL WAR.

*　　*　　*　　*　　*

THE permanent political connection of the British with Nipal commenced in 1816, when, in accordance with the Treaty of Sigauli, the Hon. E. Gardiner was appointed Resident at the Court of Kathmandu. On his arrival Maharajah Garwan Jodh Bikram Sah was on the throne, and General Bhim Sen Thappa as sole and all-powerful Minister, ably supported by the Maharani, administered all the affairs of the State.

Six months after Mr. Gardiner's arrival, the Maharajah died of small-pox, aged twenty-one, and was succeeded by his only son, Rajindra Bikram Sah, an infant of two years old. Bhim Sen retained his office of sole Minister, and strongly supported by his friend the Maharani, enjoyed, during the long minority[*]

---

[*] The long succession of minorities from 1775 until 1830 favoured the rise of eminent military ministers, such as Bahadur

which ensued, uninterrupted and unlimited power. He always used all his influence in favour of peace with the British, "a Power," as he said, "that crushed thrones like potsherds." He had been forced into the war of 1815–16, against his own better judgment, by the eagerness of the army and the excited feelings of the nation. The war being over, it was owing to his skill in negotiation that two lakhs of rupees annually were first assigned by the British Government to the Nipalese chiefs as compensation for the loss of their jagirs in the Terai; and it was entirely due to his tact and skill in dissimulation that the British Government were subsequently cajoled into restoring to the Nipalese the whole of the Terai, in lieu of these two lakhs.

Although Bhim Sen was always averse to war with the British, his pacific policy was the result of no cordiality for us, but merely of a full appreciation of our superior strength. Nothing was nearer or dearer to his heart than the independence of his country; and he was too sagacious not to perceive that a second war with the British would almost certainly be followed by the reduction of Nipal, even under the most favourable circumstances, to the condition of one of the "protected states." While, therefore, he

---

Sah, Damudar Pandi; and Bhim Sen Thappa. Ran Bahadur was an infant on his accession to the throne in 1775. Jodh Bihram Sah (1805) and Rajindra Bikram Sah (1816) were also infants on their accession to the throne.

studiously avoided every act that might lead to a rupture of the existing peace—which peace he looked upon as the best guarantee of Nipal's independence —he as steadily resisted every overture on our part to render the connection between the two nations closer, and, with great foresight, most successfully prevented our ever having any pecuniary or other direct or indirect control over the internal affairs of the State.

Now, equally as in the days of Bhim Sen, the Nipalese Darbar wish to have nothing to do with us. At the point of the bayonet they were forced to yield to the establishment of a British Resident at their Court*; but they would be as delighted now as they would have been immediately after the war, if they could dispense with the presence of that functionary among them They know however, that the withdrawal of the Resident would be immediately followed by the resumption of the Terai lands, and the probable conquest and annexation of their country. They submit, therefore, without further complaint, to a state of things which they cannot alter. Although they are still as insuperably averse as ever to any kind of intimate connection with the British Govern-

---

* At Makwanpur, General Ochterlony, by Lord Hastings' express commands, told the Gorkha Vakils that all other points of the treaty were more or less open to subsequent discussion, but that "they must take either the Resident or war." They yielded, and Lieutenant Boileau was sent as *locum tenens* until the arrival of the Resident.

ment, yet this aversion does not depend on any actual feeling of hostility towards us. But they look on us as dangerous and encroaching neighbours, and judging from the experience and fate of other states throughout India, they are firmly convinced that if once the British gain a footing (even though it be of a friendly character) within the Valley of Nipal, from that time the knell of their national independence will have struck. Acting on these principles, they distrust, and ever have distrusted, every friendly overture that is made to them; they throw obstacles in the way of anything like extensive intercourse between the two nations, and they carry their suspicions of our interested motives to such a degree, that they will not even allow a single European to travel through their hills for the purpose of collecting purely scientific information. Nothing will ever disabuse them of the belief that the British are anxious to conquer and annex Nipal. They acknowledge our supremacy in the plains, and they think that the only way to prevent that supremacy from being established in Nipal as well as in Hindustan is to keep us at a distance, and by isolating themselves from all intimate connection with us, avoid giving us the opportunity of gratifying, what they consider, the national love of foreign aggrandisement. These considerations form the real and only key to the very exclusive policy which Nipal has systematically adopted towards the British Government from the date of the last war up to the present time.

On Mr. Gardiner's assuming the position of Resident in Nipal he had rather a difficult duty to perform. Although the Nipalese had just been deprived of one-third of their dominions, they were far from being humiliated by their late defeat. On the contrary, they seemed as proud and overbearing, and as jealous of British interference, as they had been before the war.

Gardiner, however, combined in an eminent degree those qualities of firmness, courtesy, and temper which are indispensable to the success of any political officer among the natives of India. He personally won their respect; and by uniformly treating them as a perfectly independent state, he, to a certain extent, disarmed their suspicions of the policy of the British Government.

For several years after the peace of 1816 no events occurred of any importance either in the internal history or foreign policy of Nipal. Bhim Sen's family monopolised all the great offices of the State; the Rajah, being a minor, was entirely in the hands of the Minister and of his ally, the Regent Maharani, the King's step-mother. Bhim Sen, who was possessed of great perseverance as well as determination, devoted almost exclusively his time and talents to the services of the State. During the minority of the King he raised Nipal, although deprived of nearly one-third of her dominions, to nearly as strong a military position on our frontier as she had occupied before the war. He nearly doubled her internal re-

sources by careful attention to the state of her
finances, and by a judicious re-adjustment of the
national taxes. Among other changes, he resumed,
on the part of Government, to a great extent the
rent-free tenures of the Brahmans, as well as the
grants of land which had been made at various times
to the temples and other religious establishments.
This system had been commenced during the war by
Bhim Sen, who called on all Brahmans holding such
lands to come forward and assist the State, promising,
when the exigency was passed, to put them again in
possession of their tenures. Some few, perhaps, of
the holy orders were influenced by patriotic motives,
and, of their own accord, poured the contents of their
coffers into the public treasury; the vast majority de-
murred, but were compelled by the strong arm of
secular authority to disgorge their wealth, and to
place the copyrights of their own and of the Church
lands at the disposal of the State. These lands were
never restored to the Church, but were devoted solely
to defray the expenses of the army; and as a large
portion of these were in the most fertile parts of the
country, the addition to the State revenue was very
considerable.

Bhim Sen also added a good deal to the public
revenue by increasing the customs duties.* The

---

* In 1816 the customs duties only produced eighty thousand
rupees; in 1833 they produced two and a half lakhs of rupees.
This was owing to the increased commerce resulting from the in-

long minority of the King, too, was favourable to the economy of the public money by enabling the State to avoid all the expenses of a Court. Among the other means by which Nipal was enabled to repair the heavy loss consequent on our taking Kamaon, and to recover from the pecuniary involvements necessary to the late war, may be mentioned the increased value of the Terai lands as restored by us after the war.

After the war, and when our Resident was fairly settled at Kathmandu, the British Government made over the western Terai lands to Oudh, and restored the eastern Terai to Nipal. By the treaty after the war we were bound to pay two lakhs a year in pensions to the chiefs of Nipal as compensation for the loss of their jagirs in the Terai. This agreement was annulled on consideration of our giving back the Terai lands to Nipal.* Government distinctly

---

creased intercourse held by the Nipalese, now that peace was established, with the plains. It especially affected the importation of English and European articles to the exclusion of those of China and Tibet. Bhim Seen, and the chiefs generally, showed a growing inclination for British luxuries and customs.

* From the Kali river to the Rapti river (on which is Gorakhpur) the lowlands constituting the western Terai were wholly exacted from Nipal, and were made over by treaty to Oudh in 1817. Possession, however, was kept by Nipal under various pretences and evasions, and their final evacuation and the demarcation of the frontier line was not completed till 1820.

The Terai between the Rapti on the west and the Kosi on the east constitutes the eastern Terai, and was restored by us to the Nipalese.

and officially informed the Nipalese Darbar that the
lands so restored were to be received by them "as
a gratuitous boon from our Government, admitting
of no discussion." In making this restoration, our
Government were very much deceived as to the real
value of the Terai lands. Our officers reported that
the Terai only produced two lakhs a year; whereas
it has been computed subsequently that (independent
of the large assignments in land as jaigirs to the
Sardars) the amount of Terai revenue cannot bring in
less than ten or twelve lakhs annually to the Nipal
treasury. In 1834 Mr. Hodgson estimated it as
follows :—

Net revenue of land . .	Rs. 6,00,000
Elephants and ivory . .	71,000
Timber	3,00,000
Pasturage, and sundries, as drugs, dyes, &c. . . .	20,000
Total .	Rs. 9,91,000

A good deal of correspondence ensued between the
two Governments with reference to the restoration of

In 1819 Government directed the Resident to demand from the
Rajah the immediate recall of the Gorkha troops then occupying
the disputed lands which ought to have been already ceded to
Oudh, threatening, if the request were not complied with at once,
that they would withdraw the Resident and resume the whole of
the eastern Terai. The mere threat sufficed, and in 1820 the lands
were ceded to Oudh.

these lands, and subsequently as to the fixing of the exact boundary between the lands belonging to the two States   The boundary between Nipal and Oudh was not finally adjusted until 1830; and that between Nipal and the British territories remained as a matter of discussion between the two Governments for several years later

Bhim Sen took advantage of the continuance of peace, not only to improve the finances of the country, but to render the army more efficient both in numbers and in discipline   The martial feelings of the soldiery were every way encouraged; their rights and privileges were jealously preserved; but they were at the same time kept from that idleness which is so favourable to mutiny and intrigue, by strict attention to drill and discipline and by being employed in the construction of magazines, arsenals, cannon foundry, &c., and by the establishment of two large cantonments—one for the artillery and one for the line—at Kathmandu.   He had numbers of cannon founded, and manufactured extensively muskets, powder, shot, and the munitions of war

By these and other means, by consulting their prejudices as well as flattering their pride, Bhim Sen not only acquired, but retained to the last, the affections of the soldiery and of the army generally.   In 1816 Mr. Gardiner estimated the standing regular army at ten thousand men; in 1819 it was calculated at twelve thousand; and from that date it gradually increased up to 1831, when it was estimated at fifteen thousand men. At that time the military stores and arsenals, which were kept in a constant state of activity, could furnish arms and accoutrements for forty-five thousand men.

On the 1st of April 1832 Maharani Tripur (or Tripuri) Sundari, widow of Ran Bahadur, died. She had played a very important part in the politics of Nipal, and throughout a long life had preserved the character of being not only an able, but an honest and virtuous woman. She accompanied her husband in his exile to Benares; when she returned to Nipal, she upset the Regency to which Captain Knox had been accredited, had herself proclaimed Regent, induced Knox to withdraw, and succeeded in bringing about the restoration of her husband to the throne. After her husband's death in 1805, she became joint Regent with Bhim Sen, and in conjunction with that great man, to whom she ever continued a firm ally, had ruled the country up to the time of her death, in a manner that reflects the greatest credit upon their united firmness, talent, and sagacity. Her death was the first serious blow that Bhim Sen's power received. She had always supported him against the jealousy and rivalry of his brother Ranbir Singh Thappa, at that time commander-in-chief of the Nipal army, who was gaining undue influence over the young Rajah, then aged eighteen years, and was doing his best to set the young King against both Bhim Sen and his nephew Martabar Singh. Martabar Singh was then but a young man, but his talent, energy, and grasping

ambition made him, as well as his uncle, an object
of hatred to Ranbir Singh and his party, who were
jealous of the almost unlimited power of Bhim Sen.
The young King himself, being of a frivolous character, took little part in the affairs of the State;
he gave himself up to pleasure, leaving everything
connected with business to be directed by his able
Minister.

The party, however, opposed to Bhim Sen, and
headed by his brother, steadily increased in power;
but they were unable to do much against a Minister
in the hands of whose family were almost all the important offices of State, both at the capital and in
the provinces, and whose personal popularity with the
army was extreme.

In 1833 a new battalion was raised (Singh Nath),
and placed under the command of Martabar Singh;
and in the following year, 1834, he was appointed to
the government of Gorkha, with three thousand troops
under his command. About this time the Pandi
party, at the head of whom was Ranjang, son of
Damodar Pandi, began to recover their influence in
the State. They succeeded in prejudicing the Rajah
against Bhim Sen; and from this time may be dated
the commencement of the counter revolution against
the Thappas, whose power had been supreme ever
since the restoration of Ran Bahadur.

On the 19th of June 1834, a powder magazine, four
hundred yards from the British Residency, was struck
by lightning in a storm and exploded. It contained

at the time two thousand maunds (one hundred and sixty thousand pounds) of gunpowder. Of the guard on the spot, twenty-one in number, all were killed; and of a small guard of eight men at the parti near, six were killed and two miserably mutilated. Almost every window, frame, venetian, &c., in the Residency were smashed by the concussion. Damage, C. R. 1,627.

In November 1835 Martabar Singh was sent to Calcutta at the head of a complimentary mission to the Governor-General. The Rajah wished to send him to England, on an embassy to the King; but he abandoned the idea on hearing that he would be treated merely as a traveller, and would not be allowed to be the vehicle of political communication. Martabar returned to Nipal in March 1836, having been received in Calcutta with marked courtesy.

Ever since the death of the Queen Tripur Sundari in 1832, Bhim Sen's power had been on the wane. In the spring of 1837 the Rajah turned out of office some of Bhim Sen's favourites, and deprived Martabar Singh of his command of Gorkha in consequence of his refusing to hold it on reduced allowances. Martabar was succeeded by Ranjang Pandi's brother. The King at this time had a sudden fit of economy, and directed a great part of his attention to financial matters. He made the increase of his family (he had now six children), and the consequently increased household expenses of Darbar, an excuse for general retrenchments. The office of Ditha or Chief Justice, hitherto always held by an officer of the army, was given to a Brahman of legal knowledge and talent. Up to this time Bhim Sen had succeeded in excluding all civilians from appointments under Government. In the beginning of July 1837 Ranjang Pandi was restored by the Rajah to all the lands and honours formerly held by his father Damodar Pandi, and which had been confiscated in 1803.

A few days afterwards the Rajah's youngest son,* an infant of one year, died suddenly ; and it was at once given out that the child had died of poison, intended for its mother the Maharani, and given at the instigation of Bhim Sen, or some of his party. There is every reason to believe that the infant was killed by its own father, in order to obtain a basis of proceedings against Bhim Sen. On this charge, Bhim Sen, his brother Ranbir Singh, his nephew Martabar Singh, their families, the Court physician and his deputy, with a number more of the nearest relations of the Thappas, were incarcerated (the heads of the family in irons), proclaimed outcastes, and their property confiscated. They were fearfully tortured to induce them to confess, but not a syllable to criminate anyone was elicited.

---

* The Maharajah had two wives: 1st. The Maharani, an adherent of the Pandis ; she had three sons, the eldest of whom is the present King, the second is in prison at Allahabad for the conspiracy of 1851, and the third was the child whom Bhim Sen was falsely accused of poisoning. 2nd. The Junior Rani, an adherent of the Thappas, who also bore him two sons ; they and their mother are now residing in exile at Benares.

Ranjang Pandi was suddenly appointed Minister. Fearful, from this appointment, of the establishment of the Pandis in power, Fatti Jang Chauntria, Raghunath Pandit, and the junior Rani obtained from the King the liberation of Bhim Sen, Martabar, and the rest of the party. Pardon was given to the old man, who fell on his face at the Rajah's feet, in full Darbar; and public audiences were granted, and dresses of honour and caparisoned horses given to him, to Martabar, and to Bhim Sen's adopted son Shamsher Jang. Their confiscated property was returned, and they were brought back by the soldiery and people in triumph to their respective houses. Ranjang, the recognised leader of the now powerful Pandi party, was removed from the office of Minister, and Raghunath Pandit,* who was favourably inclined towards the Thappas, was elected Premier. He and his brother, Krishna Ram, were clever, well-informed men, of moderate and liberal views, but had long been living in retirement in consequence of all appointments having hitherto been conferred only on military men. Raghunath continued as ostensible Minister, but the Rajah assumed himself the immediate control and patronage of the army, which, at this time, having been increased by the raising of another battalion, now consisted of nineteen thousand

---

* He was a Brahman, and at one time filled the office of Raj Guru.

rank and file. The strength of the army at the capital was somewhat diminished, three thousand troops being marched from it to various stations in the interior and on the frontier.

In the beginning of 1838 Ranjang Pandi, through the influence of the Maharani, was appointed Commander-in-Chief; an appointment popular with the army on the whole, in consequence of the fame of his father Damodar Pandi. His brother Ramdul Pandi was made Governor of Palpa, and another brother, Karbir Pandi, Keeper of the King's Wardrobe. Bhim Sen and Martabar Singh continued at large, but out of employ. They were still very popular with the army, as was shown by the fact that many of the officers and men took their discharge from their regiments and attached themselves as private followers to their suites. The dissensions in the Palace became very violent, owing to differences between the two Queens; the Maharani insisting on the appointment of Ranjang to be Premier, while the junior Rani as warmly advocated the restoration of Bhim Sen to power.

In March 1838 Martabar Singh was sent into a sort of honourable exile, being deputed on a secret or confidential mission to Ranjit Singh, the nature of which mission was never accurately known. In May he was arrested by the British authorities as he was attempting to cross the Satlaj at night. At the end of the year he was released by the British and allowed to proceed on his journey to Lahor. As, however, he was suspected of intriguing against us, he was surrendered to our authorities by Ranjit Singh, who openly and indignantly disavowed all negotiations with Nipal, and for some years he lived within our territories, at Simla and elsewhere, under our surveillance. Ragunath Pandit, finding himself unsupported by the King, resigned the Premiership, which was conferred nominally on Pushkar Sah Chauntria (who had just returned from the embassy to Pekin), but actually upon his colleague, Ranjang Pandi, in whom all real authority was vested.

The Pandis* were now in the full possession of power; they had gained over the King to their side by flattering his weaknesses. The Maharani had ever been a firm supporter of their party; and they endeavoured to secure popularity in the army by promises of war and plunder. Their accession to power —after a thirty years' banishment to their hill estates,

---

* Runjung Pandi.
   Karbir Pandi.
   Kulraj Pandi.
   Jagat Bum Pandi.
   Dal Bahadur Pandi.
   The Raj Guru.
   Kul Chand Sahi.
   Amir Sahi.
These were the leading members of the Pandi party.

Raj Guru, who was of course a Brahman, was named Misr (at least that was the name of the division or class of Brahmans to which he belonged), and he was therefore commonly called Misr Guru.

or exile at Benares—occurred just at the time when British power in the plains was in a most disturbed state. It appeared not unlikely that the British were over-matched in their contests in China and Afghanistan, and the Darbar naturally felt inclined to take advantage of our supposed difficulties in order to advance their own interests.

Secret communications were accordingly kept up with various parts of India, especially with the Courts of Ava, Pekin, and Lahor. At the same time the Darbar appeared to be preparing for hostilities; and now that the Pandis were in the full possession of power, they greatly strengthened all the frontier posts with supplies of soldiers, guns, and ammunition. Although these apparently hostile preparations had probably no definite object, beyond that of placing the Nipalese on good vantage ground in case of any misfortune or important reverse befalling the British power in the plains, yet the British Government deemed it prudent to form a corps of observation on the frontier, as well to show the Nipalese that we were always prepared and had spare troops at our disposal, as to protect our subjects on the border in case of any actual aggression. A corps of observation was accordingly ordered in 1838 to assemble, under Colonel Oglander, to watch the Nipal frontier. This decisive measure at once brought the Darbar to a sense of their real position, and for a short time they assumed a more courteous and friendly bearing towards us.

At the beginning of 1839 Ranjang Pandi was made sole Minister, to the great disgust of the Chauntrias and other influential chiefs, as well as of the people generally, by whom he was detested. The persecutions of the Thappas were again revived, and the charge of poisoning the young prince in 1837 was brought forward against Bhim Sen. This veteran statesman, who was the only remaining obstacle in the path of the Pandis, would have been at once cut off; but the Rajah and the Pandis were afraid that, in that case, Martabar Singh would openly go over to the English, in whose power he was. Ranjang accordingly tried to lure back Martabar Singh by specious promises, in order that, once having him in his power, both uncle and nephew might be destroyed together. Foiled in this scheme by Martabar's sagacity, who detected the plot against him, Ranjang had the charge of poisoning the young prince openly revived against Bhim Sen, and forged papers and evidence were produced professing to criminate him. The old man defended himself, in open Darbar, with great spirit, asking why, if this evidence were really true, it had not been produced in 1837; and denouncing the papers as forgeries, he demanded to be confronted with his accusers. His appeal was of no use; he was surrounded by enemies. The few chiefs who were in his favour, or convinced of his innocence, sat by in silence and in fear. The Rajah denounced him as a traitor, and sent him back in chains to prison. Threats of every indignity to himself and the female members of his house were constantly made to him, with a view to induce him to commit suicide. The Court physician, who had attended the child (a Brahman, and whose life was therefore sacred), was burnt on the forehead and cheeks till his brain and jaws were exposed. The under-physician, a Niwar, was impaled alive, and his heart extracted while he was yet living. Still no evidence against Bhim Sen or any of the accused could be extorted even by these horrible atrocities, which were perpetrated not only by the order, but in the presence of the Rajah.

On the 20th of July 1839, driven to desperation, Bhim Sen attempted suicide by cutting his throat with a kukri, of which wound he died nine days afterwards. His savage enemies refused even to his corpse the ordinary funeral rites; it was dismembered and exposed about the city, and afterwards the mangled remains were thrown on the river-side as food for vultures and jackals. His very bones were not allowed to be removed that they might be buried. His family and relatives were imprisoned, and their property confiscated. A decree was also issued that none of the Thappa class should receive public employ for seven generations.

It was upon the party who perpetrated all these atrocities against the Thappas that Jang Bahadur revenged himself and them in " the massacre " of 1846. Bhim Sen being removed, no check now remained upon the conduct or policy of the Maharani and her ally, Ranjang Pandi, who was now possessed of unlimited power. A general system of extortion, injustice, and retrenchment was adopted with a view to replenish the public treasury. Ranjang and the Maharani threw all the odium of these measures upon the Rajah, hoping that, by making him unpopular, they would induce him to abdicate.

Among other means contemplated for retrenchment by the Maharani and Ranjang Pandi was a general reduction in the pay of the troops. In order to announce this to the army, a general parade of the troops was ordered on the Tandi Khel, by command of the Maharajah, on the 21st of June 1840.

On assembling, the troops, who, from private sources, were aware 'of the nature of the proclamation and had concerted measures accordingly, grounded their arms, and insisted on the redress of their grievances. These consisted in the fact that, for two years past, the soldiery, instead of being either re-enlisted at the Panjanni (or termination of the year for which they had been entertained) or else paid up and discharged, had instead been kept on in service for eight or ten months beyond the annual term, with perpetual liability to be ousted by fresh recruits coming into their places near the end of the second year, and who were yet entitled, by the usage of Nipal, to draw the entire year's pay; while the original occupant of the office, who had served his extra eight or ten months, received no pay for that broken period. In addition to this real grievance, the soldiery had been much irritated by constant rumours of contemplated reduction in their pay. Receiving no promises of redress, the troops proceeded to the house of Chauntria Pashkar Sah, the nominal Minister, situated near the British Residency, and gutted it completely. Then returning to the city, they gutted the houses of five other principal chiefs, members of the Ministry, and supposed to be connected with the authors of their grievances.

On the 22nd the Rajah himself, after repeated summonses, appeared before them and promised them full redress in every way. Shouldering their arms, the troops at once returned to their quarters without committing any further excesses.

The excitement still continuing, on the 23rd the following message was conveyed to the assembled troops from the Rajah and Rani :—

"The English Government is powerful, abounding in wealth and in all other resources for war. I have kept well with the English so long, because I am unable to cope with them. Besides, I am bound by a treaty of amity, and have now no excuse to break it; nor have I money to support a war. Troops I have, and arms and ammunition in plenty, but no money. This is the reason why I have reduced your pay. I want treasure to fight the English. Take lower pay for a year or two, and when I have some money in hand, then I will throw off the mask and indulge you with war."

To this the troops replied, by their deputies, at a

parade at which the Maharajah in person was present:

"True, the English Government is great; but care the wild dogs of Nipal (Buansu) how large is the herd they attack? They are sure to get their bellies filled. You want no money for making war; for the war shall support itself. We will plunder Lucknow and Patna. But first we must get rid of the Resident, who sees and forestalls all. We must be able, unseen, to watch the moment of attack. It will soon come; it is come. Give the word, and we will destroy the Resident, and then war will follow of course. You want an excuse for war; there is one ready made. Let us act without being watched by the Resident, and we will soon make the Ganges your boundary. Or if the English, as they say, are your friends and want peace, why do they keep possession of half your dominions (Kamaon)? Let them restore Kamaon and Sikkim. These are yours, demand them back; and if they refuse, drive out the Resident, and let us have war."

To this the Rajah asked time to consider; and so the matter dropped. The irregularities concerning their period of service were reformed, and no reduction in their pay was made. Their real grievances being thus redressed, their demands for war were not revived by the army. In this mutiny only the troops in and around the capital (about six thousand) were engaged; those in the provinces knew nothing about it. It commenced in the Sri Nath and Latur Battalions. It is believed that the real instigators of this mutiny, as well as the authors of all the wrongs of the soldiery, were the Maharani and her favourite the Prime Minister. By making the King and other chiefs unpopular with the army, at the same time that they excited a revolt among the soldiery, they hoped not only to frighten the King into abdicating in favour of the Heir-Apparent—in which case they, the Rani and the Minister, would have obtained the whole government of the country during his minority—but also to have the opportunity of ingratiating themselves with the army by coming forward to redress the very wrongs of which they themselves were the authors.

Their plans were defeated, partly by the moderation and loyalty of the troops, and partly by the Rajah having sufficient sagacity to avoid bringing matters to extremities by making them in time the full and liberal concessions which they demanded.

At the same time, Colonel Oglander's corps of observation having been removed, the Darbar recommenced their hostile intrigues against us; and emissaries were despatched throughout Rajputana and many parts of India, foretelling the coming downfall of the British power.* The attention of the Darbar

---

* Captain Karbar Khatri was arrested in Benares, in October 1840, in the act of conducting a secret mission from Nipal to Lahor, contrary to existing treaties. A quantity of jewels, intended as a present for Ranjit Sing, were found on him : they were confiscated by order of the Governor-General, and the emissary himself kept in confinement. He was subsequently released, and

was in particular directed towards Burmah, and the example set it by that State, whose insolent treatment of the British Resident at the Court of Ava had been perpetrated with impunity, suggested for a while a similar procedure at Kathmandu. Placards were posted outside the Palace, exaggerating our reverses in Afghanistan. The Darbar believed that the magnitude of our operations in Afghanistan had withdrawn our troops and crippled our power in Bengal and in the north-west. Acting on this belief, they used every means of affront, and even of intimidation, to get rid of the British Residency as being a constant check on their schemes of secret encroachment on our provinces, and of hostile intrigue against us among their and our allies. At the same time the greatest activity was maintained in the public arsenals and in the manufacture of guns and ammunition; and a census of the population fit to carry arms, *i.e.* between the ages of twelve and sixty, was made, and produced a return of four hundred thousand souls. No actual increase, however, to the strength of the army, which amounted to nineteen thousand men, occurred at this period.

In the midst of all these hostile preparations, while our traders were being oppressed, and justice denied to them in the Nipalese courts of law; while Dacoits

---

accompanied Jang Bahadur to England in 1849. He is the man who originated the conspiracy against Jang in 1851, having given out that Jang had lost his caste in England.

and Thugs were openly harboured in the Nipalese territories, and while systematic intrigue against us with powers in the plains was being adopted by the Darbar, the King, in order to blind the British Government as to his real intentions, sent a most friendly letter to the Governor-General, tendering the services of the Gorkha army in any such way as his Lordship might approve.

This state of things could not last long without coming to a crisis. In the commencement of 1840 the Darbar took forcible possession of part of the district of Ramnagar, then belonging to the British.* Friendly remonstrances were made, but were unattended to; and at last, October 1840, Government ordered the advance of a brigade, consisting of one squadron 6th Light Cavalry, 12th, 40th, and 56th Native Infantry, a detail of artillery, and a detachment of irregular cavalry, under Colonel Oliver, to-

---

* A party of about forty or fifty Gorkha sepoys, under the command of an officer, entered the Ramnagar territory, on the occasion of a large fair, at which most of the inhabitants were present, and issued a proclamation notifying that the tract of land in question (seven or eight miles wide, and twenty-five to twenty-six miles in length, lying to the south of the Someshwar range, which formed the boundary between two states), which had formerly belonged to Nipal, but had been given to Ramnagar Rajah on the occasion of his marrying a Nipalese princess, had now, on the death of that princess, been resumed by Nipal, and directing all the local authorities, on pain of severe punishment, in future not only to acknowledge the authority of the Darbar, but to pay their taxes and revenue into the treasury of Nipal.

wards the frontier to enforce, if necessary, the immediate evacuation of our territories by the Gorkha troops, and to watch the movements of the Nipalese, and protect our subjects in case of any further aggressions being made. Our force at Gorakpur was at the same time strengthened.

This had the desired effect. Seeing that we were in earnest in our demands, the Darbar reluctantly, but completely, yielded. The Gorkha troops were recalled, and ninety-one villages, which they had occupied, were restored to their rightful and original owners. At the same time the Governor-General strongly advised the Rajah, as the only means of averting war, to dismiss the Pandi Ministry, and take into his counsels men who, if not favourable, should at least not be, like the Pandis, notoriously averse to all friendly connection with the British.

Feeling how unequal the State of Nipal was to cope with the power of the British in open hostilities, the Rajah made a virtue of necessity, and, dismissing the Pandi Ministry from office, formed a kind of " coalition " cabinet, consisting of four chiefs of moderate opinions, viz. Ragunath Pandit and his brother the Raj Guru Krishna Ram, with Fath Jang Chauntria and his brother Guru Parsad. To these were afterwards added Dalbhanjan Pandi and Abhiman Rana. Guru Parsad received the name Guru as an infant; it did not imply that he had ever held, or could hold, office as a Guru. He was not a Brahman, but a Chauntra, and therefore not

21 *

eligible for the sacred office. Of this ministry Fath Jang acted as Premier.

At the request of the King, supported by the advice of the Resident, Oliver's brigade was kept on the frontier in order to give encouragement to the party in the Darbar who were supposed to be favourable to the British alliance, until February 1842, when they were withdrawn, as their presence was no longer required.

In October 1841 the Maharani, mother of the Heir-Apparent, and the lady whom Bhim Sen had so unjustly been accused of attempting to poison, died at Hitaunda, on her way to the plains. She had for several months been suffering from serious internal organic disease, but the immediate cause of her death was an attack of the severe jungle-fever, commonly called "awal." She had always been friendly to the Pandis, and opposed to the Thappas, whom she accused of having poisoned not only her own infant, but her husband's father, the late King Garwan Jodh Bikram Sah, as well as some other members of the royal family. It is now known that these charges were utterly unfounded; but it is a striking proof of the unsettled state of society at that time, of tne low tone of morality and want of protection to life which existed even in the highest circles, that such accusations should have been bandied about between the rival parties, and that they should apparently have been believed as readily as they were circulated.

No sooner was it known that the Maharani was

dead than rumours were, as a matter of course, spread about, attributing her death to poison. The junior Rani (who was an adherent of the Thappas) was suspected by some; the King himself was believed by others to have been instrumental in bringing about her death. It is now known that she died naturally; but if anyone had anything to do with accelerating her death, it was most probably the Rajah himself. " Qui s'excuse, s'accuse "; and the extreme violence which he exhibited in defending himself from the charge raises some suspicion as to his innocence.

Some months afterwards, it came to his knowledge that he had been spoken of in one of the newspapers in the plains as having poisoned his wife. Immediately coming to the Residency with the Heir-Apparent, he demanded, in the most violent manner, that our Government should find out the writer of the libel, and insisted on his receiving the most barbarous punishments, adding that, if the British Government failed to do so, " he would go to war with them." (He subsequently apologised to the Resident for his intemperate conduct and language.) Then, turning on the Heir-Apparent, the two princes began to quarrel in the most outrageous way; and not content with using offensive epithets, actually came to blows. The King then sent a letter to the Governor-General, protesting his innocence of the murder of his Queen, but adding, " I took all the care I could of her; but if some villain, unknown to me, mixed poison with her food, I know nothing about it." Then follows,

"Should the man be discovered, I will have him skinned alive, and rubbed over with salt and limes until he dies."

After the appointment of Fath Jang Chauntria as Premier in 1841, affairs continued in a very unsettled state, and were greatly complicated by the imbecility of the King, who, nevertheless, insisted upon meddling with, if not controlling, every department of the State, the ambitious intrigues of the Maharani, and the violent and extravagant conduct of the Heir-Apparent, then a lad of twelve or thirteen years of age. This young prince, who appeared to have a most ungovernable temper, as well as a most inhuman disposition, amused his leisure hours by acts of the grossest cruelty performed not only upon animals, but upon men, who were tortured and mutilated in his presence upon the slightest and often most unjust grounds, for no other object than to gratify his brutal' passions. The Rajah, instead of exercising any restraint upon these excesses of his son, constantly tried to evade all responsibility for his own acts under cover of pretended coercion on the part of the Prince, of whose violence he professed to be afraid.

Although out of office, the private and confidential intercourse of the leaders of the Pandi party continued with the King, and many of them reappeared at the Darbar in open attendance upon the Heir-Apparent, who, as he advanced in age, appeared to gain more and more influence over his father, whom he was, at the same time, most anxious to induce to abdicate in his favour.

As evidence of the warlike feelings against the British which the Pandis endeavoured to excite in the mind of the Heir-Apparent in their private intercourse with him, it may be mentioned that, in 1842, Kulraj Pandi was daily amusing the young Prince with mock fights between the English and Gorkhas. The English were represented by a set of low-caste ragamuffins dressed in British uniform, and with faces painted white, and under the command of some " Pariah," who was attired in the full-dress uniform of an English general. The Gorkhas were commanded by a son of the late Premier and by Kulraj Pandi himself. Of course these actions were all made to end in the ignominious defeat of the supposed British forces; and the poor devils who represented them were in the end often seriously, and even cruelly, maltreated by the victorious Gorkhas in order to add a little more life and piquancy to the burlesque. A little real blood being shed would be sure to make the exhibition more attractive to His Royal Highness.

The very unsatisfactory way in which the Government of the country was being conducted, resulting as much from the weakness of the Rajah as from the extravagant conduct of the Heir-Apparent, at last induced the chiefs of all parties to combine in an effort to secure not only a more effective administration of the affairs of the State, but some guarantee for the rights and liberties of themselves and of the people at large. The chiefs generally, as well as the army, were anxious that without actually deposing the King or his son, the younger and now sole surviving Rani* should be invested with full power as Regent. This proposal was vehemently opposed by the Chauntrias, and especially by Guru Parsad, who, as a branch of the royal family, thought such a step might lead to a change in the succession to the throne, and, as a party, were anxious to circumscribe, rather than enlarge, the powers of the Queen. Ragunath Pandit, brother to the Raj Guru Krishna Ram, was the chief and ablest supporter of the Queen, as Chauntria Guru Parsad was her chief opponent.

In December 1842 a general meeting of the principal chiefs and of the officers of the army was held to consider the present state of affairs, with a view to their reform. A full, free, and rather stormy discussion took place. The assembled chiefs and officers declared that they would no longer obey two masters, meaning the King and his son. They complained of the gross cruelties practised by the Heir-Apparent, which the King had apparently made no efforts to check, and of the Prince's constant acts of violence and injustice, for which the sufferers had always been refused either compensation or redress. They de-

---

* This Rani, Lakshmi Devi, had herself two sons by the King; and it was feared that, in case of her becoming Regent, she might endeavour to put aside, in favour of her own sons, the two elder princes, whose mother had died in 1841.

nounced the excessive influence of the Chauntrias over
the King, and declared that it was always exerted to
the prejudice of the Rani. It was finally determined
that a committee should be formed, with orders to
frame a set of articles of agreement for presentation
to the King, in which should be clearly set forth the
unanimous resolve of the country that measures should
be adopted for the protection of the life, the property,
and all legitimate rights, public and personal, of all
subjects of the Crown, and also to ensure an effective,
as well as a responsible, administration of the Government.

The Maharajah was very anxious that his son
should be recognised as King (Maharaj-Dhiraj), but
without his own abdication; in fact, he wished to
establish the worst form of double government—that
in which two parties should possess power, but both
of them evade responsibility. The chiefs and officers,
however, steadily refused, and the King was obliged
to yield.

At a subsequent meeting, the draft of this petition,
the " Petition of Right," as it has been called, was
submitted to the ministers, chiefs, municipal authorities from all the towns of the valley, and the whole
body of officers of the army then at Kathmandu
(eight thousand strong), and was unanimously approved of and directed to be presented to the Maharajah for signature.

On the 7th of December 1842 the draft of this
Petition of Right was carried by an immense deputa-

tion to the Rajah in open Darbar, where it was sanctioned, signed, and duly ratified by the King. In it, considerable executive authority was vested in the Rani, by whom the chiefs hoped the King would be effectively controlled.

The new rules were said to be based on those of Dherba Sah, grandfather of Prithi Narayan, and every guarantee was considered to have been taken for their effectual performance. This revolution was completed after twelve days' anxiety and deliberation among the leaders and representatives of all parties in the State, whom a common sense of wrong and danger had united in one common cause; and it is highly creditable to all parties—both those of the people and those of the Crown—that so important and exciting a struggle was concluded without any acts of violence, riot, or disturbance on either side.

In conformity to the agreement he had been bound to by the chiefs, the King, in January 1843, formally invested the Rani, Lakshmi Devi, with full political rights as Queen, promising that in all matters connected with the government of the country he would take her into his counsels, and act in accordance with her advice.

Chauntria Fath Jang Sah was continued in office as Premier, but the natural indolence of his character made him a mere tool in the hands of his able brother Guru Parsad, who was always opposed to the Queen.

CHAPTER XXIV.

1843.—But though the Maharajah, for some years past, had been entirely in the hands of the Pandis, and had uniformly supported their policy and party, various causes had of late combined to alienate him from them. The falsity of all their predictions with respect to the downfall of the British in China and Afghanistan had destroyed his confidence in their political sagacity; while their support of the Heir-Apparent in his resistance and indignities to his father, even if they did not actually instigate him to their commission, combined with the clumsy bungling manner in which they had allowed the King's name to become implicated in the false charge of having poisoned the late Queen in 1841, had made them personally obnoxious to him. In addition to these various reasons, the death of the late Maharani, who

had always been a firm adherent to the Pandis, not
only left their party unsupported by petticoat influence within the Palace, but enabled the present
Queen, who was and ever had been an ally of the
Thappas, to use all her power over her imbecile
husband for the advancement of her own friends,
and the ruin and disgrace of her political opponents.
As long as the Maharani was alive, although the
Pandis continued in favour, yet the personal as well
as political rivalry between the two queens—one an
ally of the Pandis, the other of the Thappas
—prevented either of the two great parties of the
State from becoming unduly powerful, or from mono-
polising for any length of time all the sweets of office.
But no sooner did the death of the Maharani destroy
this " balance of power " within the Palace, than the
surviving Queen, now without a rival, used all her
influence over her husband so effectually to the prejudice of her opponents, that she soon managed to get
nearly all the power of the State into the hands of
herself and her partisans. The great object of the
Queen's ambition was to set aside her two step-chil-
dren—the Heir-Apparent and his brother—and secure
the crown to the elder of her own two sons. She
knew that this scheme was impracticable as long as
either the Chauntrias or Pandis remained at the head
of the Government. The Chauntrias, as members of
the royal family, would naturally oppose any change in
the legitimate succession to the throne. The Pandis
were not only personally attached to the Heir-Appa-

rent—through whose means they hoped to be brought again into office—but they were certain to defend the interests of the late Maharani, who had always been a firm supporter of them and their party. Under these circumstances she determined to use every effort to reinstate the Thappas in power. The former leader of that powerful party, Bhim Sen, had been murdered, the present head of it, Martabar Singh, had been driven into exile, and the whole of their adherents had been most cruelly persecuted by the late Maharani and her partizans the Pandis.

She thereupon calculated that, if she could succeed in bringing back Martabar Singh to Nipal and securing to him the Premiership, a desire for vengeance on his own enemies, as well as a feeling of gratitude to her for effecting his restoration, would induce that statesman to join her party so cordially, that she hoped to make him a tool in her hands to remove, in the first place, her and his political enemies, and afterwards to set aside the children of that Maharani who had been the cause of all his and his uncle's misfortunes.

Acting on these principles, she easily convinced her imbecile husband that the Thappas were the only party on whom reliance could be placed for the proper government of the country, and that he should lose no time in persuading Martabar Singh to return to Nipal and investing him with the office of Premier.

General Martabar Singh had been living in voluntary exile in the British territories ever since 1838.

Intimation was accordingly sent to him by the Rajah, that he and the whole country were now convinced of the gross injustice which had been perpetrated against Bhim Sen and the Thappas generally, and assurances were given to him that his return to Nipal would lead not only to his own appointment as Premier, but to the restoration, to himself, to his family, and to all their adherents, of their confiscated property and titles. At the same time that he sent these messages to Martabar privately, the King publicly invested Fath Jang Chauntria with almost unlimited power as Minister, and professed the most abounded confidence in his talents and sagacity. The King wished to throw Fath Jang off his guard, and, by betraying him into some unusual stretch of power, to make him unpopular, and so prepare the way for his downfall.

Martabar Singh was too well aware of the insincerity of the King, and the insecurity of everything in Nipal, to yield at once to these alluring promises. He, however, left Simla, where he had been residing for some time on a pension of R. 1,000 a month from our Government, and came to Gorakhpur, the proximity of which place to the Nipalese frontier would enable him to communicate easily witn his friends at Kathmandu, and to ascertain from their reports the real state of feeling in the country, and what reliance he could place on the specious promises and prospects held out to him by his royal master.

As soon as it was known that he was on his way to the frontier, great anxiety was exhibited among all classes of the community for his arrival at the capital. Everyone sympathised with him in the misfortunes which he had undergone, and felt eager to atone for the indignities which had so unjustly been heaped on his late illustrious uncle. There was a general reaction in favour of the Thappas.

In February 1843 a deputation was despatched to Gorakhpur to meet him and escort him up to Nipal. In an evil hour Martabar accepted the invitation they brought him from the King, and quitting the protection of the British territories, he proceeded towards the capital of Nipal, accompanied by the deputation and a guard of honour. After halting for a few days on the confines of the valley, on the 17th of April he entered the city of Kathmandu, where he had an audience of the King, by whom he was received with the greatest distinction. He was attended on his entrance into Nipal by his nephew, Kaji Jang Bahadur, then quite a young man, who, since the downfall of Bhim Sen, had managed to elude the vengeance of the dominant party by leading a retired life, but who now took advantage of the recent change in public opinion to join his uncle on his way to Nipal, and, in attendance upon him, to come forward for the first time as a political character. This is the first appearance of Jang Bahadur on the stage of Nipalese politics, in which he has been destined to play so very prominent a part.

Martabar at once demanded to be confronted with, the former accusers of his uncle, in order that the charge of poisoning, under which his family had been ruined, might be fairly investigated. After a full investigation by a council of chiefs, the charges against Bhim Sen were declared to have been groundless; and the character and conduct of Martabar, as well as of his uncle, were declared to be cleared of all reproach. During the investigation before the Council, certain of the Pandis confessed to having perjured themselves in the prosecution of Bhim Sen, and to having wilfully deceived the King in their statements of the case, with a view to leading to Bhim Sen's overthrow. These parties were denounced by the Court as deserving of death; and a proclamation was issued by the King, vindicating the memory of Bhim Sen, and promising reparation to the Thapas as a party, and restitution to Martabar and his family of all their confiscated property.

In accordance with this verdict, the sentence of death was immediately executed upon the leaders of the Pandis, and on some of their adherents. Karbar Pandi and Kulraj Pandi, the most active members of the ministry which, under the nominal premiership of their brother, Ranjang Pandi, had murdered Bhim Sen, were beheaded. Ranjang Pandi himself was brought to the place of execution, but being at the time in a dying state, he was merely shown to the people and then removed to his own house, where he died naturally a few hours afterwards. Indar Bir Thappa and Ramham Thappa, two treacherous deserters of Bhim Sen's, and, in the hands of the

Pandis, the most active agents of mischief against their own party, were also beheaded, and with them was executed Kanak Sing Mahat, the late Chief Justice, or Ditha, who had drawn up the fictitious confession of guilt, under colour of which Bhim Sen had suffered. The Ditha is said to have been an honest man, and to have had no option as to the paper of confession, which was penned under the Rajah's own eye, and at his dictation. Bodman Karki was deprived of his lips and nose, and Bansraj Bashniat of his nose. Upwards of forty other Pandis with their families were banished to the plains, and their property confiscated.

During the remainder of the year Fath Jang continued in office as Premier, and no changes were made among his colleagues in the Cabinet.

Martabar remained out of office; he became the most influential person in the Darbar, and though the leaders of all sides paid court to him, he carefully held aloof, biding his time, and openly identified himself with none of the rival parties in the State.

The King appears to have distrusted Martabar and suspected that he was in league with the Queen, and would assist her in achieving her own objects of ambition at the expense of himself and the Heir-Apparent. For this reason, the King kept delaying to appoint Martabar as Premier, and pushed forward the Heir-Apparent,* encouraging him to take upon himself

---

* He was married in May 1843.

an undue assumption of authority, in order that the young Prince might be in a better position to defend his own and his father's rights.

At last, however, the King was obliged to yield to the constantly exerted influence of his Queen, and the loudly expressed desire of his subjects, that the existing weak Cabinet of Fath Jang should be dissolved, and that the reins of government should be placed in the hands of Martabar Singh.

On the 25th of December 1843, General Martabar Singh was formally appointed Prime Minister and Commander-in-Chief. His appointment took place in a very full Darbar, and apparently met with general approval of all parties in the State, including even the Chauntrias. (At this time Ranbir Thappa, brother to Bhim Sen, and uncle to Martabar, was living in Kathmandu in the guise and manner of a Fakir.)

Martabar's violent temper and arrogant bearing made him personally unpopular with the other Sardars, but he was most cordially supported by the whole of the army, with whom he had ever been a favourite. He soon felt the difficulty of the "double government" of the King and Heir-Apparent, and openly expressed his unwillingness to serve "two masters." His remonstrances appear to have given offence to his royal masters, and in his bearing towards them he probably arrogated to himself more than either King or Prince were disposed to concede.

In May 1844 he resigned his appointment as Minister, and expressed his desire to quit the country for the plains. He was persuaded to continue to act "until his successor should be appointed," and in October he consented formally to "officiate" as Premier, in order, as he said, "to keep the soldiery quiet." His resignation and reappointment was doubtless only a party move, to ascertain the strength of his hold on the King and on the Court. The violent excesses of the Heir-Apparent continued to cause great discontent throughout the country; among other amusements, he took to maltreating even Brahmans and cows.* His violent conduct had at first been encouraged by his father for party purposes, partly with a view to check the schemes of the Queen, and partly as a means of drawing out the opinions of the leading Sardars, and eliciting their supposed treasonable designs. His violence, however, at length became quite uncontrollable, and became the more serious as he now openly avowed his intention of making the King abdicate in his favour, and it was feared that, in the unsettled state of the country, and with so many opposing parties at Court, his wild and reckless conduct might excite a revolution.

In December 1844 the Heir-Apparent, in disgust that his father would not abdicate, suddenly left the valley with a large body of troops and a number of the leading Sirdars, and repaired to the Terai, declaring that he would not return until the throne was

---

* Sir Henry Lawrence writes that the "most fruitful sources of disturbance in Nipal are women and cows!"

vacant. The King and Martabar very shortly joined him. At Hitowara the Rajah and Prince had a violent quarrel, the latter threatening to lead the troops across the British frontier. The troops and the Sardars, headed by Martabar, sided with the Prince, and induced the King to a partial abdication; the King agreeing to remain on the throne, but investing his son with authority to issue all orders, and to enforce their obedience.

Ever since his return to Nipal, Martabar had secretly been anxious to induce the King to abdicate in favour of the Heir-Apparent. At first he proposed that, in case of the King's abdication, the Queen should be made Regent, and he himself be Premier. Gagan Singh and Abhiman Rana were in league with him to effect this change, but they were so anxious to secure all the power in their own hands, that Martabar abandoned the scheme of a Regency, and openly advocated the claims of the Heir-Apparent. This made for him a mortal enemy in Gagan Singh as well as in the Queen. The latter would have been delighted at being made Regent, as she then hoped to be able to carry out her favourite plan of setting aside the Heir-Apparent, on the plea of insanity, which the extravagance of his conduct might have easily been made to bear out. Martabar knew both father and son well; and calculated that he could control the youthful extravagances of the Prince more easily than he could the cowardly, cunning, and vacillating character of the Rajah. The sudden expedition to the Terai, and the threat to cross the British frontier with troops, was merely a ruse, done with the hope that the angry remonstrances of the British Government on the occasion of such an outrage would frighten the timid monarch into a surrender of the throne to his son. After this scene was over at Hitowara, the King, with his son, Martabar, and the whole camp, returned to Kathmandu. Before leaving the Terai, however, the Prince indulged his love of bloodshed by causing sixteen officers and soldiers, who had used threatening language to Martabar Singh, and had remonstrated against the transfer of authority from the King to his son, to be summarily executed, without trial or confession, in his presence.*

Martabar appears to have made up his mind as to which of the three rival powers at Court—the King, the Queen, and the Heir-Apparent—he should support against the other two. The King had mistrusted him all along; the Queen, in effecting his restoration to power, had calculated on obtaining a powerful but willing instrument to carry out her own views; she now found out how mistaken she was in her estimate of Martabar's character, who, though violent in temper, and vindictive too, was too loyal and high-minded a statesman to be capable of perpetrating an act of treason and gross injustice.

In advocating the King's voluntary abdication in

---

* This took place at Dhupoabasa, half-way between Bichalesh and the Cheryaghatti pass.

favour of the Heir-Apparent, he was guilty of no dis-
loyalty, but he made mortal enemies of both the Rajah
and the Queen. They concealed their resentment for
a time, from fear of the army, with whom Martabar
was a favourite; but from the date of this excursion
to Hitowara they both determined that their too
powerful and courageous Minister must be got rid of.

Kaji Jang Bahadur warmly supported his uncle in
advocating the cause of the Heir-Apparent. He could
personally bear the Prince no good will; the Prince
having frequently beaten and maltreated him, and on
one occasion made him jump into a well to escape with
his life. Jang showed his foresight and sagacity by
adhering to the side of the Prince, which he knew
would in the end be successful. He was somewhat
of a time-server, having warmly supported the Chauntrias so long as they were in possession of power.
After his return from the Terai, the King seems to
have summoned courage and retracted his abdication,
and reasserted his own position as ruler of the country,
the Prince only acting as Minister of his orders. He
arranged that he would consult with the Prince in all
matters; that the Prince should give orders to the
Minister, who should see to their execution.

The better to throw Martabar Singh off his guard,
and remove any suspicions he might entertain of secret
ill-will being felt towards him by the King or Queen,
he was publicly invested by the Rajah as Minister for
life, on the 4th of January 1845; honours were heaped
upon him by the King, and his power and services

appeared to be recognised universally.* He seemed to have reconciled father and son, and to have gained equal power over both of them. The other chiefs and Sirdars submitted to his authority without opposition, and, excepting the Thappas, he kept most of them in the background.

Despite his apparently powerful position, Martabar seems to have had misgivings as to its probable durability. On the 26th of February† he told the Resident that every minister since the days of Prithi Narayan had met with a violent death, "but he hoped that he should escape."

The Chauntrias in particular appear to have dreaded his power, and to have been apprehensive lest they should be treated by this all-powerful Minister as the Pandis had been. There is no reason to think that there was any real foundation for their alarm, but under the influence of it, whether well founded or not, Fath Jang Chauntria, who had been appointed Governor of Palpa, suddenly left his province, in company with Kaji Abhiman Rana, and proceeded towards Gaya. Martabar, apprehensive lest these and other malcontents should unite with Pandi exiles at Be-

---

* He was publicly invested by the King with some gold medals (which Martabar wore round his neck till the day of his death) recording that he had saved the life and throne of the King and of the Prince.

† In February 1845 Prince Waldemar and suite paid a visit to Nipal.

nares and other parts of the plains, ordered, on the
13th of April, Fath Jang's house and property to be
confiscated, as a punishment for his unauthorised flight
from the country.

With a view still further to increase his popularity
with the army, and probably doubting the strength of
his position, Martabar, in the spring of 1845, raised
three new regiments. This appears to have alarmed
the King, who felt that he was becoming a mere
cipher—that Martabar and the Prince really governed
the country, though they paid him the compliment of
doing so in his name. The King, urged on by the
Queen and her friends, determined at once to get rid
of Martabar, hoping thereby to recover his own
authority and position, and little foreseeing that the
removal of his courageous though free-spoken Minister
would merely transfer all authority in the State to
the hands of the Queen and her paramour, Gagan
Singh, and leave him in reality as great a cipher as
ever.

On the 17th of May 1845 General Martabar Singh
was murdered. On the 18th a deputation, with Kaji
Jang Bahadur as spokesman, was sent by the King
to report to the Resident, "that, on the previous
night, Martabar had been put to death by the Rajah,
for arrogating to himself the powers of sovereignty;

---

* These are the words of the official report by Major Lawrence.

for killing (in December 1844, at Hitowara) sixteen soldiers; for threatening to resume the lands of the Brahmans; for employing the soldiers as labourers; and for proposing to set up the second prince on the throne. That for these and other offences he had been put to death in the Palace, as His Highness feared to execute him publicly, owing to his influence with the soldiery." Although the King attributed the murder of these sixteen men at Dhupoabasa, without their having made confession, as a crime to Martabar, there is little doubt that the person who really ordered the execution was the Heir-Apparent. On this occasion Jang was as loud on the demerits of his uncle, as a month before he had been on those of the Chauntrias.

Whatever faults Martabar had committed, they were chiefly faults of temper and bearing; his public and official acts appear to have been approved of, or at least acquiesced in, by the King and all the chiefs up to the very day of his death. He was treacherously murdered from private motives of party policy; not privately executed, as the King would represent, for offences which he had committed against the State.

It appears that, on the night of the 17th, Martabar was suddenly called to the Palace, at 11 P.M., on pretence of an accident having occurred to the Queen. Suspecting nothing, he immediately obeyed the summons; and on entering the apartment in which the King and Queen were sitting together, and approaching to pay his usual respects, he was shot at from behind a trelliced screen,* one ball entering his head, and two or more, besides some small shot, entering his body. Staggering forward, he called for mercy for his mother and children; but as he spoke, he was struck to the ground from behind, and as in the agonies of death his hands were stretched out in supplication to his King, one of the attendants cut him with a sword across the wrists, and nearly severed them from his arms. His mangled remains were then let down into the street from a window, by a rope, and before daylight the corpse was despatched, by a party of soldiers, to Pashpatinath to be burnt. The road leading to the temple, about two miles distant from the Palace, was sprinkled with the blood which trickled from the numerous wounds which had been inflicted on the body.

The day before the assassination several of the Chauntrias, who for some time had been absent from the Darbar, privately visited the King, and it is supposed that they were in the Rajah's confidence, and were aware of his intentions, though they had no share in the actual commission of the murder. The man who took the chief part in the murder was Kaji Gagan Singh, the confidential attendant and reputed paramour of the Queen, and notoriously an enemy to Martabar.

---

* The murder is said to have been seen, in all its details, through the crevices of the trap-door above the staircase leading into the room in which it occurred.

A month after the murder the King sent a letter to the Governor-General, informing him of the tragedy which had occurred, and giving his reasons for its commission. After charging Martabar with treason, &c., the King said, " Therefore *I* put the said traitor Thappa to death *with my own hands*, killing him with gun and sword." On which Sir Henry Lawrence (then Resident) remarks, "Gagan Singh and four or five others killed the Minister. The Maharajah, may have mangled the corpse; but I much doubt His Highness having courage to fire a gun, much more to face his late Minister."

About the same time some people accused Jang Bahadur of having been concerned in the murder of his uncle; but at that time Jang always most positively denied the truth of the report, and it was not generally believed. Colonel Lawrence says at the time, "Poor as is my opinion of Jang's moral character, I do believe him guiltless of this murder." This view is confirmed by the fact that, immediately on hearing of their father's murder, Colonel Ranujal Thappa, Martabar's legitimate son, and Captain Ranjor Thappa, his natural son, took refuge with Jang Bahadur, which they would hardly have done had they even suspected him of being privy to their father's death. Jang assisted them in securing their father's jewels and treasure, and started them off, with some of their personal attendants, privately, under the charge of one of his brothers, to Sigauli, where they arrived safely.

Since his return from England, Jang has openly avowed that he was the person who fired the first shot at Martabar, and says that he did so, after remonstrating in vain, in consequence of the King and Queen's urgent orders. He has, on three or four occasions, shown me the identical gun which he used on the occasion.

In a letter addressed by the King (15th of August 1847), after his deposition, to the Governor-General, he says, "On General Martabar Singh's misbehaving himself, I sent for Jang Bahadur, and ordered him to kill Martabar Singh, threatening him with death if he refused to obey."

With Jang were associated in the murder Gagan Singh and Kaji Kulman Singh Thappa, though it is impossible to say exactly what part each performed. This Kulman Singh Thappa was badly wounded in the massacre at the Kot by a cut on the head; he fell to the ground, and, with great presence of mind, remained motionless in the corner where he lay, and as his head and body were covered with blood, he passed for dead, and escaped with his life. He was, and is, an adherent of the Thappa party.

Immediately after the murder, parties of soldiers, with guns, were stationed around the Darbar and at all the city outlets, the King being apprehensive that the troops might become dangerously excited on hearing of the death of their favourite leader. Everything, however, remained tranquil; and on this occasion, as on a similar one, when Bhim Sen and his friends were treated with every indignity and cruelty in 1839, and again when the Pandis were executed in 1843, not a finger or a voice was raised by the soldiery in favour of the sufferers.

The Nipalese soldiers are at all times, and under all circumstances, most singularly obedient to the "powers that be"; and they obey the constituted authority—be it Rajah, Rani, Prince, or Minister—most unhesitatingly, and without any reference to the duty required or its consequences.

Finding that there was no danger of any insurrectionary movement on the part of the army, the King assembled the troops on the Tandakhel the next day, and told them that in future he intended to take upon himself alone the entire direction of the affairs of the State. Urgent orders were sent to the plains to the exiled or absent Chauntrias and Pandis to return at once to Nipal, as he intended to make Fath Jang, Chauntria, Minister.

A company of soldiers was sent to seize Thil Bikram Thappa, Governor of Palpa, and nephew to Martabar Singh, but he succeeded in escaping to the plains.

Until Fath Jang could return, and as a temporary arrangement, Jang Bahadur was appointed to officiate as Premier. He was about the same time made a general, and given the command of three regiments.

The King found considerable difficulty in forming a Cabinet, owing to the conflicting interests and rivalries of the different candidates for office. Fath Jang had returned to Nipal, but for some time remained

in retirement, and refused to be Premier unless he
should receive such full powers, and under such
special guarantees, as the King was either unable or
unwilling to give him. Of the other leading men,
Abhiman Rana, who had returned with Fath Jang
was one candidate ; Jang Bahadur another—he appeared to have succeeded his uncle as the special
supporter of the interests of the Heir-Apparent, and
was therefore not much in favour either with the
King or Queen. The most powerful candidate, however, was Kaji Gagan Singh, who was the special
favourite of the Rani.

Several months passed in party squabbling ; the
King and Queen became reconciled, and carried on
the government together, issuing orders in military
matters through Jang Bahadur, and in all civil cases
through Gagan Singh, who had become the most influential man now in the Darbar, and was the avowed
head of the numerous party who supported the Rani's
interests.

In September 1845 Fath Jang's scruples as to ac-
cepting office were overcome by the King, and he
accepted the appointment of President or Premier of
a kind of " coalition " Cabinet consisting of himself,
Gagan Singh, Abhiman Rana, and Dalbanjan Pandi.
Gagan Singh, by the Queen's interest, was made a
General and Commander-in-Chief with the command
of the seven regiments employed about the capital,
and the charge of all the magazines and army supplies. He also superintended all the local affairs of

the Darbar. He* had got, by this arrangement, all real power into his own hands as head of the now dominant party of the Queen, and was the actual Premier in all except the name. Fath Jang's duty was to conduct the civil government of Gorkha, Palpa, and Western Nipal, and to have the management of foreign (*i.e.* British and Chinese) affairs. Abhiman Rana had charge of Eastern Nipal. While Dalbanjan Pandi, a respectable old man, had no special duty; he was merely placed in the Cabinet as a means of satisfying the Pandi party that their interests would be protected by the new Government. Jang Bahadur had no office in the Government. He was generally looked upon as a fifth or military member of the Ministry, but he was not actually in the Cabinet.

Jang's exclusion from office was the result of his being looked on by the King and Queen as a partisan of the Heir-Apparent, whose influence at this juncture was giving way before that of his step-mother, and who was known to favour Jang, while he detested the other Ministers. At the same time, Jang was known to be a man of so much energy, talent,

---

* The elevation of Gagan Sing gave great offence and caused great jealousy among the Sirdars generally, as but a few years back Gagan Sing had been but a common Darbar menial. He was originally a Chobdar, or Khuwassia, in the Queen's service; a name here given to male menial servants permitted to enter the female apartments in care of young princes, &c. Though discontented, the Sirdars could not openly oppose the favourite of the day.

and daring, that the Court could not afford to make an enemy of him ; he was therefore allowed to retain the rank of general, with the command of the three regiments previously given to him. But he had no actual office in the Government.

The new Cabinet professed very friendly sentiments towards the British Government, and the Maharajah formally offered the use of his army in the event of hostilities occurring between the British and the Sikhs. He repeated the offer on hearing of the battles of Mudki and Firozeshahr. The Lahor Government applied to the Nipalese to assist them by making a diversion in our rear, in the Terai or towards Oudh. The King sent an answer that " when the Sikhs had taken Delhi it would be time enough to think of it." At the time of the Panjab war, individuals might, and did, talk arrogantly of war ; but no party, nor people of influence, ever thought of serious collision with the British.

After hearing of the victory of Sobraon the Rajah made a formal request to the Governor-General, " that the British Government, in this day of its triumph, and augmented possessions, should give something out of its abundance to its poor friend of Nipal, which had been so staunch, and offered her troops so often." He modestly asked for Kamaon, or some territory in the Terai yielding two or two and a half lakhs !

CHAPTER XXV.

For upwards of a year after the murder of Martabar Singh no material changes occurred in the state of parties and politics at Kathmandu. Unavowed jealousies naturally existed among the Ministers, but nothing occurred which seemed likely to lead to a " breach of the peace."

There were three distinct parties at the capital :—

1st. *The party of the Queen*, who was anxious to secure the crown for her own son, and meantime the Regency for herself. This party, by far the most powerful, was led by General Gagan Singh, Commander-in-Chief. Although a parvenu, his personal demeanour was not arrogant, but his birth and previous occupation made him unpopular with the other chiefs ; while his notorious amour with the Queen made him an object of jealousy and dislike to the King and royal family. He always openly used the name and authority of the Queen, whose agent he professed to be, and on whom he was constantly in attendance.

2nd. *The party of the Heir-Apparent.*—The Prince was now comparatively quiet, and his party neither numerous nor strong. His chief partisan, Jang Bahadur, was growing lukewarm, and seemed half inclined to join the Queen's side.

3rd. *The party of the Rajah.*—This included the Chauntrias and many of the more quiet and least ambitious of the chiefs. The King, though weak and vacillating himself, had hitherto succeeded in playing the rival parties so cleverly one against the other that things had, on the whole, turned out very much to his own profit and advantage. His chief stay was on Fath Jang, a high-minded and unambitious chief, who was then evidently waiting for events, and though nominally Premier, took very little part in any of the business of Government except that belonging to the foreign department. General Abhiman Rana followed the lead of Fath Jang, and confined his attention to civil affairs. He was a sensible, well-disposed man, but of no great energy or ability.

The Rajah apparently kept now on good terms both with the Queen and the Prince; but the amour of the former with Gagan Singh, not only as affecting his personal honour, but as giving too much power to the faction opposed to his own interests, made him determine on destroying General Gagan Singh.* He

---

* This account of the causes which led to Gagan Singh's death, and of the parties who brought it about, was given to Colonel

dissembled, however, so cleverly that the Queen even never suspected him of feeling any jealousy on the subject, nor of being in any way implicated in the death of her lover. The King secretly pointed out to his two sons the disgrace attaching to the royal house from the intimacy notoriously existing between the Queen and her favourite Minister, adding that he was powerless against the lady, but that the two princes had better avenge the family honour, and adopt some measures to have Gagan Singh destroyed. The younger prince (Mihla Sahib) being quite a lad, was allowed to go about without restraint or suspicion, and had become very intimate with Fath Jang's family. To Fath Jang he disclosed the scheme, and by his assistance he managed to secure a man, named Lal Jha, who undertook to shoot the General.*

Thoresby, in 1847, in conversation, by the Heir-Apparent after he had ascended the throne. It accounts for some apparent inconsistencies as to the origin of the massacre at the Kot, and may be believed as true.

* Lal Jha was an intriguing mischievous Brahman—a notorious scoundrel—who had frequently been confined, but had always managed to escape for want of positive evidence against him. After the murder of Gagan he escaped to Bettiah, where he met Kaji Jagat Bam Pandi, of the Kalapandar, an exile, who engaged him in a plot to return to Nipal and kill Jang Bahadur. On the road to Nipal, through the Terai, he and his accomplices were seized by the "awal" fever, but managed to get on to Kathmandu, where Lal Jha was arrested as a suspicious character. He sank under the "awal," and when near his death he publicly confessed that he had killed Gagan Sing, and had come back to kill Jang Bahadur, having been promised promotion and rewards by Jagat Bam Pandi if he succeeded in doing so.

23 *

Besides Fath Jang, General Abhiman Singh Rana, Kaji Dalbanjan Pandi, and Bir Kishor Pandi were all privy to the scheme, as, of course, was the King himself, who had originated the whole. Jang Bahadur, as being supposed to be inclined to the Queen's side, was kept in perfect ignorance of everything connected with the plot.

On the night of the 14th of September 1846, at 10 P.M., General Gagan Singh, while engaged in prayer in a chamber in his own house, was killed by a shot fired at him through an open window from an adjoining roof of the building. The shot was fired by Lal Jha, who, in the confusion that ensued, managed to escape from the city, and proceeding direct to the plains, arrived safely at Bettiah.

The news of this murder was immediately carried to the Queen, at her palace, Hanuman Dhoka, by the General's son, Captain Wazir Singh. The Queen at once set out on foot for the late General's house, attended by only four female servants. After viewing the corpse of her lover, she vowed vengeance on his murderers, promised him a funeral at the public expense, and forbad his three widows to perform satti. Then taking the sword of state (to which, as a sort of Regent, she was entitled) in her own hand, she proceeded to the Kot, or Court of Assembly for Military Purposes, and ordered the bugles to be sounded for the collection of the troops, and messengers to be sent to summon an immediate assembly of all the civil and military functionaries of the State.

Meantime, Jang Bahadur, having heard of what had passed, arrived at the Kot, in company of his brothers, at the head of the three regiments under his command. He stated that, as General Gagan Singh and himself had been together the Rani's especial servants, and, as Gagan Singh was now murdered, he felt that his own life was also in danger from the same quarter; and that as the Queen's own life and that of her sons were probably in danger, he advised that an immediate and strict examination into all the circumstances of the case should be instituted, and that severe punishment should be inflicted on all those who should be proved to be guilty. At the same time he urged on the Queen that, as the King had already, in January 1843, invested her with full political authority in all affairs of the State, she should now act entirely on her own responsibility.

While Jang was conversing with the Queen, General Abhiman Singh Rana had gone to the Palace and brought the King to the Kot, where, meantime, all the sardars and officers of the State, mostly unarmed, had assembled in pursuance of the Queen's orders—with the exception of Fath Jang Chauntria and his relatives, who had not yet arrived. Remarking their absence, the Queen sent Jang's brother Bam Bahadur to summon them without delay. At the same time she ordered General Abhiman Singh Rana to have Kaji Bir Kishor Pandi put in irons, as she suspected him of being a party, if not a principal, to the murder of the General. The order was immediately executed, the Kaji strongly asserting his own innocence. Enraged at his continued denials of all knowledge of the crime, the Queen ordered General Abhiman Rana to cut off his head. The General referred to the King, who was present, for his orders; but the King, knowing well who was the real criminal, would not sanction such an execution without the trial or confession of the prisoner. The General, therefore, refused to obey the Rani, as her orders were in defiance of those of the King, and left the Queen's presence.

The Rani at once sent for Jang, and ordered an immediate council to be held without waiting for the return of Bam and the Chauntrias. The King, however, only too glad of an excuse for postponing the stormy discussion which he knew would arise, and in which he was afraid it might transpire that he himself was the author, and the Chauntrias the abettors, of the late murder, said that no council would be safe, nor investigation complete, without Fath Jang's presence and 'prudence to guide it, and rode off in company with Kaji Badrinar Singh (Jang's brother) to Fath Jang's house. After delaying some time there, he sent off Fath Jang to the Kot in company with his son Kharak Bikram Sah and his two brothers—Sirdar Bir Bahadur Sah and Captain Ransher Sah—with some other members of the family, as well as with Bam Bahadur and Badrinar Singh.

The King himself then, afraid to be present at the investigation ordered by the Rani, with his usual cowardice, slunk away alone, and repaired to the

British Residency under the pretext of wishing to inform the Resident, whom the event in no way concerned, of the murder of Gagan Singh. It being past midnight, an interview was not effected, and the King returned towards the Kot. On reaching its neighbourhood, the gutter in the street was crimson from the blood flowing from the inside of the Kot. So sudden had been the massacre. The people about persuaded the King to retire, out of harm's way, into his Hanuman Dhoka Palace.

On the approach of Fath Jang and his party to the Kot, they were met by General Jang Bahadur, who was now acting as agent for the Queen. After relating to the Chauntrias all that had occurred, and how Abhiman Rana had refused to execute Bir Kishor Pandi although ordered to do so by the Rani, whose authority was now supreme, he proposed, as a means of appeasing the infuriated Queen and so bringing matters into a tranquil state, that both Abhiman Rana and the Pandi should be summarily executed; and he offered, with Fath Jang's approval, to effect their deaths at once. In which case, he added, Fath Jang should continue as Premier, while he, Jang, would be Commander-in-Chief, and would act under Fath Jang's orders.

It is evident, from this proposal, that neither the Queen nor her spokesman, Jang, at that time suspected the Chauntrias of being privy to Gagan Singh's death; and also that at that time Jang had no idea or anticipation of the massacre which was about to ensue, which was not premeditated by anyone, but arose suddenly and unexpectedly out of an accidental collision between a few individuals, at a time when the passions of all were strongly excited by the tragic event which had just occurred, and to investigate which they were then assembled.

Fath Jang, however, refused to be a party to this plan, and proposed that the Pandi should be fairly tried, and, if found guilty, punished; but he thought that Abhiman Rana had only done his duty. In making this proposal, Fath Jang well knew that no evidence could be brought against the Pandi; and he probably calculated that, during the trial, time would be gained, during which he and the other Ministers, who were privy to the murder, might adopt measures of defence against the Queen and her partisans. Had the King but had the courage to have been present to support with his authority and approval the reasonable proposal of his minister and friend, there can be no doubt that the whole affair would have been quietly settled, and the subsequent bloodshed avoided. Throughout the whole proceedings the King exhibited the greatest weakness, cowardice, and irresolution; and on him, not on Jang, ought the responsibility and blame of the subsequent slaughter to be fixed.

This conversation between Jang and Fath Jang took place in the quadrangle surrounding the building of the Kot. When it was over, Fath Jang went into the lower room on the ground floor, where Abhiman Singh Rana was sitting, and Jang went up to the Rani on the second or upper floor. It is sup-

posed that Fath Jang repeated to Abhiman Singh
what Jang had just said to him; for Abhiman Singh
immediately sent for the officers of his three regiments and desired them to be on the alert, and to load
their muskets with balled cartridges. Jang, seeing
from the window that the men were loading, directed
the Rani's attention to the fact. She immediately
left him and descended, sword in hand, to the large
western apartment, where Fath Jang, Abhiman Singh,
Dalbanjan Pandi, and the other Sirdars, with some of
Jang's brothers, were assembled. Addressing them
all, she called out, "Who has killed my faithful
General Gagan Singh? Name him quickly." No
one answered, but Fath Jang promised a full investigation. Much enraged, the Rani tried to use her own
sword on Bir Kishor Pandi, who was in irons, but
the three ministers restrained her, and trying to
pacify her, followed her from the hall towards the
upper story. The Rani mounted the dark and narrow
staircase alone, the three ministers waiting at the
foot of it (it is a steep narrow ladder rather than a
staircase, dark, and surmounted by a trap-door), and
preparing to follow her as soon as she had reached
the second story, when suddenly shots were fired
within the building, and Fath Jang and Dalbanjan
Pandi fell dead, and Abhiman Singh Rana wounded.
Abhiman Singh, exclaiming "This is Jang's treachery," staggered back to the hall, and endeavoured
to get out of it to join his regiment, which was outside the building, in the surrounding quadrangle; but

Krishna Bahadur, with one stroke of his sword, nearly cut him in two, and he fell dead. This occurred in the presence of a number of Sirdars, Kajis, and other officers, among whom was Kharak Bikram Sah, son of Fath Jang, and several other Chauntrias.

Hearing of his father's death in the adjoining passage-room, and seeing Abhiman Singh cut down before his eyes, Kharak Bikram Sah hastily drew his kukery, and rushing on Bam Bahadur, inflicted a gash across his head, and another across the head of Krishna Bahadur; then having cut down a sepoy, he turned again upon Bam Bahadur, who, quite unprepared for this sudden melée, was somewhat stunned by the blow on his head, and half blinded by the blood which was streaming over his face, was endeavouring to draw his talwar from its sheath, in which it was fastened by a twisted knot. Kharak Bikram Sah's hand was upraised, and in another instant he would have cut down Bam, who was incapable of defending himself from his sword being entangled, when Jang Bahadur (who had been upstairs till now, but on hearing the noise below had rushed down) entering the apartment, and seeing his brother's danger, seized a rifle and shot Kharak Bikram Sah through the chest, and he, staggering backwards, was despatched by a sword-cut from Deher Shamshir, Jang's youngest brother. This was Jang's first appearance on the scene of bloodshed; he had been above at its commencement, waiting for and upon the Rani, and only came down on hearing the firing below.

The unpremeditated origin of the disturbance is confirmed by the fact of Bam being unarmed, except with his talwar, which he had not even taken the precaution to have ready for use, and which he had not time to draw in self-defence, before he was attacked. Who fired the first and fatal shots on the three Sardars (Fath Jang, Dalbanjan Pandi, and Abhiman Rana) as they followed the Queen out of the apartment, is unknown.* There had been high words passing below among the Sardars of different parties as the Queen withdrew, and it is probable that in the excitement of the wrangling, one or more of Jang's younger brothers, who were present, on seeing Abhiman Rana's soldiers loading their muskets in accordance with that General's orders, imagined that this

---

* In reporting to the Resident his own nomination to the office of Sole Premier on the 16th of September (two days after the massacre), and giving an account of the matter, Jang stated that on the Council being assembled to investigate into the death of Gagan Sing, the Queen publicly accused all the ministers by name as accomplices in the murder, and she called out to Gagan Sing's regiment to seize them, and she would have put them all to death *en masse*. Great confusion followed; the ministers mutually recriminated each other, swords were drawn, and the first blood was shed by Fath Jang's son, who attacked and wounded Bam Bahadur. He said that Fath Jang himself and the other ministers were killed, not at the outbreak, but during the progress of the slaughter. Jang says that had he not restrained her she would have put the Heir-Apparent and his brother to death at the time of the massacre, and imprisoned the Rajah. He always maintains that the massacre originated entirely in the violent and outrageous conduct of the Queen, who, holding supreme power at the time, ought to be held responsible for it.

was preliminary to some treachery against them or Jang, and rashly gave the order to fire on General Abhiman Rana. In the heat of the moment this order being obeyed by more than one excited partisan, several shots were fired at the General at the same instant, and Chauntria Fath Jang and Dalbanjan Pandi, who were standing at the time close to him, fell dead by the same discharge by which he was mortally wounded.

Blood having thus been shed, the fierce passions of those present were excited beyond all control. Everyone distrusted his neighbour, and, in self-defence, all who had arms drew them and prepared, if necessary, to sell their lives as dearly as possible. The confusion was extreme in the small, low, and badly lighted apartments and passages of the building. In an instant swords were used, more blood was shed, and a promiscuous melée ensued, which, as a large number of the assembly were unarmed, soon became a slaughter rather than a fight. A party of Jang's followers and personal attendants, armed with double-barrelled guns, forced their way into the building, determined to defend their master and his brothers to the last. Round them those of the Thappa party rallied, and, with Jang at their head, commenced firing on all who seemed opposed to them. It was a moment when Jang felt that all who were not friends to him must be enemies, and all present who were not members of, or known to be attached to, his party were ruthlessly shot or cut down. Some were saved by Jang's brothers, who put them out of the Kot by a small doorway at its back.

As soon as the death of Abhiman Rana was known, his troops and followers, in alarm, fled; so that Jang's own corps, named after Kali Baksh, had little difficulty in gaining possession of the quadrangle surrounding the Kot, the outlets of which they secured, and then opening their fire, they picked off, with little danger or loss to themselves, all members of the assembly, armed or unarmed, who were opposed to them. Those who took refuge inside the Kot were shot or cut down by the party who had rallied round Jang in person; those who came out into the quadrangle were at once slaughtered by the men of his regiment, who were in possession of it on every side. The massacre was quickly over, as resistance was feeble and unavailing. While it lasted, the Queen stood at the open window of the uppermost story, urging on the soldiers, and calling out to them, "Kill and destroy my enemies." The bodies of the slain were heaped up together, without reference to rank, and nearly filled the small quadrangle surrounding the Kot.

Before the slaughter was well over, the Queen conferred the office of Premier and Commander-in-Chief upon General Jang Bahadur; and he presented to her his nazar of acknowledgment. The Queen remained in the upper story of the Kot, a calm and unmoved witness of the horrors that were perpetrated below, till daybreak, when Jang conducted her to the Hanuman Dhoka Palace, and then he proceeded to present his nazar, and pay his respects as Premier, to the King and the prince. The King angrily demanded of him, " By whose order have so many chiefs and officers of the State been slaughtered ? " Jang replied, " Everything has been done by the orders of the Queen, to whom your Majesty yourself made over sovereign power."

The King hastily repaired to the Rani for an explanation of her conduct, but he found that royal tigress, who, when inflamed by the passion of revenge, had been an unmoved spectator of the past night's bloody massacre, now overcome by the natural feelings of her sex, and absorbed in grief at the loss of her lover. An angry altercation ensued, in which the Queen assured him that the only way to avoid further bloodshed would be to place the elder of her own two sons upon the throne. No satisfactory agreement being come to, the King, fearful for his own life, left her and accompanied by Sardar Bhowani Singh and Captain Karbar Khatri, started towards Patan, with the intention of proceeding to Benares.

As soon as the first outbreak of grief was over, the Queen sent for Jang and for Kaji Birdhig Bashniat, and ordered them to confiscate the property of all the Sardars and officers who had been killed or had fled, and to expel their families, wives, and children from the country*; and also to put the Heir-

---

* This order was executed to the letter. Each individual was allowed to carry away one bundle only of his personal property

Apparent and his brother under strict surveillance, and allow no one to approach them.

Karbar Khatri, who had been appointed by the Queen to act as a spy on the King's movements, having reported that the King, while *en route* to Patan, had held a private conversation with Bhowani Singh on the Tandi Khel, at which he was not allowed to be within hearing, the Queen sent a Subadar and fifty soldiers with strict orders to cut off and bring back with them Bhowani Singh's head. He was killed on the road, in the presence of the King, who made no effort to prevent the outrage, but continued his course to Patan, from which city, however, he was, after much difficulty, persuaded by one of Jang's brothers to return at night to the palace at Kathmandu.

For eight days all the troops and guns at the capital were kept in readiness around the Darbar, and at the different city gates, while hundreds of those connected either with those who had been killed, or with those who had fled, and all who were suspected of disaffection, were expelled the city. On the eighth day, order and tranquillity being entirely

---

or clothing. A few days afterwards, by Jang's influence and mediation, the expelled families of the fallen chiefs, mostly Chauntras, the male branches of which family were nearly exterminated in the fray, were recalled; but they refused to return, and proceeded on to the plains. All persons detected remaining concealed in Nipal, after ten days, were threatened with death.

re-established, Jang removed the troops to their own
quarters, and directed his attention more exclusively
to the performance of his general duties as Minister.

In an official report made to the Resident by Jang
Bahadur, the number of Sardars and military officers
killed in the massacre of the 14th and 15th of September was thirty-one. This did not include a considerable number of soldiers and others of no note
who were accidentally killed during the melée. A
great many more either absconded or concealed themselves. To this number may be added about twenty
more, of no great note, who were executed in November as members of the Bushniat conspiracy. Of
the Sardars killed at the massacre, the following were
the only men of any rank or importance in the State :
General Gagan Singh ; Fath Jang Sah, Chauntria, and
his son Kharak Bikram Sah; General Abhiman Singh
Rana; Kaji Dalbanjan Pandi; Kaji Ranjor Singh
Thappa, a son of the famous General Amar Singh who
commanded at Ramghar and Malaun in the Nipal
war of 1814–15; and Sardar Bhowani Singh. To
these may be added Bhir Dhuj Bashniat, who was
killed on the 31st of October. None of the others
who were killed had taken any prominent part in the
politics of the day.

The Panjanni occurring just at this time, Jang
had the opportunity—of which he, of course, freely
availed himself—of turning out of office, and from
the ranks of the army, any men who were disaffected
to his own interests, at the same time that he could,

and did, enrol and promote all his own family, friends, and relations.

The Heir-Apparent and his brother were still kept in confinement within their own portion of the Palace; but Jang himself visited them daily, and two of his brothers were constantly in attendance on them, as Jang knew that they required protection from the evil designs of the Queen. In fact, the Queen continually urged Jang to put the two princes to death, and place her eldest son on the throne. He steadily evaded her request, and took every precaution to preserve their lives.*

At last, Bhir Dhuj Bashniat told the Rani that Jang had been long attached to the Heir-Apparent, and now that he was Minister there was no chance of his consenting to injure him. He therefore proposed to the Queen, as a preliminary measure towards the completion of her designs, that Jang should be destroyed. As he promised his own active assistance in this plot, she conferred on him secretly a grant of the Wazirat, to be openly assumed on Jang's death.† Wazir Singh, eldest son of the late Gagan

---

* After the massacre the Rani, with Jang as Minister, really possessed and exercised supreme power; but the government was professed to be carried on by the King, Queen, and Heir-Apparent jointly (*tinon Sarkar*).

† The Bashniat conspiracy against Jang was originally to have been effected in the following manner. Jang and his brothers were to have been induced, on some pretext, to sleep in the apartments of the King and the two princes. The conspirators were

Singh, and who, on his father's death, had been
made a general, was a party to this arrangement,
which was made in the presence also of a Pandit
named Bijni Raj.* This Pandit revealed the whole
transaction to Jang, who quietly redoubled his precautionary measures for the safety of himself and the
Heir-Apparent.

On the morning of the 31st of October 1846, Wazir
Singh secretly took his regiment, with muskets loaded,
to the Kot, and concealed the men in the interior of
the building. Meantime the Queen sent Bhir Dhuj
to summon Jang to her presence in the Palace, whence
she proposed that they should proceed together to the
Kot. Jang, aware of the plot against him, immediately collected all his relatives, partisans, and
attendants, armed with guns, and was proceeding
towards the Darbar, when he met Bhir Dhuj in the
street. The latter, greatly alarmed at this sudden

---

then to have found some means of murdering the King and his
sons, and were then to have accused Jang and his brothers of the
deed, when their execution would have followed of course immediately. The elder of the Rani's own sons would then have been
placed on the throne, she herself made Regent, and Bhir Dhuj
Bashniat minister. It was probably either from feeling the difficulty of carrying out this plot successfully, or from some mis-
giving as to whether Jang did not suspect it, that the conspirators
altered their plan and endeavoured to allure Jang into the Kot,
where, had he arrived, there would have been another bloody
massacre of himself, his brothers, and their adherents.

* This Pandit was rewarded by Jang with the office of Raj
Guru, which he has ever since held.

rencontre, and suspecting his designs were discovered, put his hands together in a most respectful manner, and said that the Queen wished Jang to meet her in the Kot directly. "How can that be?" replied Jang. "As *you* have been appointed Minister, what can I be wanted for?" Bhir Dhuj, trembling with fear, gave no answer, and Jang made a sign to Captain Rana Mir Adhikari, who shot the traitor dead on the spot.

Jang immediately repaired to the Palace, and placing his turban at the feet of the King and Heir-Apparent, who happened to be together, requested either to be dismissed from his post at once as unworthy to hold it, or else to be invested with full authority to put to death all the enemies of the Heir-Apparent. The power asked for was at once granted by the King, who embraced Jang, and desired him to destroy all enemies of his son and of the throne, and to adopt any measures necessary for the safety of the State.

Quitting the Palace, Jang ordered the bugles to be sounded to warn all the troops to get under arms; after which, all those who had taken any part in the counsels of Bir Dhuj Bashniat were sought for and put to death. About fourteen or fifteen Bashniats and some four or five petty military officers suffered death. General Wazir Singh had taken timely flight, and escaped to the plains.*

---

* In August 1856, on the occasion of Jang Bahadur refusing the Premiership, when the ex-Maharajah was recounting Jang Bahadur's services to the State as a ground for conferring extra

24 *

In the evening Jang waited on the Maharani. by order of the Heir-Apparent, with a message that, as she had become his bitter enemy, her residence in Nipal was no longer desirable, and that she and her two sons must prepare to quit the country for the plains without delay.

Alarmed at the failure of all her plots, she made no demur; and leaving the Palace for the house of a friend, she commenced preparations for her departure. She succeeded in persuading her irresolute husband to accompany her, professedly on a pilgrimage in order to expiate the bloodshed of the 14th of September; and on the 23rd of November 1846 she, the King, and their two sons, started for Benares, the Heir-Apparent remaining in Nipal as Regent during the absence of his father.

Immediately after the detection of the Bhir Dhuj Bashniat conspiracy, Jang was formally re-confirmed by the King in the office of sole Premier, and honorary titles were conferred upon him and his family, as

---

honours upon him, he declared (although it has hitherto been repeatedly denied by Jang Bahadur and his brothers) that the massacre at the Kot in September 1846 was a premeditated affair, and was planned and carried out under written instructions sent from time to time by himself (the ex-King) to Jang Bahadur, who assembled the Sirdars on that evening .in order that he might put to death all who were supposed to be disaffected, or to have been engaged in the murder of Gagan Sing. He also added that it was to Jang Bahadur "that the State was indebted" for the massacre of the thirteen Bashniats in and about the Maharani's apartments on the night of the 31st October following.

a mark of the royal gratitude. "Rana Ji" was added to his family name of Konwe, and the jagirs formerly held by his grand-uncle, Bhim Sen, were restored to him. Jang appointed his own brothers and nearest relatives and friends to all the offices about the Darbar, or connected with the command of the army or government of the country.

The Queen and party arrived safely at Benares, and the King, having completed his pilgrimage and paid the usual devotions and customary fees at the shrines of the Holy City, it was expected that he would have returned to Nipal immediately. After some delay, he quitted Benares, leaving the Queen and her two sons behind him. He was accompanied as far as Govindganj, where he dismissed them, by a large number of the malcontent exiles, among whom were Guru Parsad Chauntria and Guru Rangunath Pandit.

The King arrived at Sigauli on the 25th of March, and for some time seemed uncertain as to whether or not he should return to Nipal. He continued to correspond with the Rani at Benares, who through Guru Parsad's agency easily gained him over to her views, and engaged him in a plot to reintroduce the exiles and refugees, who were to murder Jang and upset his government, as a necessary preliminary for her own return to Nipal in company with the King, whom she was most anxious to join at Sigauli. Several letters were sent by the Heir-Apparent and his brother, as well as by Jang, endeavouring to persuade the King to return at once to Kathmandu; but they

clearly told him that, after what had passed, it was
quite impossible that the Rani should be allowed to
re-enter Nipal, and that when he returned to his
capital he must leave her behind him in the plains.
He was informed also that it had been intimated to the
troops that as long as the King was absent from the
country no orders could be received from him, but that
the Heir-Apparent must be looked on as sole and
supreme authority. Nothing, however, seemed able to
make him break away from the influence which the
Rani and her able and intriguing partisans had established over him. He tried at one time tampering
with the troops and conspiring against Jang's life; at
another, letters full of flattery, cajolery, and false promises to his sons as well as to the very Minister whose
life he wished to take, and whose government he was
plotting to subvert.

Time passed on in these unsatisfactory negotiations,
till at length, on the 12th of May, two men were
arrested, having in their possession a document which
they had received from Chauntria Guru Parsad and
Kaji Jagat Bam Pandi, signed and sealed by the King,
and calling upon his " eight thousand troops and fifty-
six lakhs of subjects " to seize or kill the Minister
and all connected with him. This brought matters
to a crisis. All the troops were assembled, and the
King's orders read to them by Jang, who told them
" that most of them were acquainted with the merits
of the late events, that they had now received orders
direct from the King, and that he himself was Minister

and stood before them, and they could do to him as they thought proper." The troops, however, refused to recognise the validity of the order, and demanded for the safety of the country that the Heir-Apparent should be placed on the throne. The Prince was accordingly, on the 12th day of May 1847, proclaimed King, with the usual forms and amidst general acclamation. In the proclamation it was stated that "the Maharajah Raj Indra Bikram Sah having taken up his residence abroad, and also having exhibited, by the inconsistency of his conduct on various occasions, decided symptoms of insanity, which rendered it impossible that confidence could any longer be placed in him, he was to be considered as having abdicated the throne, and his son, Surindra Bikram Sah had accordingly succeeded him as Ruler of Nipal." A letter to this effect, entering fully into the reasons which induced them to place the Heir-Apparent on the throne, signed by three hundred and seventy Sardars, Kajis, military officers of different grades, and all the servants of the Government present in the capital, was sent to the King at Sigauli. In the course of it they say—"Your Highness, uniting with the Kala Pandis, caused General Bhim Sen Thappa to be murdered; then joining the party of the Thappas, you had the Pandis put to death. Afterwards in conjunction with the Rani, you caused the death of Martabar Singh; again, contrary to all precedent in your dynasty of fourteen generations, you gave absolute power to the Maharani, and so caused the massacre at the Kot; and now, lastly, you are sending orders for the murder of the present Minister, for no offence whatever."

It was not intended to exclude the King from the country, should he wish to return, but it was quite determined that he should have no share in the administration of affairs, nor possess any public authority. He was offered a handsome allowance if he preferred remaining in the plains to returning to Nipal. No commotion was excited by these events. The country was tired of party quarrels and of palace intrigues; they had had more than enough of massacres and revolutions; and they welcomed this as a final settlement which they hoped would secure to them the blessings of an undisputed succession to the throne, and a firm administration of the affairs of the State.

On hearing of what had occurred at Kathmandu, most of the Sardars and others in attendance on the King at Sigauli, left him and returned to Nipal, some with, some without, his permission. Numbers of the exiles collected in the neighbourhood of Bettiah, under the lead of Rangunath Pandi, and in communication with the ex-King, and with his sanction continued their plots against the life of Jang Bahadur.

Some parties of these exiles, taking advantage of their situation as refugees within the British territories, having made preparations apparently to annoy, if not to plunder, the Nipalese Terai, a regiment of four hundred men, under Captain Sanak Singh, were sent down from the capital to attack the marauders and defend the frontier. But it having been ascertained that, instead of a mere plundering party, Guru Parsad Chauntria and Jagat Bam Pandi had collected a large force of men of all sorts, four more regiments, under General Bam Bahadur, and accompanied by the second prince (Mihla Sahib), left Kathmandu on the 26th of July for the Terai, to be near at hand in case of need. It soon appeared that Guru Rangunath Pandi had come over from Benares with messages from the Queen, and had entirely gained over the King and persuaded him to join the rebel camp, and that the ex-King had suddenly left Sigauli on the 23rd and gone to Alu in the Nipal Terai, where Guru Parsad and his men were encamped. Rangunath himself, to be out of harm's way, returned to Benares after the ex-King's departure for the frontier. The King had evidently been misled most grossly as to the support he was likely to receive in thus entering his country again at the head of an armed force. He expected that the troops would flock to his standard from all quarters, and that he should return to Nipal in triumph.

On the 26th of July, Captain Sanak Singh with his regiment, about four hundred strong, reached Simra Basa, and the next day marched to Bissaulia, where he heard that the ex-King was encamped at the village of Alu with fifteen hundred or sixteen hundred men of all sorts. On the night of the 27th he marched towards Alu or Ulu, and reached it at 3 A.M. of the 28th. He immediately commenced an attack upon it, the ex-King having his quarters in a kutcherry in the village. In consequence of the darkness, considerable confusion prevailed on both sides; little opposition was made; the assailants pressed on, killing all who came in their way, and soon made a prisoner of the ex-King. On the King's side between fifty and sixty were killed; among them was the maternal uncle of the King. Guru Parsad, Bir Bikram Sah, and Jagat Bam Pandi, with many other exiles, basely fled at the commencement of the action, crossed the frontier, and escaped towards Benares. On the side of the assailants none were killed, and only five or six wounded.

The ex-King was conducted as a State prisoner to Makwanpur and thence *via* Sisaghari to Thankot. He entered the capital on the 8th of August under a royal salute, was received with every attention and respect, and then sent on to Bhatgaon, where arrangements for his future residence in the old Darbar, as a retired sovereign under surveillance, had been made. No kind of sympathy was shown to him by the people or army in any part of his journey through the country since he crossed the frontier, and he bitterly accused the leading exiles in the plains for the gross manner in which they had deceived him as to the public feeling in his favour.

The ex-King professed to acquiesce entirely in all the arrangements which had been made during his absence for the government of the country. Shortly after his return, however, he was detected tampering with some of those who were allowed to visit him, and he was accordingly placed under stricter surveillance, but he still continued to reside at Bhatgaon. The public tranquillity was not again disturbed; the new King was recognised as such by the British Government, and his position was much strengthened by a son and heir being born to him on the 30th of November 1847.

CHAPTER XXVI.

HISTORY OF NIPAL—(*continued*).

1848.—IN April letters were intercepted from Chauntria Guru Parsad, then at Benares, instigating certain parties in Nipal to assassinate, under promise of reward, Jang Bahadur, and also the Raj Guru Bijai Raj Pandit.

In May, when it became probable that there would be a second war in the Punjab, Jang Bahadur volunteered the services of eight regiments, under his own personal command, to assist the British in the approaching campaign. The offer was renewed in October, but in each case was declined with suitable acknowledgments.

In making this offer it is impossible to suppose that the Minister was influenced by any sincere or active desire to see the British power increased in the northwest. He probably thought it a good opportunity to bring his name personally before the British Government under favourable circumstances, and that, in making an offer which he must have known would be refused, he should get the credit with the British Government of at least friendly intentions, and naturally hoped that in this way he might win the support of the British Government, and by being looked upon as their friend he might strengthen his own position in the Nipalese Darbar. It is probable also that, although the mission to England was not then talked of publicly, it was privately in contemplation at that time, and that Jang thought that the offer of his and his army's services would ensure his receiving a cordial and flattering welcome on his arrival in England.

In December the senior Rani presented the King with a second son. At the close of the month (22nd), the King, Minister, and principal Sardars, accompanied by twelve or thirteen regiments, each six hundred strong, and by forty-one guns, started for the Terai, professedly on a shooting excursion. After reaching Bissaulia, they turned to the east along the skirts of the forest, in quest of game. Fever, however, (from which the Minister himself suffered severely,) broke out among the troops ; several deaths occurred ; sport was scarce ; the party became disgusted and discouraged, and in the beginning of January the camp broke up and returned to Kathmandu.

The unexpected approach of so large a body of troops and guns to the British frontier at this critical time, when the news of the disastrous affair of Ramnugar had just been received, caused considerable sensation throughout the whole of India. It was generally believed that this was a preconcerted movement on the part of the Nipalese, with a view to create a diversion in favour of the Sikhs, by obliging the Indian Government to collect a force on the Nipalese frontier, and so preventing their sending up additional troops towards the Panjab. With whatever object the expedition was made, there is no doubt it had this effect for a short time and to a limited extent. Strong remonstrances to the Darbar were emphatically and immediately made by the Governor-General as to the impropriety of so large a force remaining at this juncture in the Terai; these remonstrances, added to the sickness which prevailed in the camp, certainly accelerated the return of the King and party to Kathmandu.

Colonel Thoresby, then Resident, always maintained that it was a purely hunting expedition, and that the presence of so large a body of troops was from a desire partly to add to the splendour of the royal cortége, but chiefly because, in the then unsettled state of Nipalese politics and parties, the Minister was afraid to leave them behind him for fear of treacnery, and a counter revolution against himself and party during his absence in the Terai. It is impossible for us now to account with any certainty for the motives by which the Minister was actuated.

The reasons assigned by Colonel Thoresby are probably true, but in addition to them it is highly probable, and quite consistent with the wily character of the Gorkhas, that though the Minister and Darbar had no wish to assist the Sikhs openly, yet they thought that by making this hostile demonstration, under pretence of shooting, at this critical time, they should, by exciting alarm among the British, increase their own prestige throughout India, place themselves on a vantage ground in case of any subsequent differences or discussions between the British and the Nipalese Governments, and, above all, by adding to the belief in the power and resources of Nipal, should ensure a more favourable reception for the Minister when he should make his contemplated visit to England.

1849.—In April, the ex-Rani, Chanda Kunwar of Lahor, having escaped from the fortress of Chunar, where she had been confined since the conclusion of the Panjab war, unexpectedly arrived in Nipal. At Chunar she substituted a female slave for herself, in the place where she was supposed to be, and escaped without difficulty. She was not missed for several days. Meantime, she went down the river to Patna in a boat; thence, sometimes on foot, sometimes riding a hired tattoo, or carried in a hired dooly, she made her way, without molestation or suspicion, through the country until she reached the frontier of Nipal. She passed herself off everywhere as a "Bairagini," or female Gusain, in progress to join her husband Gusain, who was ill in Nipal. She was accompanied by no females, but merely by two Panjabi male servants.

Once within the territory of Nipal she was of course safe from pursuit. Her escape from Chunar and coming on to Nipal was known to no one here until she sent word on from Hetowara, stating who she was, and asking for a hospitable reception. A day or two afterwards, the 29th of April, she arrived at Kathmandu. She was knocked up by fatigue, but escaped the " awal."

The Darbar appeared somewhat embarrassed by her presence, but at once said that they could not incur the odium of a breach of hospitality by surrendering her to the British authorities as a prisoner. They promised, however, that she should be vigilantly watched, and should have a guard constantly about her to prevent her escaping or carrying on any clandestine intrigues. A house within Jang's own garden was assigned to her to live in, and an allowance of about C. R. 800 a month given to her, besides grain for her household, which was subsequently arranged to consist of two Panjabi women, four Panjabi men, and two Gorkhali women, supplied by the Darbar to be constantly about her person. About a year after her arrival in Nipal, the King was anxious that she should appear in open Darbar to thank him for his hospitality; he was, however, dissuaded from the project by the advice of the Resident. On occasion of proposing it, Bam Bahadur (then officiating as Minister) said that neither custom of her caste nor family usage need prevent her, although a Hindu, from appearing in public.

In the autumn of 1849 it was finally arranged that a mission, headed by Jang Bahadur, should be sent to England, "to carry the King's respects and assurances of friendship to the Queen; to see the greatness and prosperity of the country, and the state of the people; and to ascertain how far the application of the arts and sciences was available to the comforts and conveniences of life." As Hindus they did not appear to consider that their caste was anyway endangered by the voyage; they said that they could as easily be purified at Benares on their return from England as those always are who come back from the embassies which are periodically sent to China.

On the 3rd of November Dr. Login left Nipal for the plains; he reached Sigauli in thirty hours, having gone partly on pony, mostly on foot; he escaped the awal, but died, after a few hours' illness, of cholera at Dinapore.

Towards the close of the year, some disturbances having occurred (about Drs. Campbell and Hooker) in Sikhim, the Darbar at once offered the assistance and services of their local troops on the Sikhim frontier. Near the frontier are three small forts, Ilamgarh, Dubagarh, and Dhunkota, attached to each of which is a small body of Kiranti and Limbu local troops, in all about seven hundred. The offer of the Darbar was politely declined.

(About this time Gulab Singh of Kashmir wished to obtain a number of Hindu idols from Nipal. Colonel Thoresby says the best can be procured from Jaipur, which is celebrated for its supply of marble idols which it sends to all parts of India. In Nipal the idols are carved out of common sandstone, and are mostly only in relief. They are only made to order, no supplies of them being kept on hand for sale.)

1850.—On the 15th of January Jang Bahadur's mission left Kathmandu *en route* for England. It consisted of—

> General Jang Bahadur Kunwar Ranaji, Minister and Commander-in-Chief.
> Colonel Jagat Shamsher, Minister and Commander-in-Chief.
> Colonel Dihar Shamsher, Minister and Commander-in-Chief.
> Barra Captain Ranmir Singh Adhikari.
> Kaji Karbar Khatri.
> Kaji Delhi Singh Bashniat.
> Kaji Hemdah Singh Thappa.
> Lieutenant Lal Singh Khatri.
> Lieutenant Karbar Khatri.
> Lieutenant Bhim Sen Rana.
> One bard or doctor, one Niwar artist, two subahs, one subahdar, and four cooks and domestic servants.

General Bam Bahadur, Jang's second brother, was appointed to officiate as Minister and Commander-in-Chief during his elder brother's absence.

During this year there was a good deal of correspondence about the affairs of the ex-Rani of Nipal, then resident with her two sons at Benares. It appeared that when the ex-King and Queen left Kathmandu for Benares in November 1846, the King took with him from the public treasury ten or twelve lakhs, in cash and jewels. On his returning to Nipal in 1847, he left this money with his wife and sons at Benares. Her behaviour shortly after with Dalbahadur, an exile from Nipal, caused open scandal. She squandered large sums of money on him, and not only neglected, but helped in corrupting, her sons, both by her precepts and her practices. After a time, to stop the scandal which arose, the British Government took possession of the cash balance that remained, and sold the jewels and effects. The whole together realised upwards of six lakhs of rupees; this was invested in the 5 per cents. for the benefit of the Rani and her sons, who were to live on the interest, the whole being under the control of the agent to the Governor-General at Benares. (On Jang's return from England, in passing through Benares, he made a new arrangement about this money, as the previous one had given rise to much discussion and dissatisfaction. He divided the whole sum into three lots, and gave one to the mother and one to each of the sons. At the same time, he offered the boys liberal provisions if they liked to return to Nipal, but they declined doing so; the option was not given to the ex-Queen, as it was considered quite out of the question to allow her ever again to enter the country.)

On the 24th of May 1850, a salute of twenty-one guns was spontaneously fired by the Darbar's orders in honour of the birthday of the Queen of England. It was the first time such a compliment was ever paid, but it has been done regularly ever since.

In October, the senior Maharani of the King, and mother of his only two sons, died, and public mourning for one year was enjoined.

1851.—On the 6th of February Jang Bahadur with his mission reached Kathmandū on their return from England; the King and his father (the ex-King), and a large party of Sardars went out to meet him on the banks of the Baghmatti river. A few days after, a complimentary letter to the Maharajah from the Queen of England was presented in full Darbar, under a salute of twenty-one guns, by Jang, who had brought the letter with him. Jang resumed his post of Minister, and entered on his duties from the day of his arrival, without any opposition, and everything appeared to have settled down into its usual state of order and tranquillity.

On the 16th of February, a conspiracy against the life of the Minister was detected. General Bam Bahadur, near midnight of the 16th, went to Thappatalli, his brother's residence; and after sitting over the fire for some time in silence, he suddenly burst into tears, and told Jang that he had a secret in his mind which had made him sleepless for two nights past; that he had delayed revealing it till now from fear that, although he himself was conscious of his own

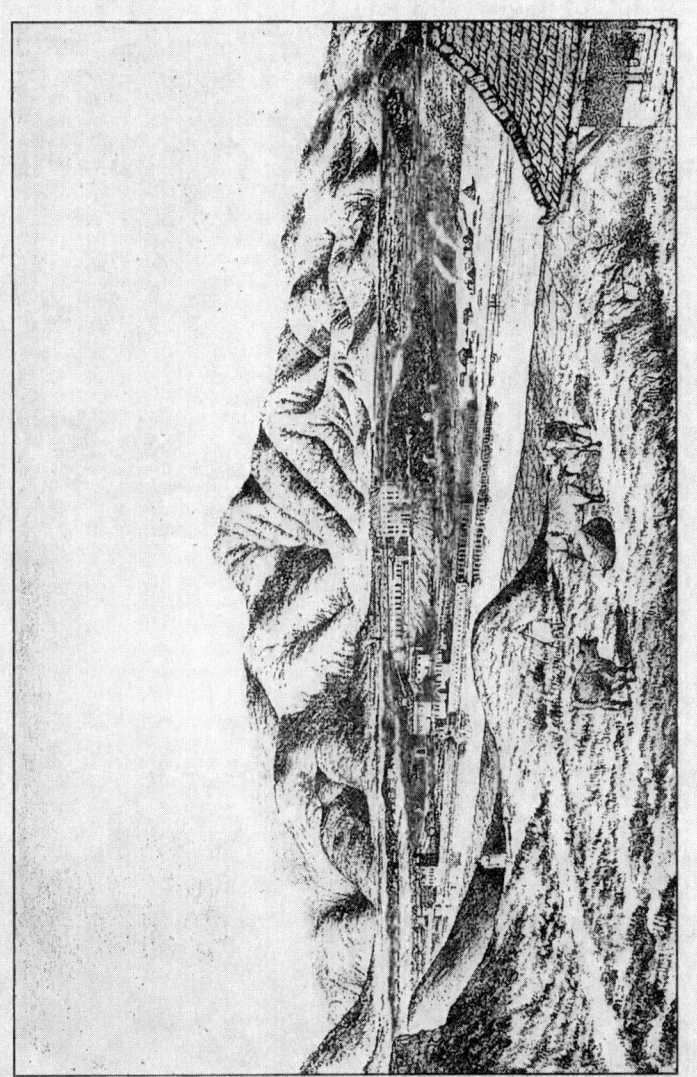

THAPPATALI, THE RESIDENCE OF MAHARAJA JANG BAHADUR

innocence, Jang might suspect that he (Bam) was as guilty as the others ; and that now Jang would only just have time to save his life, as there was a conspiracy on foot by which Jang was to be shot the next day by a hired assassin, while on the high road from his own house to the Darbar. He then entered into all the details which were known to him.

It appeared that two days before, General Badri Nur Singh Kunwar Ranaji (Jang's younger brother) and General Jai Bahadur Kunwar Ranaji (his first cousin), had visited Bam, and after informing him, on the authority of Kaji Karbar Khatri, that Jang had lost his caste in England, by eating meat and drinking wine with and from the hands of Europeans, as well as by various other acts incompatible with his caste as a Hindu, they told him that they were determined to take Jang's life, to subvert his Government, and get all power into their own hands ; that the Muhila Sahib (the King's younger brother) was a party to the scheme, and that they, the conspirators, only wanted his (Bam's) assistance and consent, and they were prepared to carry the plot into immediate execution, and in event of its success, Bam himself should be appointed Premier. Bam, with characteristic craft, professed to enter into all their views, but begged for a day or two's delay before the assassination should take place. With great tact and skill he drew out from the conspirators all the details of their plan, professing all along to be most anxious to assist and further them. Once master of all the facts, he determined to reveal the whole to Jang, and not only save his life and so frustrate the plot, but secure the arrest of all the conspirators. His courage, however, for two days failed him; he felt acutely the painful position in which he was placed—he had the lives of his two brothers in his hands; and he could only save the life of the elder one by betraying the guilty and so ensuring the capital punishment of the younger. His difficulty was increased by feeling that Jang would naturally suspect, and would probably accuse him of having been originally a party to the plot, and of having only now abandoned it and betrayed his companions in consequence either of having been unable " to screw his courage to the sticking point," or else of having had misgivings as to the probable success of the conspiracy, or perhaps from having quarrelled with the others as to the ultimate division of power and place and patronage in case the conspiracy should be successful. In any case his motives and conduct would be liable to be suspected. His sense of duty, however, prevailed, and after two days' hesitation he revealed the whole to Jang near midnight of the 16th of February, it having been arranged that the assassination should take place on the morning of the 17th.

Jang, Bam, and a few followers, all armed, immediately repaired to the Kot, assembled the guards, and before the intelligence could be circulated so as to put them on the alert, despatched parties, each one hundred strong, to the residences of the accused, with orders neither to ask nor answer any questions, but to cut down any or all who resisted, and to bring the Mubila Sahib, the two generals (either alive or dead), and Kaji Karbar Khatri without delay to the Kot. Colonel Jagat Shamsher was sent to arrest Jai Bahadur, while Barra Captain Rana Mir Adhikari, Jang's oldest as well as most undaunted and well-tried friend, was despatched to secure the most formidable of the conspirators, General Badrinar Singh. Colonel Dher Shamsher, meantime, was ordered to charge all the guards throughout the city with men from his own corps, and to collect and keep in readiness a body of Jang's own regiments, sufficient, if necessary, to bear down any opposition which might be attempted. With such secrecy and promptness, however, were all these orders executed, that no opposition in any quarter was attempted, the tranquillity of the capital was undisturbed, and within two hours from the time when they were delivered, all four prisoners, heavily ironed, were brought to the Kot, where, in the interim, Jang had assembled a number of the Sardars, and the King and his father, the ex-King, had arrived and were holding a Darbar to deliberate on the guilt of the accused. At first the prisoners stoutly denied their guilt, and the examination having lasted till morning without eliciting a confession, the Darbar was adjourned. During the following day, however, a paper clearly implicating them all was found, and having been produced, they fully acknowledged their guilt and confessed to having conspired to put to death the Prime Minister and to cause a revolt against the existing government of the country. The first question, as to their guilt, having been settled, the nature of their punishment had to be decided.

A grand Council was assembled, at which the King and his father, the ex-King, were present. Neither the King nor his father voted on the subject, but they said that whatever punishment should be awarded on the other prisoners, the Muhila Sahib should receive and suffer the same. The Darbar at first unanimously determined that the prisoners should be put to death, but to this decision Jang, who was the only dissentient, would not consent. After further deliberation, the Darbar agreed to spare their lives on condition that they were deprived of eye-sight. The Darbar considered it necessary to deprive them of eye-sight, and so make them helpless, as the only means of securing those who had voted on the matter, or who had taken any part in the proceedings, from the future vengeance of the prisoners, in case they should ever regain their liberty, either by escaping from prison, or in course of any subsequent revolution or change of parties, a contingency in Nipal which may at any moment occur. The Darbar were especially afraid of the future vengeance of General Badrinar Singh, should he ever regain his liberty. He was a man of considerable talent, great energy and activity, and of a very violent and vindictive disposition. He was known, also, to possess great personal influence over the troops.

Jang, however, determined not to yield to the severe

measures recommended by the Darbar, and in this humane decision he was strongly supported by the tears and supplications of his mother, a lady of irreproachable character, of great judgment and decision, and who has always possessed very great influence over Jang Bahadur, and who has always exercised that influence on the side of clemency and mercy.

Considerations of policy as well as of humanity doubtless had some weight on this occasion with the Minister. In a state where the tenure of power is always so uncertain as it must be in Nipal, Jang could not but be aware that great odium might hereafter attach to any maltreatment of the person of a member of the royal family, especially when that member was heir-presumptive to the throne. He was therefore peculiarly unwilling to revive in the present case a punishment which had not been practised in Nipal, even on the lowest criminals, for many years past. Considerable discussion took place, but no decision was come to. At last Jang, as a "tertium quid," persuaded the Darbar to apply to the friendly aid of the British Government to confine them in the fortress either of Chunar or of Allahabad, for the term of their natural lives. By this plan he hoped not only to save their lives and eye-sight, but to obviate any danger of their escape, and of the disturbances which would be certain to ensue should they regain their liberty. His own life also he felt would never be secure so long as the prisoners remained confined in their own country, where their presence might and would probably at any

time excite discontent, and act as a point of union to
those in the state who were disaffected to the present
authorities. The general feeling of the army, as well
as of the Darbar, was to put the prisoners to death,
and so fearful were the Darbar of the prisoners'
escape, that for their own protection they firmly ad-
hered to their determination to enforce the decree of
death or blinding against the prisoners, unless the
British Government could be induced to undertake
their custody, and they openly and officially announced
that if, " within a month," the Governor-General
should not accede to Jang's request to confine them
within British territory, the law must take its course
and their eye-sight be destroyed. Meantime, the prisoners, Prince Upindra Bikram Sah, General Badrinar
Singh Kunwar Ranaji, and General Jai Bahadur Kunwar Ranaji, remained as prisoners at the Kot,
guarded by a whole regiment, under a colonel, two
captains, and a proportion of subaltern officers. It
was found necessary to keep Badrinar Singh's hands
bound, as he would undoubtedly have attempted to
commit suicide. The other two prisoners were confined in separate rooms and strictly watched, but were
not bound in any way.

After considerable delay, which obliged the Darbar
to extend their period of one to a period of two
months, for the question to be settled in, the British
Government at last consented to take charge of the
prisoners by confining them at Allahabad for five
years, the Government promising to take every pre-

caution for their security, but at the same time stating clearly that they would not be responsible that they did not escape. One rupee a day was fixed on as subsistence allowance for each of the three prisoners, and one rupee for the servants, five of whom were allowed to accompany them from Nipal, on condition of their sharing their imprisonment, as they could not be allowed to go outside the fort. All necessary clothing to be sent from Nipal. These expenses, and the pay of a sergeant to look after the prisoners, the Darbar agreed to defray. The prisoners left Kathmandu for the plains on the 24th of June 1851, under the custody of a captain and fifty sepoys. In consequence of its being the season when the ordinary road through the Terai was closed, from the prevalence of the " awal" fever, the party, after arriving at Sisaghari, did not descend into the valley of the Rapti river, but following a footpath over a spur at the back of the Phulchoak mountain, descended towards Makwanpur, where they slept, and whence on the following day they were all carried by a dak of elephants to Bissaulia, thus running through the malarious district in one day. By adopting these precautions not a single man of the whole party contracted the fever. The same course, and with the same impunity, was followed, in the ensuing August, with a Mussulman native doctor attached to the Residency, and who, in consequence of an offence against the Nipalese laws of caste, was sent as a prisoner to the plains in the height of the most unhealthy season of the year.

In consequence of the manner in which the conspiracy had been revealed, before the time had arrived for its actual execution, no other Sardars were proved to have been implicated in it; though there can be little doubt that, had the plot been allowed to proceed a little further before it was detected, and especially had it at its outbreak been successful in destroying Jang, a numerous party among the Sardars and in the army, would have been found more or less involved in it. Such a plot would never have been so nearly matured, had not the ringleaders of it felt that there was a large party in the state ready to support them when the moment for action should arrive. Besides those who felt a personal dislike of the Minister, who were jealous at his success and envious of his power, there were very many unsuccessful candidates for office in the state or in the army, very many disappointed and unprincipled political adventurers, who would have been only too glad to assist in bringing about any revolution, from the hope that they should be able in some way to benefit themselves during the confusion and disturbances with which it would necessarily be attended. Such men as these eagerly availed themselves of the statements made by Kaji Karbar Khatri, that Jang had lost his caste while in England, to enlist into a crusade against the Minister numbers of bigoted Hindus who were greatly scandalised at the reports that Jang, by his free intercourse with Europeans and his adoption of many of their practices, had disregarded prejudices and violated laws which were always looked upon in Nipal as peculiarly sacred. Many did not scruple to insinuate that he had sold himself to the hated Faringhi; and that in order to increase his own power and strengthen his own position he was under a secret understanding with the British, which would probably at some future, and perhaps at no very remote, period, endanger the liberty and independence of the country.

Jang told Mr. Erskine (the Resident) that the disaffection was not general in the army. Among those who were opposed to him, several had told the conspirators, when they urged them to join in the plot, that they were afraid of the Minister, and that they would do nothing until they saw Jang's head severed from his body. It was in consequence of this feeling that Badrinar Singh, who always took up every matter with his whole soul, had proposed that in the event of Jang being shot his head should be at once cut off, and he promised that he himself would carry the head in his own hands and exhibit it to the assembled troops on the Tandikhel, as " the head of a traitor." From this we may infer that, at first, the conspirators intended only to subvert Jang's government, but that, finding they could do nothing with the army as long as he was alive, they plotted afterwards to take his life also.

Men influenced more or less by some or all of these feelings must have formed a large and influential party in the country. Such a party in the Darbar was known to have existed for some time, and to have been under the guidance of General Jai Bahadur* as its leader. This faction, with Jai Bahadur at its head, was well known, even while Jang was in England, to be anxious to embarrass, even if they should not succeed in upsetting, the government of the Minister. General Badrinar Singh was induced to join this party in their intrigues against the Minister, in consequence of a disgraceful *exposé* having just taken place, in which he was detected by Jang (immediately after his return to Nipal) in taking a bribe of twelve thousand rupees to obtain the restoration to office of a subah in the Terai, who for peculation had been removed from his appointment by Jang, just before his departure for England. During Jang's absence in England, Badrinar Singh was "Superintendent of all the Civil Courts," and in that capacity was peculiarly open to offers of bribery and corruption. The Muhila Sahib, a weak young man, was easily persuaded to fall into the schemes of the conspirators, who flattered his vanity by holding out to him visions of superseding his brother on the throne, and excited his animosity personally against Jang by making him discontented with the annual allowance which the Minister had assigned to him for his maintenance. There is reason also to believe that some jealousy of a bitter and domestic nature had been excited in his mind by his

---

* Jai Bahadur was "Superintendent of Changra Duties" during Jang's visit to England.

learning that, during the Minister's absence in England, he had on two or three occasions sent private and confidential letters to one of the Prince's wives.

The Prince and the two Generals were the only Sardars who were proved to be concerned in the plot; there was no reason to believe that Kaji Karbar Khatri knew anything of the plans of the conspirators. He had been taken to England by Jang, because he was looked upon as a dangerous and disaffected intriguer; he owed no goodwill to the Minister, in consequence of having been accused by him of having helped himself to a large amount of property out of the King's toshakhana, two or three years before, when he had charge of it; and he had gratified his spite, on returning to Nipal, by informing those who he knew were most hostile to Jang, that the Minister when in England had lost his caste in various ways, among other instances by eating meat and drinking wine with Europeans. He had been guilty of gross and malicious perjury, but had no share in the counsels of the conspirators, who had merely used him as a tool, on whose evidence they could found their charges against the Minister. On the day when the prisoners were arrested he was confronted with them, and on being unable to substantiate his assertions, he was subjected, as a punishment, to a disgusting degradation from the hands of two drummers of low caste, and in the presence of a large assembly of spectators, by which his honour and dignity were outraged and his own caste destroyed. He was confined to his own house for a year, but no other punishment was inflicted upon him.* At the end of the year, by the order of the King, who is supreme in such matters, he was forgiven, his caste restored to him, and he was allowed again to appear in public.

This affair of the conspiracy having been settled, and the prisoners removed to the plains, the Minister employed himself seriously in revising and mitigating the extreme severity of the Penal Code. Capital punishment was abolished for all offences except murder. Mutilation was also abolished as a common punishment, and the power of employing it reserved only for special and extraordinary cases. He could not interfere, however, to suppress the practice of satti, except by discouraging it whenever he had an opportunity of doing so; nor could he venture to oppose the prejudices of the military classes by depriving a husband, whose honour had been aggrieved, of the right of summary revenge on the person of his wife's seducer.

In July 1851 the King suddenly professed an extreme anxiety to retire into private life, by abdicating

---

* This punishment was strictly in accordance with the principles of Nipalese law by which, when possible in criminal cases, punishment is inflicted on the offending organ. As in a case of perjury his tongue was the offending member, and the punishment accordingly was inflicted upon his mouth. In 1852 a man who had been guilty of malicious slander against the Minister had his tongue, as the offending organ, cut out before the assembled troops.

the throne in favour of his only son, a child of three years of age. The only reason he assigned for this desire was his grief at the death of his Queen, nine months before. There is reason, however, to believe that he was disgusted by the constant surveillance which it was considered necessary to exercise over him, especially on occasions of his going about the valley, to Pashpattinath, Shambhunath, and elsewhere. On these occasions he wished to go in private and unattended, or with only one or two of his own picked attendants. It was not deemed prudent to indulge him in this fancy, as it was believed that there only too many Sardars who would have been ready to avail themselves of these opportunities of secret interviews with the King, and that they might easily work on his weak and excitable mind and betray him into acts of violence or treachery. To obviate this, Jang had insisted on the King's never appearing in public without being attended by a suitable retinue, many or most of whom were of course trustworthy agents and allies of the Minister.

The King, however, was after some little difficulty induced to give up all idea of abdication, and to consent never to go about *incognito*, nor without a suitable retinue of attendants.

At a private darbar held on the occasion, at which beside the King, Jang, Bam, the Resident and suite, no one was present, Jang in the course of an address to the King reminded him of having twice saved his life—first, from the ex-Queen about six years before;

secondly, by preventing the accomplishment of the recent plot for his own assassination, which, Jang said, if successful, would have been shortly followed by the violent death of the King. The King fully admitted the truth of what he said. Jang finished his lecture, for such it was, by contrasting his own conduct as Minister with that of Martabar Singh. Martabar, he said, had allowed the King (then Heir-Apparent) to indulge in many inhuman practices, such as chopping off the limbs of innocent and respectable persons, and throwing live slave-girls down wells, "which practices, however," added Jang, looking at the King with a menacing look, under which the latter quailed, "I never have permitted and I never will permit to take place."

Jang informed the Resident that, in the event of the death of the King and Heir-Apparent, without direct male heirs, it was intended either to place on the throne, according to the English custom, one of the daughters of the King, or to select a male successor by the voice of the National Council. He added that the nature of his offence, as a leader in the late conspiracy, would for ever preclude the Muhila Sahib, though Heir-Presumptive, from coming to the throne.

On the 22nd of September 1851 another son was born to the King.

In December, everything at the capital being quiet, the King and Minister, accompanied by a large party of Sardars, and with two regiments of infantry, went to the Tarai on an elephant and rhinoceros hunting excursion. Their route was to the west, along the valley of the Rapti, and in the neighbourhood of Chitaun.

CHAPTER XXVII.

HISTORY OF NIPAL—(*continued*).

1852.—On the 24th of May (as on the same day in
1851) a salute of twenty-one guns was fired by the
orders of the Darbar in honour of the English Queen's
birthday. This custom was introduced by Jang and
is regularly practised. In the following November,
on hearing of the death of "his friend" the Duke
of Wellington, Jang ordered eighty-three minute
guns to be fired, to evince his sympathy with the
British Government on the sad occasion.

In November a conspiracy was detected for the
assassination of Jang Bahadur, his brothers, and their
immediate adherents. Captain Bhutu Bashniat (elder
brother of Kaji Delhi Singh) was the ringleader, and
was the only man of any mark against whom anything
was proved ; but there is every reason to suppose

that many influential parties were more or less implicated. A few subordinates were seized. The prisoners
having confessed their guilt, were sentenced to death,
but the punishment was commuted to confinement in
the malarious district of Chitaun on the Rapti in the
Terai. No further investigations were made, as it was
thought more judicious to let the matter rest. This
affair being settled quietly, the King, Minister, and
a large escort proceeded to the Terai on a hunting
excursion.

1853.—The King returned to the capital in January,
but Jang, with his two youngest brothers and a small
suite, proceeded on to Kamaon on a pilgrimage to
Badrinath and Kedarnath. Bam Bahadur officiated
as Minister during his absence.

In April the portraits of the Queen and Prince
Albert, which had been promised when Jang was in
England, and which he was commissioned to present
to the Maharajah, arrived at Kathmandu; they were
opened under a royal salute. The King professed
himself much gratified, and declared, in a letter to
the Queen acknowledging their safe arrival, that he
would never lose sight of them, but they should
always remain in his apartments, and be visited every
day. A few months afterwards they were removed
from the Palace and sent off to Thappatalli, where
they have remained ever since.

In May (on the 27th) Jang, accompanied by his
two youngest brothers, with Sautaram Captar, arrived
at Kathmandu on their return from their trip to

Kamaon. They left Aliganj, eighteen miles on the other side of Sigauli, at midnight, Sigauli at 2 A.M., and Jang arrived at his own house (Thappatalli) between 3 and 4 P.M., having in the very hottest time of the year, just before the setting in of the rains, ridden on horseback one hundred and three miles in fifteen and a half to sixteen hours. From Aliganj to Kathmandu he had twelve horses on the road, and he rode the whole way, with the exception of the last two or three miles, when he happened to meet a palanquin and was brought home in it.

His three companions tailed off somewhat, but they all arrived in the course of the night, none of the four having been more than twenty-four hours on the road. They had ten horses apiece from Sigauli to Kathmandu. Kaji Hendal Thappa and Delhi Singh came on leisurely; they dawked by night to Bichakoh, whence elephants brought them on the next day to Bamphedi; they slept at Sisagharri, and came into Kathmandu on the 3rd day.

Although the season, from drought, was an unusually hot one, yet not one of the party suffered from awal fever, or any illness whatever.

There had been that spring an unusual scarcity of rain, and the crops had suffered in consequence very much; prayers of all sorts had been made for rain, but with no effect; as a "dernier ressort," Bam, at the advice of the Brahmans, ordered that every cow in the valley should on a certain day be taken to the banks of the Baghmatti, and there the sacred animal's milk should be poured into the sacred stream and offered to the Deity as a means of appeasing his wrath and obtaining a fall of rain. Even this measure failed, and the people were in despair on account of their rice crops. Fortunately, however, Jang suddenly and unexpectedly made his appearance, and on that very afternoon there was a thunderstorm and a very heavy fall of rain. The coincidence was so striking that it is not surprising that the people attributed the blessing to Jang's " fortunate star."

In September General Jai Bahadur, one of the State prisoners confined at Allahabad for the conspiracy of 1851 against Jang, died in prison of cholera. Jang's mother, fearful that Badrinar Singh might also die in a foreign land, persuaded Jang to apply to the British Government to have him and the King's brother surrendered to the Nipalese Government. They were given up immediately, and returned to Nipal, arriving at Kathmandu in January 1854, while the King and Jang were absent in the Eastern Terai on a shooting excursion. They remained in honourable confinement in their own houses until March, when Jang having seen them, Badrinar Singh was sent to Palpa, to live with his own son (a lad of fourteen), who was appointed Governor of that province, and who was made responsible for his good conduct. He was allowed to take all his family and property with him, to be at large, and to go where he liked shooting, &c., within a circuit of ten miles from Palpa, but he was not to leave the district. Badrinar, of course, professed before quitting Kathmandu to be very loyal and penitent.

The King's brother was sent to Bhatgaon, and apartments given to him in the Darbar Kot. At the end of the year, however, he was allowed to return to the capital and take up his residence in his old quarters on the Thandi Khel.

On the 15th of March (the last day of the Huli) Jang's statue on the Thandi Khel was inaugurated with great show. There was a review of all the troops and artillery, with firing, &c. &c. On the following evening there were general festivities; grand display of fireworks; all the troops were feasted, as were numbers of the common people; Niwar dancing, &c. &c. The Thandi Khel, covered with the tents of all the officers, with there fireworks, dancing, &c. &c., going on, looked somewhat like Greenwich or Camberwell Fair.

On the 8th of May 1854, the eldest daughter of the Maharajah (by his senior Rani, a daughter of the Gulmi Rajah), a child aged six years, was married to Jang's eldest son, aged eight years.

On the evening of the 8th the bridegroom, beautifully dressed, seated in a palki, and having a gold kalas (a sacred vessel containing holy water used by Goru on that and other religious occasions) carried before him, on the head of the oldest female servant in his father's establishment, was carried in procession to the Darbar, being the residence of the bride's parents. The Maharajah, as the bride's father, met the bridegroom at the Thandi Khel, and escorted him to the Darbar. The procession was a very gay one; regiments marching before and behind, bands playing, Niwars dancing, and fireworks and muskets being discharged in all directions.

That night the marriage ceremonies were celebrated between the bride and bridegroom; the bride remaining during the night with her family and female relations.

On the following day, the 9th, in the evening, the bridegroom took the bride home to his father's house at Thappatalli. There was a similar procession to that of the day before. The bride was in a palki, with kalas carried before her, and surrounded by a crowd of female attendants, gaily attired and waving fans of chowry-tail and peacock's feathers, in their best attire. The bridegroom's father followed behind his wife's.

To give *éclat* to the scene, a grand parade of all the troops at the capital was held at the Thandi Khel, the artillery and infantry discharging repeated volleys as the procession with the happy couple appeared on the ground.

On these occasions all the female attendants get fees, but the bearer of the kalas gets much the largest. The bride generally remains five days and nights in the house of her husband, during which time " puja " is daily made by the Brahmans to the kalas. At the end of five days the bride returns to her family, and remains with them until she is old enough to go and live with her husband. The husband occasionally visits her while she is thus staying with her parents. When the time arrives for her permanently going to her husband, she is conducted by him to her future home with considerable pomp, and with procession, &c., much the same as at the first wedding.

In this instance, the King's daughter only remained one day and night at Thappatalli with her husband, and then returned to the Palace, but this was an exception to the usual rule.

A few days afterwards, Jang was married to the youngest sister of Fath Jang Sah Chauntria, who was murdered at the Kot in 1847.

She and her elder brother and their mother had been residing in exile at Bettiah since the massacre, but these were allowed to return to Nipal in the spring of this year; the son was given the rank and the jagir of a Kaji; and the girl, aged twenty-three, married to Jang as a further means of cementing the close family alliance between the Minister and the Royal Family. At this wedding Jang took the kalas in procession to the bride's house, where the wedding was celebrated with great feasting, &c.; but the bride, as usual, remained for the night with her own family. The next day Jang brought her back to Thappatalli, where she remained for good.

The kalas is only used by the Gorkhas and not by the Niwars, either Hindu or Buddhist, at weddings. It is, however, used by Niwars on other occasions, as of making or confirming a priest. It is considered a most sacred object, and no one is allowed to touch it; puja is made to it. The carrying it, and receiving the fee for doing so, is the perquisite of the female who has been longest in the family of the bridegroom. In a royal wedding she receives one hundred rupees; poorer people give from three to five rupees as an average. In some few cases lately, certain wealthy Hindu Niwars (as Siddimah Subah, also the Fat Darbar Munshi) have been allowed to carry the kalas at their recent weddings, but it has been conferred on them by the State as a privilege; they have in fact, on payment of a fee, been raised (?) from the rank of Niwar to that of Parbattiah.

On occasion of this wedding, the bride, as eldest daughter of the King, received as dowry the results of a "capitation tax" on the inhabitants of the valley and neighbouring districts. This tax was sold by Jang to a Niwar at Patni, who paid 2,70,000 rupees, or £27,000, cash to him for it, all raised above that sum being the Niwar's profit; the tax was expected to realize about three lakhs altogether. On the marriage of the eldest princess, it is always customary to levy a capitation tax in order to raise her dowry, but this is not done with the younger princesses, their dowry being paid cash from the Government Treasury.

May 22nd.—The Embassy which had left Nipal in 1852 for Pekin with the quinquennial tribute from the Nipalese to the Chinese Government, arrived at

Balaji under the charge of Bhim Sen Rana, Lieutenant; all the other Sirdars who started with it from Nipal died on the road to or from China. The mission, especially during its return, had been treated very unceremoniously by the Chinese authorities along the road they had to traverse—coolies were not provided regularly nor provisions either. Many of their followers were beaten or otherwise maltreated, and all claims for redress disregarded. Every obstacle was thrown in their way, in consequence of which treatment the whole trip, which ought not to have exceeded eighteen months, was protracted till near two years.

On their arrival at Nayakot, all the members of the Mission received back their caste by a written order from the Guru; they had to pay certain fees and perform certain ceremonies for a prescribed number of days. They brought back with them about one hundred China and Pumi ponies. They halted a day or two at Balaji till they had an audience of the Minister, on which occasion the Lieutenant and his companions were all dressed in silk robes and sable caps given them at Pekin by the Celestial Emperor. They brought back a letter from the Emperor of China to the King of Nipal, which was presented to the King in full Darbar, with a salute of twenty-one guns.

May 24th.—Salute of twenty-four guns fired in honour of the Queen's birthday.

The greater part of this year was occupied by the

Darbar in making extensive preparations for their projected invasion of Tibet. The following were the causes which led to the quarrel between the Nipalese and the Tibetans. For several years past the Nipalese had had many causes of complaint against the Tibetan authorities at Lhassa. Niwar and Kashmiri merchants, and other subjects of Nipal resident at Lhassa, had in various ways been maltreated, and all their applications for justice or redress had been disregarded. Blood even had been shed in more cases than one, but still the Tibetan authorities had uniformly turned a deaf ear to every remonstrance that was made to them, either by the Nipalese Vakil on the spot, or by letters from the Darbar officially sent to them from Kathmandu.

The Darbar, finding that their remonstrances to the Tibetan Kajis were unattended to, addressed the Chinese Ambah, and requested his interference to obtain for them reparation for the injuries received by their subjects at Lhassa, as well as the punishment of such Tibetans or Chinese as should be proved to have committed offences against the persons or property of subjects of Nipal resident in or passing through Lhassa.

These applications from the Darbar were treated with silent contempt. The Nipalese then sent petitions, containing a full statement of their grievances, to the Ambah, requesting him to transmit them to his imperial master at Pekin, but still the Darbar did not obtain either an answer to their remonstrance, or even any acknowledgment of their letters having been received.

While the feelings of the Nipalese were naturally irritated by these continual slights, they heard of the maltreatment of their embassy on its return frcm Pekin, and of its detention at Llassa in consequence of the local authorities having thrown obstacles in the way of its advance by seizing and imprisoning some of its followers, as well as by refusing to supply the Mission with the requisite carriage and provisions.

This appears to have decided the Darbar to give up further remonstrances, and to adopt such decisive measures as would at once revenge their own wounded pride and obtain ample redress for the many insults and injuries inflicted on their subjects.

With this object they determined on seizing all that portion of Tibet which lies to the south of the Kerang and Kuti passes, and which extends from the snowy range to the mountains which are immediately to the north of the Valley of Nipal.

This district originally belonged to the Nipalese, but in 1792, when the Chinese army invaded Nipal, the Botya inhabitants of these mountains threw off their allegiance to the Gorkhas and joined the invaders, and these wild regions have ever since been annexed to Tibet, and as such have formed part of the Chinese Empire.*

---

* They were given over to the authorities of Lhassa by the Chinese, as a grant for the benefit of Buddhist temples and the support of Buddhist monasteries in Tibet.

The present appeared to the Darbar a favourable opportunity for recovering their former territory, and at the same time for revenging themselves on the Tibetans for the numerous insults and injuries which they and their subjects had sustained through a long series of years.

The Darbar was encouraged in this design by knowing the straits to which the Emperor of China was reduced in the contest with his rebellious subjects under Tientch, and they calculated on this rebellion for keeping the Chinese army so well employed in the neighbourhood of the capital, that they would not be able to afford any material assistance in repelling attacks on their territory in so distant a quarter as Tibet. Anticipating the success of the rebels under Tientch, and the consequent downfall of the Manchu dynasty, the Darbar determined to take advantage of the anarchy and confusion attending this civil war, not only to throw off the yoke of allegiance to China which had long been galling to their pride, but, by seizing and permanently annexing to Nipal a considerable portion of Tibet, to be beforehand in appropriating their share of the plunder which would follow the probable break-up of the present Celestial Empire.

For this purpose the army was this year largely increased by raising several new regiments; numbers of new guns and mortars were cast, thousands of new muskets were manufactured, and the whole department of the artillery was brought into a state of efficiency for active service.

To obviate the inconvenience of the entire absence of a commissariat in Nipal, the Government ordered the collection of enormous stores of grain and food near the frontier, and purchased from the plains several thousands of small tents for the use of the army in the field. At the same time, carriage for the guns, ammunition, tents, baggage, &c., was supplied by the enlistment into the public service of a whole army of kalassies and coolies, who were apportioned in certain numbers to every regiment and to every gun, and whose duty it was to accompany that regiment or that gun on the march and to remain with it as long as their services are required. All the arsenals, magazines, &c. &c., were brought into the greatest activity by the employment of thousands of workmen in preparing ammunition, knapsacks, gun-carriages, boxes, &c. &c. &c., for the use of the army, and every possible preparation was made for advancing into Tibet as soon as the severity of the winter should be over, and while the passes across the snow should be sufficiently open for the passage of the army with its guns, baggage, &c.

In order to occupy the territory which the Darbar proposed to wrest from the Tibetans, it would be necessary to take permanent possession of the Kerang, and also of the Kuti pass. It was not, however, proposed to despatch the forces whose business it would be to occupy these passes until the spring of 1855, as the vicinity of these passes to the capital would always enable the Government, if it were necessary, to send off troops at a moment's notice in sufficient numbers to repel any attacks which might be made upon Nipal in those directions.

In the meantime, it was thought prudent that detachments should be stationed at various points leading to the other principal passes into Tibet, so as to command them, and prevent the possibility of any sudden invasion of Nipal by a Tibetan or Chinese army. For this purpose a large force was ordered to assemble at Dhankuta, near the Sikhim frontier,* in order to protect the eastern provinces, and by its detachments to close and to command the Wallanchun and Hatia passes. Another still larger force was collected at Jumlah, to which all the Chaubisia and Baisia Rajahs were directed to send contingents, in order to protect the western provinces of Nipal, and to command the important pass of Tahbhas or Yari, leading directly into central Tibet, as well as that of Muktinath leading to Mastang.

---

* Jang would have liked to have sent a division through Sikhim into Tibet, but the treaty with the British prevented its even being officially proposed. The authorities at Lhassa forbade the Sikkim Rajah to interfere, and ordered him to close the roads and stop all communication between Sikhim and Nipal; and they threatened, in case of his disobedience, to confiscate the two taluks, Dobta and Sareh, which the Rajah held in Tibet, and which lie on the road from Nipal to Digarchi. Meantime, as a precautionary measure, a portion of the Tibetan army had occupied these two taluks temporarily or during the continuance of the war. The Sikhim Rajah agreed to these terms, and closed all the roads between Sikhim and Nipal.—(Campbell's Letter to Government, July 20, 1855.)

I.   **27**

The standing army at the capital was considered
sufficient for the protection of the valley and the
districts to the north of it from any chance of attack
from either Kerang or Kuti.

END OF VOL. I.